New Frontiers in Regional Science: Asian Perspectives

Volume 35

Editor in Chief
Yoshiro Higano, University of Tsukuba

New Frontiers in Regional Science: Asian Perspectives

This series is a constellation of works by scholars in the field of regional science and in related disciplines specifically focusing on dynamism in Asia.

Asia is the most dynamic part of the world. Japan, Korea, Taiwan, and Singapore experienced rapid and miracle economic growth in the 1970s. Malaysia, Indonesia, and Thailand followed in the 1980s. China, India, and Vietnam are now rising countries in Asia and are even leading the world economy. Due to their rapid economic development and growth, Asian countries continue to face a variety of urgent issues including regional and institutional unbalanced growth, environmental problems, poverty amidst prosperity, an ageing society, the collapse of the bubble economy, and deflation, among others.

Asian countries are diversified as they have their own cultural, historical, and geographical as well as political conditions. Due to this fact, scholars specializing in regional science as an inter- and multi-discipline have taken leading roles in providing mitigating policy proposals based on robust interdisciplinary analysis of multifaceted regional issues and subjects in Asia. This series not only will present unique research results from Asia that are unfamiliar in other parts of the world because of language barriers, but also will publish advanced research results from those regions that have focused on regional and urban issues in Asia from different perspectives.

The series aims to expand the frontiers of regional science through diffusion of intrinsically developed and advanced modern regional science methodologies in Asia and other areas of the world. Readers will be inspired to realize that regional and urban issues in the world are so vast that their established methodologies still have space for development and refinement, and to understand the importance of the interdisciplinary and multidisciplinary approach that is inherent in regional science for analyzing and resolving urgent regional and urban issues in Asia.

Topics under consideration in this series include the theory of social cost and benefit analysis and criteria of public investments, socio-economic vulnerability against disasters, food security and policy, agro-food systems in China, industrial clustering in Asia, comprehensive management of water environment and resources in a river basin, the international trade bloc and food security, migration and labor market in Asia, land policy and local property tax, Information and Communication Technology planning, consumer "shop-around" movements, and regeneration of downtowns, among others.

Researchers who are interested in publishing their books in this Series should obtain a proposal form from Yoshiro Higano (Editor in Chief, higano@jsrsai.jp) and return the completed form to him.

Editor in Chief
Yoshiro Higano, University of Tsukuba

Managing Editors
Makoto Tawada (General Managing Editor), Aichi Gakuin University
Kiyoko Hagihara, Bukkyo University
Lily Kiminami, Niigata University

Editorial Board
Yasuhiro Sakai (Advisor Chief Japan), Shiga University
Yasuhide Okuyama, University of Kitakyushu
Zheng Wang, Chinese Academy of Sciences
Hiroyuki Shibusawa, Toyohashi University of Technology
Saburo Saito, Fukuoka University
Makoto Okamura, Hiroshima University
Moriki Hosoe, Kumamoto Gakuen University
Budy Prasetyo Resosudarmo, Crawford School of Public Policy, ANU
Shin-Kun Peng, Academia Sinica
Geoffrey John Dennis Hewings, University of Illinois
Euijune Kim, Seoul National University
Srijit Mishra, Indira Gandhi Institute of Development Research
Amitrajeet A. Batabyal, Rochester Institute of Technology
Yizhi Wang, Shanghai Academy of Social Sciences
Daniel Shefer, Technion - Israel Institute of Technology
Akira Kiminami, The University of Tokyo
Jorge Serrano, National University of Mexico
Binh Tran-Nam, UNSW Sydney, RMIT University Vietnam
Ngoc Anh Nguyen, Development and Policies Research Center
Thai-Ha Le, RMIT University Vietnam

Advisory Board
Peter Nijkamp (Chair, Ex Officio Member of Editorial Board), Tinbergen Institute
Rachel S. Franklin, Brown University
Mark D. Partridge, Ohio State University
Jacques Poot, University of Waikato
Aura Reggiani, University of Bologna

More information about this series at http://www.springer.com/series/13039

Chisato Asahi
Editor

Building Resilient Regions

 Springer

Editor
Chisato Asahi
Department of Urban Science and Policy,
Faculty of Urban Environmental Sciences
Tokyo Metropolitan University
Hachioji, Tokyo, Japan

ISSN 2199-5974 ISSN 2199-5982 (electronic)
New Frontiers in Regional Science: Asian Perspectives
ISBN 978-981-13-7621-4 ISBN 978-981-13-7619-1 (eBook)
https://doi.org/10.1007/978-981-13-7619-1

© Springer Nature Singapore Pte Ltd. 2019
This work is subject to copyright. All rights are reserved by the Publisher, whether the whole or part of the material is concerned, specifically the rights of translation, reprinting, reuse of illustrations, recitation, broadcasting, reproduction on microfilms or in any other physical way, and transmission or information storage and retrieval, electronic adaptation, computer software, or by similar or dissimilar methodology now known or hereafter developed.
The use of general descriptive names, registered names, trademarks, service marks, etc. in this publication does not imply, even in the absence of a specific statement, that such names are exempt from the relevant protective laws and regulations and therefore free for general use.
The publisher, the authors, and the editors are safe to assume that the advice and information in this book are believed to be true and accurate at the date of publication. Neither the publisher nor the authors or the editors give a warranty, express or implied, with respect to the material contained herein or for any errors or omissions that may have been made. The publisher remains neutral with regard to jurisdictional claims in published maps and institutional affiliations.

This Springer imprint is published by the registered company Springer Nature Singapore Pte Ltd.
The registered company address is: 152 Beach Road, #21-01/04 Gateway East, Singapore 189721, Singapore

Preface

The concept of resilience within a context of sustainability is closely related to risk and vulnerability. Risk is defined by hazard, exposure, and vulnerability. In order to achieve a sustainable society, common frameworks for managing risk components have been built, mainly in the fields of climate change and disaster research. The extent to which an area or people exposed to risks are more likely to suffer damage determines the state of their sustained well-being. It is important to ask ourselves who exactly is faced with that risk and to address their vulnerability. Similarly, if we return resilience to its context of well-being in relation to sustainability, it can be said that resilience has a magnitude of power to restore a sense of well-being to people suffering from damages. That is, the components of resilience are regarded as the magnitude and speed at which well-being, degraded by the damage, recovers.

In Japan today, building resilience is important in a dual sense. First, the socio-economic structure of Japan is in the midst of long-term changes due to a declining birthrate and an aging population. These changes have caused problems throughout social systems that had so far seen periods of high economic growth and stable growth, resulting in a long-term decline of overall well-being through economic slowdown and social distortion. Second, Japan is one of the most disaster-prone countries in the world, which reduces a population's well-being. The Great Hanshin-Awaji Earthquake of 1995 and the Great East Japan Earthquake of 2011 resulted in enormous damage, with 6,437 and 22,199 dead and missing, respectively. In addition, damage caused by earthquakes, volcanoes, storms, and floods occurs every year.

The two issues described above are also closely related to each other from a regional standpoint. Japan's economic growth has been achieved through urbanization, that is, the massive migration from rural areas to metropolitan areas. On the other hand, local economies and local communities in rural areas that have historically supplied labor to cities have become vulnerable due to depopulation. In addition, there are many regions where the hazard of disasters has increased because forestry and agricultural practices essential to restoring ecosystems were ruined. In urban areas, rapid aging of the population and aging of urban facilities resulted in a dilution of local communities, a decrease in disaster-response abilities, and a decline in the well-being of urban inhabitants. These are common problems in many Asian countries facing economic growth, urbanization, and a higher disaster risk.

This book aims to approach, in a multidimensional way, the question of how regions with increased vulnerability can hold on to resilience, that is, the potential power to recover well-being. The basic viewpoint of this book is that regional resilience should be built on the basis of individual well-being and that the goal, plans, action, analysis, and evaluation for managing resilience are always considered from the point of view of an individual's well-being, and not sacrificed by other members of the region or other regions. This view is in line with the "no one will be left behind," a philosophy from "Transforming our World: The 2030 Agenda for Sustainable Development" adopted at the United Nations Sustainable Development Summit 2015.

This book consists of four parts: (1) From Vulnerable to Resilient: A Framework for Regional Context, (2) Case Study and Issues, (3) Design and Policy for a Resilient Regional System, and (4) Evaluation of Regional Vulnerability and Resilience.

One of the distinguishing features of this book is a bottom-up approach to introducing cases: first, we discuss a region's resilience and then follow with theoretical management and evaluation. Using the basis of individual well-being, we recognize that challenges to regional resilience are diverse. By overviewing the case first, we emphasize the plurality of regional issues and examine which solutions contribute to the construction of resilience.

Another approach featured in the book is viewing regional resilience through the integrated frameworks of geo-, eco-, and socio-environment (GES) systems shown in Chap. 1. This GES framework enables us to comprehensively understand the cases, policies, and evaluations for resilience described in Chap. 3 and beyond. For example, the case studies in Part 2 demonstrate effective approaches to recognize and utilize endowments from GES frameworks, in order to enhance regional resources. In Part 3, practical management tools for damages to socio-, eco-, or geo-systems (such as waste and contamination) are discussed, as well as an analysis of the role of parks in converting disaster damage from GES into greater resilience. In Part 4, evaluations that visualize both damage to and endowments from geo- and ecosystems based on individual well-being are explained, demonstrating the case for economic and reconstruction evaluation. Furthermore, comprehensive analysis of smart city projects presents an integrated and explicit viewpoint to evaluate GES relationships.

Many academic experts in urban science contributed invaluably to this book. Their areas of expertise represent a wide scope, from disaster prevention to civil engineering, environment, green spaces, regional development, economic, financial, real estate expertise, and so on. I thank all the authors for their enthusiastic contributions to the challenging aims of this book and for their patience during the long editing process. In particular, Professor Kiyoko Hagihara has led the discussion throughout this book, contributing outstanding ideas accumulated through her interdisciplinary approach to economics and engineering within environmental and regional issues.

Preface

I would also like to express my gratitude to the editorial board at the Japan Section of the Regional Science Association, for including this volume as one of the epochal series of New Frontiers in Regional Science: Asian Perspective, and, in particular, Professor Yoshiro Higano, who kindly reviewed the contents of this volume as editor in chief.

I hope that this book will serve even a little in building the resilience of all regions suffering from structural problems of urbanization and disaster vulnerability.

Hachioji, Japan
Chisato Asahi

February, 2019

Contents

Part I From Vulnerable to Resilient: A Framework for Regional Context

1 Sustainability and Vulnerability: Well-Being in the Geo-, Eco- and Socio-environment 3
Kiyoko Hagihara and Yoshimi Hagihara

2 Building Resilience for Vulnerability 17
Fumiko Kimura

Part II Case Study and Issues

3 Sustainable Activities for Rural Development 37
Shingo Yokoyama

4 Small Activities to Transmit Environmental and Cultural Resources: The Case of the Takasegawa River in Kyoto 53
Noriko Horie

5 Management of Depopulated Areas Viewed as Concept of GES Environment: The Case of Kumogahata in Kyoto 69
Yoshinori Ida and Kiyoko Hagihara

6 Resident's Awareness About Inheritance of Greenery in Gardens 87
Shogo Mizukami

Part III Design and Policy for a Resilient Regional System

7 Types of Social Enterprises and Various Social Problems 107
Fumiko Kimura, Kiyoko Hagihara, Noriko Horie, and Chisato Asahi

8 Overviews of Waste Management Policies in Japan 125
Shigeru Fujioka

9   Methods of Environmental Risk Management for Land
    Contamination Problems: Suggestions for Japan.............. 149
    Miwa Ebisu and Kiyoko Hagihara

10 The Role of Parks in the Inheritance of Regional Memories
    of Disasters... 177
    Noriko Horie

11 Measuring the Public Supply of Private Hedges for Disaster
    Prevention.. 193
    Noriko Horie

Part IV   Evaluation of Regional Vulnerability and Resilience

12 Environmental Valuation Considering Dual Aspects
    of an Urban Waterside Area............................. 205
    Kiyoko Hagihara and Susumu Shimizu

13 Economic Evaluation of Risk Premium of Social Overhead
    Capital in Consideration of the Decision-Making Process
    Under Risk.. 223
    Chisato Asahi and Kiyoko Hagihara

14 A Study of Nishihara Village's Disaster Response
    in the Kumamoto Earthquake and the Disaster Victims'
    Perception of Life Recovery and Assessment of Health.......... 245
    Sotaro Tsuboi

15 Smart Cities for Recovery and Reconstruction
    in the Aftermath of a Disaster........................... 261
    Yoriko Tsuchiya

Part I
From Vulnerable to Resilient:
A Framework for Regional Context

Chapter 1
Sustainability and Vulnerability: Well-Being in the Geo-, Eco- and Socio-environment

Kiyoko Hagihara and Yoshimi Hagihara

Abstract The process for realizing sustainability must be carefully considered. Equity, vulnerability and well-being are important factors. Concepts in sustainability and vulnerability are complementary and closely related; mitigating the vulnerability of the human-environment system can increase its resilience or sustainability. First, sustainable development necessarily requires the integration of social, economic and environmental goals. Integration begins with the recognition that the environment and society are closely linked. There are three layers of environment that are relevant, that is, the Geo-environment, the Eco-environment and the Socio-environment. Second, well-being consists of multiple factors and is defined as hierarchical in this study. Third, sustainability is considered from the perspective of the fundamental theory of welfare economics. Fourth, a social-environmental analysis in Bangladesh is shown regarding vulnerability. Finally, the results of the social-environmental analysis demonstrate that it is necessary to take the diverse character of the social environment in different areas into account.

Keywords Sustainability · Vulnerability · Resilience · Geo-, Eco- and Socio-environment · Well-being

1.1 Introduction

The concept of sustainability should be the first consideration in environmental governance. Sustainable development was defined by the World Commission on Environment and Development in 1987 (WCED 1987), that is, sustainable

---

K. Hagihara (✉)
Tokyo Metropolitan University, Tokyo, Japan
e-mail: khagi@tb3.so-net.ne.jp

Y. Hagihara
Kyoto University, Kyoto, Japan
e-mail: y-hagi@gf7.so-net.ne.jp

© Springer Nature Singapore Pte Ltd. 2019
C. Asahi (ed.), *Building Resilient Regions*, New Frontiers in Regional Science: Asian Perspectives 35, https://doi.org/10.1007/978-981-13-7619-1_1

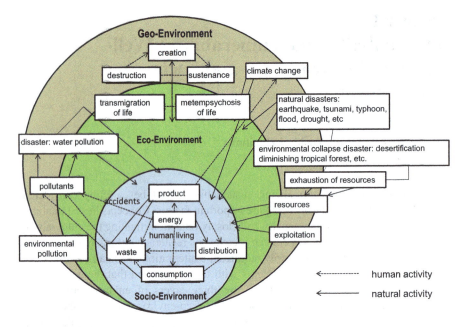

Fig. 1.1 GES (Geo-, Eco- and Socio-) environment

development is development that meets the needs of the present without compromising the ability of future generations to meet their own needs. However, it is difficult to define the word 'development' exactly and to determine the needs of future generations. The interpretations of the word must be different between developed countries and developing countries.

A process for realizing sustainability must be carefully considered. In the process, equity, vulnerability, social marginalization and well-being must be considered. If we ignore social marginalization, vulnerability and the uneven distribution of benefits from economic development, then we risk sowing the seeds of future conflict (Adger and Jordan 2009). The concepts of sustainability and vulnerability are complementary and closely related; mitigating the vulnerability of the human-environment system can increase its resilience or sustainability. Vulnerability refers to the relationship between poverty, risk and efforts to manage risk.

Sustainable development necessarily requires the integration of social, economic and environmental goals. Integration begins with the recognition that the environment and society are closely linked.

There are three relevant environmental layers (Fig. 1.1): the Geo-environment where the law of geophysics governs, for example, climate change and natural disasters such as earthquakes, floods, droughts and typhoons; the Eco-environment where the law of ecology governs, for example, ecosystem functions and services; and the Socio-environment where rules of society govern, for example, human well-being (Hagihara et al. 1995, 1998; Hagihara and Hagihara 2004; Hagihara 2008). If the geological space where the Geo-environment exists is the entire earth, the

Eco-environment cannot exist without the Geo-environment, and the Socio-environment cannot exist without the Geo- and Eco-environments. Humans are members of the Geo-, Eco- and Socio-environments. Conceptions such as resilience and vulnerability are also important aspects in every layer.

The components of well-being that must be sustainable are discussed below. First, well-being consists of multiple factors. Well-being is defined as hierarchical in this study. Second, sustainability is considered from the perspective of the fundamental theory of welfare economics. Third, the concept of vulnerability is defined. Fourth, the social-environmental analysis in Bangladesh is shown regarding vulnerability. Finally, the results of a social-environmental analysis demonstrate that it is necessary to consider the diverse character of the social environment in different areas.

1.2 Sustainability and Well-Being

As mentioned, it is difficult to define the word 'sustainability' exactly. Thus, the elasticity of the concept has given rise to questions such as 'Sustainability of what?', 'Sustainability for whom?' and 'How is sustainability put into effect?'

1.2.1 Sustainability of What and for Whom?

Sen's ideas (e.g. see Sen 1984) have recently influenced the sustainability framework. For example, Deaton refers to Sen's concepts of 'capabilities' and uses the term 'well-being' to refer to all the things that are good for a person and that contribute to a good life. Well-being includes material well-being such as income and wealth; physical and psychological well-being, represented by health and happiness; and education and the ability to participate in civil society through democracy and the rule of law (Deaton 2013). Stiglitz et al. (2009) demonstrated that well-being is a pluralistic concept and its various aspects should be considered simultaneously.

Well-being, therefore, consists of multiple factors. Moreover, well-being is considered hierarchical in nature, or as a pyramid in this study. That is, human welfare consists of three levels: the first level includes income, health and a safe environment; the second level is composed of a convenient and comfortable environment; the third level includes the realization of a meaningful life, fruitful communication, taking enjoyment in pastimes and a flourishing natural environment (see Fig. 1.2). The following is a more detailed description of the structure of well-being: at the first level as the base of well-being, people can enjoy safety and a secure life supplied with various kinds of infrastructure including traffic, roads, energy, housing, municipal water, sewerage systems, parks and less pollution. These are critical elements for regional survivability. For individuals within the region, it means continued life, and for communities within the region, it means their continued

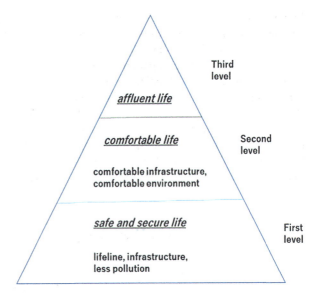

Fig. 1.2 Structure of well-being

ability to function as a community. The cumulative result of sustained actions to strengthen these capacities over time creates resilience. Thus, regional resilience is brought about through enabling survivability. At the second level, people can enjoy a comfortable life such as having a comfortable traffic system, comfortable housing and comfortable surroundings including green vegetation, clean water and healthy soil. At the third level, people can enjoy an affluent lifestyle, that is, people can enjoy rich surroundings, be in close contact with each other, participate in building up their community and so on. The first level is always the first priority in society whether in developed or developing countries. Consequently, 'sustainability of what' means well-being by securing the first level of welfare.

The sustainability agenda covers intergenerational justice, resource use, pollution, urban and rural planning, participation, poverty and social inclusion. A social state refers to a particular allocation of resources. The ranking of a social state is inevitably a normative procedure; it involves making value judgments. The normative analysis of economic efficiency proceeds with only individualism and the Pareto principle as value judgments. There is an important relationship between resource allocations generated by the market economy and those ranked highly by the Pareto criterion. This relationship is summarized in what are referred to as the two basic theorems of welfare economics.

One of the welfare criteria is Pareto Optimality, which requires that no one is made worse off, and at least one individual believes that they are better off after a policy decision. The problem with this is that most policy changes make some people better off and some people worse off simultaneously. Modern welfare economics is now based upon the Kaldor-Hicks principle of potential compensation called the potential Pareto principle. That is, if those who gain from a policy gain sufficiently to compensate for those who lose, the policy is an improvement regardless of whether compensation is actually paid. However, in applying the potential Pareto principle, it is possible that a policy could actually lower the sum of utilities if people with different levels of wealth have different marginal utilities of money. If the low-wealth person's marginal utility of money is higher than that of the high-wealth person, then it is possible that the utility loss of the low-wealth person could outweigh the utility gain of the high-wealth person.

The potential compensation criterion is useful in separating efficiency and equity but has meant that discussions of actual compensation have been avoided on the grounds that equity issues are outside the economists' realm (e.g. see Hagihara et al. 2013).

Furthermore, even though a Pareto-optimal state is reached, this in no way implies that an equitable society in terms of income distribution is achieved. Rather it will be a more likely result that wealthier person and the poorer person are still the same situation after reaching the Pareto-optimal state (Just et al. 2004). An additional example of this apparent contradiction is a statement from the Resilience Alliance, a research organization founded in 1999. It states that 'resilience is the the capacity of a social-ecological system to absorb or withstand perturbations and other stressors such that the system *remains within the same regime, essentially maintaining its structure and functions'*. This statement by the Resilience Alliance therefore also seems to contradict the aim of achieving societal equity.

According to the economic literature, sustainable development is economic and social development that maintains a certain minimum level of human welfare for present and future generation of humans, in the sense of either maximizing welfare over time or meeting the demands of distributional justice between generations. However, if sustainability is also concerned with equity in distribution over generations, then it raises the same question as to what it is we are supposed to be distributing equally. The question 'Equity of what?' is directly related to the common question among environmental activists and advocates, 'Sustainability of what?' (O'Neill et al. 2008; Munda 2005). Much of the environmental valuation literature is concerned with the issue of sustainability; however, they ignore income distribution (e.g. see Hanley and Spash 1993; Hanley 2001; Hanley and Barbier 2009). Yet a sense of fairness is a critical factor in economic decisions (Gowdy 2004).

Cost-benefit analysis (CBA) is a common method used to aid decision-making (e.g. Nas 1996; Hanley and Barbier 2009). It has been widely used as an evaluation tool for public policymaking by governments in Japan and worldwide.

Although CBA is adequate to evaluate the efficiency of the policy in question, it does not take into account the equity issues and sustainability aspects of the policy. Therefore, multicriteria analysis (MCA), which includes participatory multicriteria analysis, has been proposed to evaluate policies (Munda 2005; Kallis et al. 2006). Sustainability raises a set of issues based on the civil rights of current and future generations as well as respect for ecological systems (Messner 2006). MCA takes into account a much wider variety of methods than CBA (e.g. see Nijkamp 1977; Figueira et al. 2005; Getzner et al. 2005; Vincke 1992). An essential characteristic of MCA is the consideration of various evaluation criteria, which are weighted during the analysis. In MCA approaches, diverse quantitative, qualitative and fuzzy criteria can be defined to reflect different kinds of effects as well as trade-offs and synergies. Even CBA results can be included in MCA.

Recently, there has been a push for greater public participation and the inclusion of non-governmental stakeholders in project appraisal. There are different methods for including participation, such as scenario workshops, mediated modelling and social multicriteria evaluation (Munda 2005). However, some difficulties have been identified for participatory MCA. Several methodological issues and questions are still subject to debate, such as the following: What MCA method and which participatory approach should be selected for a particular evaluation problem? Who should determine the criteria? Who decides on the weightings? Who is to be included in the participation process? How can objective results be attained (Messner 2006)?

1.2.2 Sustainability and Vulnerability

Concepts in sustainability and vulnerability are complementary and closely related; mitigating the vulnerability of the human-environment system can increase its resilience or sustainability of that same system (Pearsall 2010; The Resilience Alliance 2017).

As noted, any process for realizing sustainability must be carefully considered. Equity, vulnerability and well-being, for example, must be taken into account. If we ignore social marginalization, vulnerability and the uneven distribution of benefits from human development, then we risk sowing the seeds of future conflict and witnessing the breakdown of collective responsibility. In other words, the processes of decision-making directly affect the sustainability of its outcomes.

If the first level of the above-defined well-being is vulnerable, survivability as well as sustainability may not be attained. As indicated in the 2030 Agenda for Sustainable Development, Goals 1–3 seem to be fundamentals of survivability (UN 2015). Goal 1 states that end poverty in all its forms everywhere; Goal 2 states that end hunger, achieve food security and improved nutrition and promote sustainable agriculture; and Goal 3 states that ensure healthy lives and promote well-being for all at all ages, respectively.

The extent of vulnerability depends on hazard. Therefore, vulnerability is defined as the concepts of hazard and risk and the ability to cope with hazard and risk as follows:

$$\text{Vulnerability} = f \ (\text{peril}, \text{coping} : \text{hazard})$$

where coping implies both the characteristics of risk and the individual's ability to respond to the risk (Hagihara and Asahi 2016).

Considering the Pareto-optimal state that we mentioned above, we must pay attention to the perspective that, even after the improvement of resilience, there are still difference among people with respect to their survivability. Thus, building community and regional resilience, while at the same time maintaining vulnerability among residents, is out of the question. In addition, it also brings in a question pertaining to sustainability: 'for what and for whom?'

1.3 Social-Environmental Survey in Bangladesh

Bangladesh has long been recognized as one of the countries that are most vulnerable to the arsenic-contaminated groundwater. Bangladesh is one of the world's poorest countries, and it continues to suffer from many kinds of disasters such as cyclones, floods, droughts and saltwater ingression and disadvantages such as infectious diseases and a low literacy rate (Hagihara et al. 2003). The Bangladeshi people cannot adopt countermeasures themselves against arsenic contamination because their resources are stretched by severe poverty and several natural disasters that afflict the country periodically. Thus, the Bangladeshi people currently depend on economic and technical aids from other countries and international institutions.

However, some of the arsenic-removal equipment provided by foreign institutions is too inconvenient for daily use. Thus, the arsenic contamination of drinking water in Bangladesh can be regarded as a typical combination of natural disaster and social-environmental disaster. The purpose of the survey discussed in this study was to reveal the relationship between arsenic contamination and the residents' social environment and to suggest acceptable alternatives to improve their above-mentioned first level of well-being, that is, to alleviate their unhappiness (Fukushima et al. 2016).

Two villages, Azimpur and Glora, were selected as the survey areas. Azimpur is one of the most seriously arsenic-contaminated areas. It also faces several economic problems. On the other hand, these issues are not as serious in Glora. We devised a questionnaire based on the KJ Method and Interpretive Structural Modelling (ISM) (Hagihara 2008) and translated it into the local language, Bengali. The questionnaire items consisted of 5 large items, each of which includes small items, and the number of total items was 57 items. Thus the questionnaire consisted of items on:

1. Personal data (e.g. sex, number of family members, literacy rate and so on)
2. How local residents obtain drinking water (e.g. 'carrying drinking water is physically taxing')
3. Current awareness regarding drinking water (e.g. whether local residents are aware that arsenic is injurious to health)
4. The possibility of pursuing options to improve drinking water safety (e.g. 'I do not mind bearing the expense to improve drinking water safety)
5. Local residents' concerns in daily life (e.g. worries about maintaining/securing a job)

These items are constituent elements of the above-mentioned well-being. We conducted the questionnaire survey between September and November 2003. As a result, 110 samples for Azimpur and 103 samples for Glora were obtained by the questionnaire survey.

The result of a simple aggregation of samples obtained from the questionnaire surveys indicates comparatively large differences between Azimpur and Glora in terms of people's literacy rate and occupations, the colours of the signs on the wells ('green' means it is not contaminated, and 'red' means it is contaminated), the awareness about and actions concerning drinking water use and the ease of obtaining medicine. These results are to be expected because the people in Azimpur are poorer than those in Glora and the groundwater in Glora is more contaminated by arsenic. However, the people in both villages have almost the same extent of knowledge and concern about arsenic contamination, and many people are willing to pay either in monetary terms or physically burden to improve the situation. Further, most of the people surveyed are currently concerned about many issues including jobs and earning a steady income. The survey results demonstrate that the community and media are vital sources of information for the people in Azimpur while those in Glora tend to rely more on the media to obtain information.

In order to analyse the relationships among all items in the questionnaire, Cramer's Coefficient of Relationship (Cramer 1946) was applied to all 213 samples obtained from the two villages. Cramer's Coefficient of Relationship uses χ^2-value to analyse the relationship between two items. Cramer's Coefficient of Relationship, ϕ, is described as below:

$$\phi = \chi^2 / \{N(k-1)\}^{1/2} \tag{1.1}$$

where χ^2 is χ^2-value, N is the sample number and k is the number of less category, or option in two items. The value of ϕ ranges between 0 and 1.0.

As a result of Cramer's Coefficient of Relationship, for example, 'own well is used for drinking and/or cooking purposes' is strongly related to 'use of some option to mitigate the problems caused by arsenic contamination' and 'use safe well' and so on.

1.4 The Unhappiness Function of Local People in Bangladesh

We first attempted to construct well-being, that is, people's happiness function. However, we found that it was better to construct the unhappiness function rather than a happiness function for people's well-being. Therefore, we derived the unhappiness function of local people in Bangladesh.

We used one type of multicriteria analysis (MCA) that can deal with well-being which we have already defined both quantitatively and qualitatively. As mentioned above, an essential characteristic of MCA is its explicit consideration of various evaluation criteria explicitly, which are weighted during the analysis. In MCA approaches, diverse quantitative, qualitative and fuzzy criteria can be defined to reflect different kinds of effects as well as trade-offs and synergies.

1 Sustainability and Vulnerability: Well-Being in the Geo-, Eco- and...

Table 1.1 Score for items on each axis (Azimpur)

1st axis		2nd axis		3rd axis	
'51a'	−0.083	'51a'	−0.064	'17'	−0.083
'51c'	−0.051	'51b'	−0.026	'3'	−0.065
'53'	−0.030	'53'	−0.011	'15'	−0.042
'3'	−0.017	'3'	−0.007	'53'	−0.010
'7'	0.003	'7'	−0.001	'51a'	−0.008
'51b'	0.053	'17'	−0.001	'51c'	0.018
'17'	0.078	'15'	0.022	'7'	0.044
'15'	0.089	'51c'	0.166	'51b'	0.083

Table 1.2 Interpretation of the results of Table 1.1 and contribution ratios

	Azimpur	Glora
1st axis	Satisfaction with water	Worry about and satisfaction with water
	25.2%	28.1%
2nd axis	Worries about daily life and water	Worries about daily life and water
	20.8%	19.4%
3rd axis	Rich life	Rich life
	15.0%	15.9%

Hayashi's Quantification Theory Type II (Yasuda and Unno 1977; Hagihara 2008) was applied to obtain the main factors for people's satisfaction with the drinking water that is currently available in both villages. Seven items were selected as the factors affecting people's satisfaction with drinking water as follows: '3, literacy'; '7, number of family members'; '17, carrying drinking water is a physical burden'; '32, own well is used for drinking and/or cooking purposes'; '34, use of some option to mitigate the problems caused by arsenic contamination'; '41, do not mind bearing a cost for getting safe water'; and '51a, worry about arsenic contamination'. From the above factors, important factors were selected as follows: '51a', '7', '17' and '32' in Azimpur and '34' and '51a' in Glora. Then, a discriminant function of the satisfaction for each village was modelled.

Hayashi's Quantification Theory Type III was applied to evaluate people's unhappiness. We referred to the above analysis the result of discriminant function of the satisfaction, to identify the factors that are supposed to constitute to the unhappiness as follows: '3, literacy'; '7, fewer family members'; '15, satisfied with the current drinking water'; '17, do not feel physical burden to carry drinking water'; '51a, worry about arsenic contamination'; '51b, worry about job and income'; '51c, worry about too many things'; and '53, easy access to medicines'.

Table 1.1 shows the results of the analysis for Azimpur. Table 1.2 explains the meanings of the results for the three axes in Table 1.1.

The contribution ratio represents how an axis integrates the data. Therefore, the contribution ratio indicates the importance of the axis (Hagihara 2008). Two unhappiness functions were modelled for Azimpur and Glora using Eqs. 1.2 and 1.3 respectively, as follows:

$$D_{Ai} = -\frac{25.2}{l_i} \sum_{j=1}^{8} \delta_i(j)x_{1j} + \frac{20.8}{l_i} \sum_{j=1}^{8} \delta_i(j)x_{2j} + \frac{15.0}{l_i} \sum_{j=1}^{8} \delta_i(j)x_{3j} \qquad (1.2)$$

$$D_{Gi} = -\frac{28.1}{l_i} \sum_{j=1}^{8} \delta_i(j)x_{1j} + \frac{19.4}{l_i} \sum_{j=1}^{8} \delta_i(j)x_{2j} - \frac{15.9}{l_i} \sum_{j=1}^{8} \delta(j)x_{3j} \qquad (1.3)$$

where

$$\delta_i(j) = \begin{cases} 1 \ (\text{sample } i \text{ responds to item } j) \\ 0 \ (\text{sample } i \text{ does not responds to item } j) \end{cases}$$

subscript A means Azimpur and subscript G means Glora, respectively; i is the sample serial number; j is the item number; l_i is the number of items to which sample i responds 'yes' to the 8 items; and x_{rj} is the score of the item j for the rth axis, which is obtained by Hayashi's Quantification Theory Type III.

If a certain person's D_i is positive and the absolute value is large, he/she is relatively unhappy. If D_i is negative and the absolute value is large, he/she is not relatively unhappy.

In order to assess the strength of the contribution of the items towards the unhappiness, the item scores x_j were calculated using Eqs. 1.4 and 1.5 in Azimpur and Glora, respectively as follows:

$$\text{Azimpur} \qquad x_j = -25.2x_{1j} + 20.8x_{2j} + 15.0x_{3j} \qquad (1.4)$$

$$\text{Glora} \qquad x_j = -28.1x_{1j} + 19.4x_{2j} - 15.9x_{3j} \qquad (1.5)$$

where x_{kj} is the score of item j for the kth axis.

Table 1.3 shows the item scores that directly contribute to the unhappiness.

According to Table 1.3, addressing the issues posed by items '15' and '17', which are related to the current drinking water situation, would mitigate the unhappiness in Azimpur. Therefore, in order to mitigate the unhappiness, it is important to improve the current drinking water situation. However, the same logic/action does not apply to Glora. In both villages, the results of the analyses for item '51c' indicate that the people are very unhappy. Thus, we can conclude that other social-environmental

Table 1.3 Scores combined with contribution rate

j	Items	Azimpur x_j	Glora x_j	j	Items	Azimpur x_j	Glora x_j
1	'3'	−0.69417	0.107076	5	'51a'	0.626394	−1.34232
2	'7'	0.555727	−2.16949	6	'51b'	−0.61212	−1.09315
3	'15'	−2.41378	1.299371	7	'51c'	4.995888	4.615948
4	'17'	−3.22323	0.396022	8	'53'	0.388253	−1.64643
Total contribution rate		60.9%	63.4%			60.9%	63.4%

problems would be also significant issues constituting local people's unhappiness and mitigating the problems posed by arsenic in drinking water will not be enough to allay their unhappiness.

The items that are important towards improving people's satisfaction with drinking water in both villages are as follows: '51a, worry about arsenic contamination'; '7, fewer family members'; '17, carrying drinking water is not a physical burden'; '32, own well is used for drinking and/or cooking purposes' in Azimpur; '34, use some options to mitigate the problems caused by arsenic contamination'; and '51a, worry about arsenic contamination' in Glora.

1.5 Ways to Improve Local People's Well-Being

We presumed a particular scenario to consider the changes in satisfaction with drinking water and the unhappiness. The scenario consisted of releasing people from the physical burden of carrying water and from worrying about arsenic contamination.

The extent of satisfaction was evaluated using Eqs. 1.2 and 1.3 for each village. The averages of D_i, which are defined in Eqs.1.4 and 1.5, were used as the thresholds to classify whether sample i is unhappy for each village. Therefore, we presumed that if D_i takes a value above the average, the sample i is unhappy. Conversely, if D_i takes a value below the average, the sample i is not unhappy. The thresholds and equations are fixed throughout the scenario analysis.

We set the condition for the scenario as follows: 'A' shows the number of samples that were satisfied with the currently available drinking water and were not unhappy, and 'B' shows the number of samples that were unsatisfied with the currently available drinking water and were unhappy.

The application of this scenario has led to a significant change; in Azimpur, the people in Group 'B' (unsatisfied and unhappy) move to Group 'A' (satisfied and happy). In contrast, there is little change in Glora. The results can be explained as follows. In Azimpur, mitigating the issues posed by items '17' and '51a' (carrying water is a physical burden and worry about arsenic contamination, respectively) strongly increases satisfaction with drinking water. Moreover, addressing the issues posed by items '15' and '17' (satisfied with currently available drinking water and carrying water is a physical burden, respectively) strongly mitigates unhappiness. In contrast, the two items play smaller roles in people's satisfaction with drinking water in Glora. Moreover, the issues indicated by the people's responses to items '15, satisfied with currently available drinking water' and '17, carrying water is not a physical burden' relatively increase unhappiness.

According to the results, mitigation of the physical burden and allaying the worry about arsenic problems provide significant results for the case of Azimpur only. It is very important for the people living in Azimpur to easily obtain safe drinking water. However, this is not so for the people in Glora, where the contamination is not as serious. Consequently, in order to suggest an acceptable alternative to improve their situation, we must consider not a stereotyped way but a tailored way for each area.

1.6 Concluding Remarks

The concept of sustainability should be the first consideration for environmental governance. The concept should include sustainability of what, sustainability for whom and the process to realize sustainability. The ability to cope with various environmental disasters should be taking into account, and vulnerability is a key factor in coping with such disasters. The concepts of sustainability and vulnerability are complementary and closely related. 'Vulnerability' is defined in this study as the concepts of hazard and risk and the ability to cope with hazard and risk. For example, poverty is the major cause of the inability to cope with disasters. Together with hierarchical well-being and the welfare theory, both sustainability and survivability should be considered in a developing country such as Bangladesh in particular.

Arsenic-contaminated groundwater in Bangladesh is a typical combination of natural and social-environmental disaster. Measures for removing arsenic from drinking water have been provided by other countries and international organizations. However, the Bangladeshi people have embraced only a few such measures. We studied the possible reasons for this situation and believe that local peoples do not accept many of the measures, because the temporal proposals and techniques to reduce the contamination have been promoted by other countries without any consideration of the local people's traditional ways of life. Therefore, local peoples are reluctant to become accustomed to these techniques.

Together with the concept of the GES environment, hierarchical well-being and the welfare theory, vulnerability in water resources in Bangladesh was considered. We analysed the relationship between arsenic contamination and the social environment in two villages. We conclude that the factors constituting satisfaction with the currently available drinking water and that contribute to unhappiness differ between the villages of Azimpur and Glora. Therefore, we must create an appropriate approach that is an acceptable alternative for each village, rather than a single solution for both problems to improve people's well-being in these villages.

References

Adger WN, Jordan A (2009) Governing sustainability. Cambridge University Press, Cambridge
Cramer H (1946) Mathematical methods of statistics. Princeton University Press, Princeton
Deaton A (2013) The great escape. Princeton University Press, Princeton
Figueira J, Greco S, Ehrgott M (eds) (2005) Multiple criteria decision analysis: state of the art surveys. Springer, New York

Fukushima Y, Hagihara Y, Hagihara K (2016) Social environment analysis regarding arsenic-contaminated drinking water in Bangladesh. In: Hagihara K, Asahi C (eds) Coping with regional vulnerability. Springer, Tokyo, pp 197–215

Getzner M, Spash CL, Stagl S (2005) Alternatives for environmental valuation. Routledge, Oxford

Gowdy JM (2004) The revolution in welfare economics and its implications for environmental valuation and policy. Land Econ 80(2):239–257

Hagihara Y (2008) Adaptive system planning methodology for environment risk management. Kyoto University Press, Kyoto. (in Japanese)

Hagihara K, Asahi C e (2016) Coping with regional vulnerability: preventing and mitigating damages from environmental disasters. Springer, Tokyo

Hagihara K, Hagihara Y (2004) The role of environmental valuation in public policy making: the case of urban waterside area in Japan. Environ Plann C Gov Policy 22:3–13

Hagihara Y, Takahashi K, Hagihara K (1995) A methodology of spatial planning for waterside area. Stud Reg Sci 25(2):19–45

Hagihara Y, Hagihara K, Takahashi K (1998) Urban environment and waterside planning. Keiso Shobo, Tokyo. (in Japanese)

Hagihara Y, Hagihara K, Hoque B, Yamamura S, Hatayama M, Sakamoto M, Miyagishima K (2003) A study on disaster problems in Bangladesh from natural and social aspects. In: The annals of the disaster prevention research institute. Kyoto University, No 46B, pp 15–30 (in Japanese)

Hagihara K et al (2013) Fundamental theory for environmental decision aiding. Keiso Shobo, Tokyo. (in Japanese)

Hanley N (2001) Cost-benefit analysis and environmental policymaking. Environ Plann C Gov Policy 19:103–118. https://doi.org/10.1068/c3s

Hanley N, Barbier EB (2009) Pricing nature: cost-benefit analysis and environmental policy. Edward Elgar, Cheltenham

Hanley N, Spash CL (1993) Cost-benefit analysis and the environment. Edward Elgar, Cheltenham

Just RE, Hueth DL, Schmitz A (2004) The welfare economics of public policy. Edward Elgar, Cheltenham

Kallis G, Videira N, Antunes P, Pereira AG, Spash CL, Coccossis H, Quintana SC, del Moral L, Hatzilacou D, Lobo G, Mexa A, Paneque P, Mateos BP, Santos R (2006) Participatory methods for water resources planning. Environ Plann C Gov Policy 24:215–234. https://doi.org/10.1068/c04102s

Messner F (2006) Applying participatory multicriteria methods to river basin management: improving the implementation of the water framework directive. Environ Plann C: Gov Policy 24:159–167. https://doi.org/10.1068/c2402ed

Munda G (2005) Multiple criteria decision analysis and sustainable development. In: Figueira J, Greco S, Ehrgott M (eds) Multiple criteria decision analysis: state of the art surveys. Springer, New York, pp 953–986

Nas TF (1996) Cost-benefit analysis: theory and application. Sage, London

Nijkamp P (1977) Theory and application of environmental economics. North-Holland, Amsterdam; Translated by Fujioka A, Hagihara K, Kanesawa T, et al. 1985, Kankyo-keizaigaku no Riron to Ouyo (Keiso Shobo, Tokyo)

O'Neill JH, Holland A, Light A (2008) Environmental values. Routledge, London

Pearsall H (2010) From brown to green? assessing social vulnerability to environmental gentrification in New York city. Envir Plann C Gov Policy 28:872–886

Sen A (1984) Commodities and capabilities. Oxford India Paperbacks/Oxford University Press, Kolkata

Stiglitz J, Sen A, Fitoussi J-P (2009) Report by the commission on the measurement of economic performance and social Progress. www.stiglitz-sen-fitoussi.fr

The Resilience Alliance (2017) Key Concept/Resilience (2017, March 20). Retrieved from http://www.resalliance.org/resilience

United Nations (2015) Transforming our world: the 2030 Agenda for Sustainable Development A/70/L.1

Vincke P (1992) Multicriteria decision-aid. Wiley, Chichester

World Commission on Environment and Development (1987) Our common future. Oxford University Press, Oxford

Yasuda S, Unno M (1977) Shakai toukeigaku (Social statistics). Maruzen, Tokyo. (in Japanese)

Chapter 2
Building Resilience for Vulnerability

Fumiko Kimura

Abstract Vulnerability has been discussed in various situations, including regional management policy. The global economic crisis has caused much confusion, with events such as the Lehman shock, the destructive influence of natural disasters, and so on; the concept of resilience is said to be effective in absorbing these shocks in a flexible manner. The aim of this chapter is to determine how to build resilience in individuals and organisations working on various tasks; examples of how to enhance resilience will be examined. The first two sections provide an overview of the transition of concepts as applicable to multiple fields, as resilience concepts are used in various fields. These concepts are based on the two aspects of continuity and recovery when facing environmental changes. The third section presents specific examples of resilience. The paper discusses reports of the recovery process from disasters; regions rich in social capital recovered from the crisis efficiently and effectively through collaborative work and activities. In other words, social capital is a recovery engine. The concept of Resilience Engineering is becoming more sophisticated through its application to fields requiring improved safety measures, including air traffic control and medical safety. The fourth section details the act of building resilience. The chapter concludes by summarizing that individuals and organisations need to build resilience, predict the extent of the impact on the environmental change in advance, and cope with actions to minimize the impact of the disaster. It is necessary to prepare a recovery plan to overcome such influences.

Keywords Resilience · Vulnerability · Social capital

F. Kimura (✉)
Division of Correspondence Education, SOKA University, Tokyo, Japan
e-mail: fkimura@soka.ac.jp

© Springer Nature Singapore Pte Ltd. 2019
C. Asahi (ed.), *Building Resilient Regions*, New Frontiers in Regional Science: Asian Perspectives 35, https://doi.org/10.1007/978-981-13-7619-1_2

2.1 Introduction

In recent years, vulnerability has been discussed in various situations. An insufficient safety net has caused many social problems, including a high unemployment rate for young people, expansion of the income gap, expansion of the fiscal deficit, and the reduction of social welfare due to financial difficulties related to the budget. In addition, although 6 years have passed since the Great East Japan Earthquake, the convergence process of the Fukushima Daiichi nuclear power plant still cannot be seen. The global economic crisis has caused much confusion, with events such as the Lehman shock, the destructive influence of natural disasters, and so on. The concept of resilience is said to be an effective characteristic that is necessary while constructing organisations, institutions, and systems that must absorb these shocks in a flexible manner and adapt to changes in circumstances under a wide range of conditions (Zolli and Healy 2012).

In the fields of information engineering and statistics, robustness has been used as a way to deal with vulnerability. Recently, however, the idea of resilience has attracted attention as a solution to vulnerability and has been pointed out in various scenarios. Resilience is said to be 'the ability of external forces to return to their original state' or 'the ability to recover from difficulties by people' (Zolli and Healy 2012). As for buildings and structures, there are examples where the viewpoint shifts from earthquake-resistant structures to seismic isolation structures with regard to earthquakes. Resilience has its origin in physics and was initially defined as 'the power to repel distortion caused by external force'. Furthermore, in modern times, it is used as 'the capacity of a system, enterprise, or a person to maintain in core purpose and integrity in the face of dramatically changed circumstances' (Zolli and Healy 2012).

The aim of this chapter is to determine how to build resilience in individuals and organisations working on various tasks; examples of how to enhance resilience will be examined. The next section gives an overview of the transition of concepts based on resilience, along with the etymology and terms related to resilience, how terms are used, various applied fields, and changes in the concepts. The following section then examines concrete examples of resilience; the fourth section presents what individuals and organisations need to build resilience.

2.2 Concepts

2.2.1 What Is Resilience?

2.2.1.1 Term

The concept of resilience is illustrated by the movement of a ball in a round container, as shown in Fig. 2.1. When the force externally applied is weak (arrow with broken line), the ball moves somewhat but stays inside and eventually returns to its original position. However, when a strong force (solid arrow) is added, it cannot

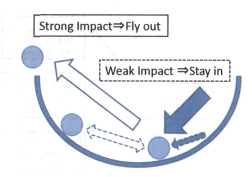

Fig. 2.1 Resilience and vulnerability

stay inside but rather jumps out and moves to a new place. Elements such as resistance from the ball (difficulty in rolling), the shape of the container (deep or shallow), the strength of the applied force, and so forth are related; these elements determine whether the ball ultimately stays inside or goes outside of the container. Vulnerability is present even when no external force is applied; if even a small amount of external force is added, movement will cause the ball to change from the current position.

Resilience is used in various fields and has varying definitions as applicable to each field. In civil engineering, resilience means the ability to recover structures such as buildings after being damaged. In the event of an emergency due to an earthquake or flood, it indicates the speed at which the lifeline recovers from the damage. In an ecological sense, resiliency means the power of the ecosystem to avoid an unrecoverable state. In the field of medicine, it is said that 'resilience helps you recover from a difficult situation that makes you sick, or from the disease itself'. This is an idea that will clarify the curing power of nature and the flow that points to its therapeutic application (Otsuka 2012). In addition, psychology implies that it is the ability of individuals to deal effectively with trauma. Furthermore, in business situations, it is often used to improve the organisation so that a business continuity plan (BCP) is possible.

These definitions are based on the two aspects of its function when facing a change in the environment: continuity and recovery. In this way, variations of the definition of resilience are used in different fields, so it is difficult to strictly define. Terms related to resilience include 'robustness', 'redundancy', 'recovery to the original state', etc. Zolli and Healy (2012) regards these terms as 'not resilience'; rather, resilience can be defined by the statement, 'We are going to achieve our objective while changing ourselves in a fluid manner according to a constantly changing environment'. Resilience and related fields are shown in Fig. 2.2.

2.2.1.2 Etymology

Kato (2009) discusses the organising terms such as resilience, stress, and vulnerability from the perspective of psychiatry. Resilience was originally a term of physics with the presence of stress. Stress means 'distortion due to external force', and

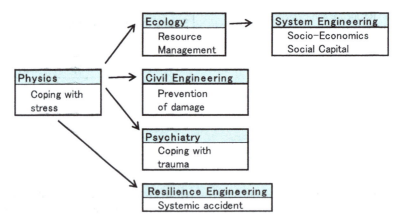

Fig. 2.2 Fields of resilience

resilience began to be used as 'force to repel distortion caused by external force' against it. In the UK, it was used meaning 'bouncing off and bouncing back' from the 1600s, and in the 1800s, the meaning became the 'original shape, returning force to place, flexibility' after being compressed. In French, the verb *resilier* meaning 'bouncing off, returning' dates back to the Middle Ages, originating from the Latin *resilire*, etymologically meaning 'to bounce again'. More recently in the 1900s, the noun resilience has been used in the field of physics meaning of 'impact strength'.

Handoh and Kubota (2012) show a transition from physics to ecology to system theory. Resilience was defined as 'the ability of a system to change the system in order to maintain the same function, configuration and feedback mechanism against shocks such as disturbance, to absorb the disturbance and reconstruct it'.

2.2.2 Development and Definition of the Resilience Concept

As mentioned earlier, resilience concepts are used in various fields; in this chapter, the transition of use from ecology to the socioeconomic field (Kohsaka 2012), psychiatry (Kato 2009, 2012), and Resilience Engineering (Hollnagel et al. 2006) is examined.

2.2.2.1 Ecology and Socioeconomic Field

In the field of ecology, Holling (1973) advocated resilience. Discussions began with analyses of two kinds of relationships in which some species eat and eat other species over time, until the numerical value settles to a state of equilibrium. A pattern has been found that the numerical value rapidly changes, but it settles at a certain point at a certain time. It is also a category of resilience that together with the process by which the natural environment and the ecosystem are regenerated under external forces, human society has coped and responded, and are trying to remember such lessons. Kohsaka (2012) showed how various organisations such as volunteers, unions, companies, and their associations responded to the earthquake disaster and became the power of regeneration. Additionally, it can be pointed out that there is a change in thinking about resource management in the background of the change in concepts.

In resource management prior to the introduction of resilience concepts, it was central to the discussion that grasping resources as a steady state, efficiently managing them, and distributing them optimally were policies that were implemented based on the experts' plan. However, as ecosystems often change from the initial state due to natural disasters and changes in society and the economy, plans led by experts and administrations often do not last long. On the other hand, as local residents participate in decision-making, their detailed knowledge and empirical rules pertaining to local ecosystems and resources are reflected in planning and other decisions. In this way, Kohsaka points out that resilience concepts related to ecology have appeared. In other words, because ecosystems and communities dynamically change, focusing on flexibility and voluntarily maintaining the function of the system are important.

Handoh and Kubota (2012) introduced Holling's assertion that system stability and resilience are different concepts and organised the transition between concepts. In ecology, resilience and resistance were mathematically defined as a concept expressing stability. The resilience in this case strongly means recovery speed and indicates the act of maintaining the original state. Therefore, the resilience process of the system needs to be observed on a time scale longer than the resistance process itself. Resilience implies that flexibility is more significant than the robustness of the system in order to change.

The Resilience Centre (RC) at Stockholm University in Sweden defines resilience as the 'ability to continuously change and adapt the system to the extent that it does not go beyond the boundary that cannot be recovered' (Kohsaka 2012). Furthermore, Handoh and Kubota (2012) said that the concept of resilience will be refined by the Resilience Alliance (hereinafter referred to as RA) established in 1999 and introduced it as follows.

RA proposes a resilience thinking method and shows the following four attributes as resilience features:

(a) Latitude: Allowable range in which resilience works even if the system changes. Changes beyond the tolerance range are difficult to recover or irretrievable.
(b) Resistance: The difficulty of changing the system (it is regarded as reciprocal of the sensitivity).
(c) Precariousness: The risk of the current state of the system.
(d) Panarchy: The extent to which one hierarchical level is affected by other levels in the hierarchical structure of the system.

RA defines resilience, adaptability, and the concept of transformability. This concept is regarded as the ability to create a new system when the current system cannot be maintained. The evolution of living things can also be said to be the ability to transform living things.

2.2.2.2 Resilience in Modern Psychiatry

The field of psychiatry, in addition to ecosystems, distinguishes between resistance and resilience. Resistance indicates psychological immunity (ability to resist distress, damage, and dysfunction). That is, resilience is a process of escaping from the trauma that society experiences through emergency situations, group disasters, and so forth. An explanation from Kato (2009) is summarized as follows. The process of using resilience in psychiatry can be roughly divided into (1) defence factors and recovery factors and (2) processes for defence and recovery. Defence factors are further divided into individual-specific and group characteristics. When considering resilience as a process for defence and recovery, resilience can be interpreted as 'coping behaviours', 'self-healing', and so on.

In the field of paediatric psychiatry, much of the early research on resilience was done in the 1970s (Oshima and Abe 2009). The resilience concept originates in the observation and treatment of orphans in the UK; it began with a long-term observation of children who were high risk or who had endured trauma. In France, attention was focused mainly on the medical sector, child psychiatry, and clinical psychology and in particular those from facilities and teams who see injured children early on. A cohort study of high-risk children with environmentally unstable factors such as poverty, violence, and parental pathology was conducted, and reports that one third of those had become competent, reliable, considerable adults are introduced.

A long-standing follow-up study focused on children who were judged to be at risk due to an unfavourable living environment (poverty, parent's mental illness, etc.) was conducted. As a result, it was confirmed that there was a child who grew admirably even though they grew up in an adverse living environment and a child with a lower occurrence rate of psychopathology. From this, factors that seem to promote health and comfort such as good self-respect and social support were identified. Based on the above, since the 1980s, research on resilience has been introduced into adult psychiatry as a concept implicating defence factors and resistance to mental illness (Den 2009).

Furthermore, resilience concepts have included not only adversity but also stress in life (Den 2009). Recently, studies on acute posttraumatic stress disorder (PTSD) resulting from events such as battle, assault, accident, natural disaster, etc. are increasing. According to Den (2009), in the American papers of 1995, 50% to 60% of Americans are exposed to some traumatic experience, but only 8% to 20% are reported to have PTSD. With the expansion of the concept of resilience, 'defence factors' have been drawing attention, along with risk factors of PTSD. Research results based on 750 pilots who did not develop depression or PTSD while receiving extreme stress during the Vietnam War as clinical studies investigating resilience factors have been reported. This research cites resilience factors as optimism, altruism, having social support with others, having a sense of mission, and having undergone some kind of training. In modern medicine, it is pointed out that building resilience is an important point of treatment because treatment for PTSD has not been established yet.

2.2.2.3 Resilience Engineering

The concept of Resilience Engineering (hereinafter referred to as RE) was proposed in 2001 as a countermeasure to the trade-off between efficiency and safety, and the first meeting was held in Sweden in 2004. The concept of RE is a complementary approach to the existing approaches to safety. This way of thinking is becoming more sophisticated through the application to fields requiring better measures for safety issues such as air traffic control and medical safety. The conventional idea of safety is 'a state where things are not going bad' (Safety-I). RE advocates transformation to a new way of thinking: 'to ensure that things go in the right direction' (Safety-II) (Hollnagel et al. 2006). In RE, the elements of resilience are ① ability to prevent bad things, ② ability to prevent bad things from getting worse, and ③ ability to recover from bad things that happen. Its objective is to ensure that organisations, technologies, and systems can deal with changes in the situation and continue their activities; changes in the situation are said to include the unexpected.

RE defines resiliency as 'the ability of an organisation (or system) to respond as quickly as possible to external disturbance as much as possible and restore it from its impact so that it will have minimal impact on dynamic stability'. In other words, it is the ability of the system to adjust its functions before, during, and after a change or disturbance, maintaining the necessary actions in any expected or unexpected situation. Hollnagel et al. (2006) presents real-world examples of resilient systems, such as in the dynamic change in environment, continuation of motion adaptive to change, avoidance of catastrophic state, adaptive and active correction for activity purposes, and processes leading to steady-state restoration.

2.2.2.4 Definition

Although various definitions are given with respect to the fields further described below, it can be seen that the importance is placed on the processes for maintenance of function and purpose (Table 2.1). This chapter focuses on the process and adopts the definition used in ecology (resilience centre), the 'ability to continuously change and adapt the system to the extent that it does not exceed the boundary that cannot be recovered'. In particular, it is an examination that emphasizes the ability to adapt to change.

2.3 Case Studies

In this section, two case studies describe the roles and functions of resilience. One case examines the role of social capital (SC) in the process of recovery from disasters in the socioeconomic field, and the other is Resilience Engineering (RE) which is a response to organisational accidents.

Table 2.1 Definitions of resilience

Field/proponent	Definition
Physics	Force to repel distortion due to external force
Ecology	The ability of the system to continuously change and adapt within a range not exceeding the boundary line (which will not be recoverable)
Civil engineering	Prevention of damage
Psychiatry	Protective factors and resistance to mental illness
System Engineering (Socio/Economics)	The ability of the system to respond to changes from the outside, to maintain its own function and structure while absorbing shock
Resilience Engineering	Ability to ensure that an organisation (or system) has only minimal impact on dynamic stability by responding to disturbances as early as possible and recovering from the impact
Zolli	Force that when faced with an externally applied force returns to its original state. Ability for people to recover from difficulties
Aldrich	Recovery of disaster-struck communities and the presence (or absence) of such a capacity

2.3.1 Recovery Process from Disaster and the Role of SC

Aldrich (2012) focused on the recovery of communities struck by disaster and the presence (or absence) of the capacity to do this; he calls this resilience. He defined community recovery as *the process of repopulation by survivors – who may have fled or been evacuated – and new residents along with the gradual resumption of normal daily routines for those occupants.* He focused on two critical concepts (disasters and social capital) together to understand how social resources influence post-disaster recovery. Using studies of four major disasters (1923 Tokyo and 1995 Kobe earthquakes, 2004 Indian Ocean Tsunami, and 2005 Hurricane Katrina), it uncovered how social networks and connections form the core engine of recovery after the most devastating of events.

Putnum (1995) defined the SC with three elements of 'trust', 'norm', and 'network'. In addition, bonding, bridging, and linking are shown as three dimensions of SC, and Aldrich uses these three dimensions his analysis (Aldrich 2012).

2.3.1.1 Tokyo Earthquake, 1923

In the aftermath of the Tokyo Earthquake (Great Kanto Earthquake), the recovery level of the population varied greatly depending on the district. Therefore, Aldrich (2012) analysed the relationship between the population recovery rate and the voting rate as a proxy variable of SC. In the elections of 1922 and 1933, districts with high voting rates and many demonstrations showed resilience.

Strong connections and trust among residents help them overcome collective action problems that may prevent other neighbourhoods from effectively rebounding. However, strong social networks can bring negative externalities alongside the benefits of tighter bonds. After the 1923 quake, mainland Japanese residents organised horrific attacks against Koreans across the capital. If bonding social capital was strong in certain neighbourhoods but bridging social capital was lacking, the panic of the fires and quakes, combined with existing prejudices and rumours of poisoning, may have inflamed local residents who sought to attack those 'outside' of their groups. Such investigations would further our understanding of the 'dark side' of social capital (Putnam 1995).

In the Tokyo area, it was reported that the number of 'neighbourhood associations' in neighbouring organisations increased from 452 to 986 from 1922 to 1933 following the earthquake. In addition, the Tokyo urban planner hopes to set up meeting places so that young people, women, retirees, and others have a space for community activities. This plan allows elementary schools and neighbouring parks to fulfil the role the church plays in the West.

2.3.1.2 Kobe Earthquake

Regarding the recovery from the Kobe Earthquake (Great Hanshin-Awaji Earthquake) that took place on January 17, 1995, Aldrich (2012) presents that this process occurred over 18 years (1990–2008) in Kobe City, nine wards (Tarumi, Nada, Kita, Suma, Higashinada, Nagata, Hyogo, Chuo, and Nishi). The population has almost recovered as of 2007, but some of the wards remained at low levels. As a concrete example, Aldrich compared two districts of the same degree. In the Nagata A district, less than 10% of residents were natives, and 35% of residents rented their homes; additionally, they had a tendency to rely on leaders (cadres), and hollowing out was seen. On the other hand, in the Fukushima B area, 75% of inhabitants were born and raised in Fukushima, and the proportion of rental housing was 16%. Support from traditional social ties and strong bonds promoting interaction, collaboration, and information transmission are factors that, according to SC, determine the recovery rate as a whole.

Using the number of established NPOs as a surrogate index of SC, Aldrich revealed the role of SC in the disaster recovery process by comparing two additional locations: the Mano district (SC high) and the Mikura district (SC low). Many owners of condominiums were in a difficult state without reconstruction progress or the formation of repair agreements. But in areas where the SC was high, people were overcoming this state not only through repairs but also through the construction of new housing complexes. Immediately after the disaster in the Mano district, they entered discussions on 'joint rebuilding', and old detached houses were rebuilt into fire- and seismic-resistant multifamily houses; this points out the importance of the 'neighbourhood association'.

There were 300 earthquake victims living in tents in the park and over 120 people experiencing the 'lonely death' by living away from the community in a temporary housing area. There were many people saying, 'I knew little of the neighbourhood residents before the disaster', but since 1995, Kobe City has called for the establishment of solidarity through a program aimed at increasing trust and participation. Volunteers totalling 630,000 to 1 million people were involved in the support of this area.

The Japanese government promoted the registration of NPOs and NGOs, and 1995 came to be called 'the first year of volunteers'. However, an essential element of the recovery was that the network of residents in the communities within the disaster area was more important than the short-term outsiders. In the case of Kobe, unlike the Tokyo Earthquake of 1923, Aldrich (2012) reported that no negative externalities of strong social ties were seen.

2.3.1.3 Tsunami in the Indian Ocean

During the tsunami in the Indian Ocean, which was caused by a seabed earthquake in 2004, 230,000 people were killed throughout India, Indonesia, Sri Lanka, and Thailand. In the example of an Indian fishing village in Tamil Nadu, aside from the confusing time immediately after the disaster, the government was able to create and maintain a list of the dead and injured, along with a list of necessary supplies for reconstruction, food, and daily necessities that would be distributed equally to the people. In the well-organized villages such as in Tamil Nadu, the 'uur panchayats (resident's organisation)' served both as an institutionalized form of bonding SC and a source of linking SC connecting residents to each other.

However, those who were not members of the main group within the village, such as widows, Dalits, Muslims, and other peripheral groups, were excluded from distribution of goods. Additionally, in the village without SC, restoration did not occur. Since these villages were missing from the map of the recovery process, they could not cooperate with NPOs and NGOs and were not consulted by the Indian government. Many villages damaged by the tsunami could hardly receive aid supplies. Therefore, it is necessary to take steps to strengthen the SC.

In addition, Aldrich (2012) conducted quantitative analyses using 62 villages and data from 1600 people; he found that villagers who attend ceremonial occasions are deeply embedded in social relations and resilience is strengthened through this and access to resources is possible even after a tsunami occurs. Standard disaster assistance procedures focus on repairing physical infrastructure damage, but SC is essential for disaster recovery. SC brings a solution to common problems, but in particular, negative externality is involved when people who do not belong to the group, people other than the main members of the local organisation, are involved. In other words, although SC is a benefit for some, it may have a negative impact on others.

2.3.1.4 Hurricane Katrina

Even though 5 years have passed since Hurricane Katrina (2005), Lower Ninth Word remains a ghost town, and only the population in one quarter of the area has recovered (Aldrich 2012). Among them, Village de L'Est (a village where Vietnamese residents live) was deeply affected and struggled with poverty; however, the population recovery rate was 90%, and businesses reopened within 2 years after the disaster. In this village district activists tried to maintain strong ties between residents during and after evacuation. In other words, Father Vien and other leaders led the residents to evacuation centres in preparation for the hurricane, took pictures of all the members, and confirmed their safety to distant family and friends. Furthermore, he set up a Vietnamese radio station and informed refugees of the rebuilding plan for the village. In this way, the SC fulfilled the role of private insurance, and the multi-type SC strengthened the community's resilience.

2.3.1.5 The Role of SC

The result of the examination of the previously discussed four disasters showed that the SC is an engine of recovery. Next, the results are shown (Table 2.2).

Table 2.2 Recovery from disaster and social capital

Disaster	Survey target	Data	Findings of survey
Tokyo Earthquake 1923	1922~1933	Unit: Range of police box (1.97 km^2) District: 31 Proxy variable of SC: Voting rate	Relationship between population growth rate and voter rate Yamanote was recovering faster than the downtown (SC) Above average: Population increase of 7%, below average: Population increase of 0% Possibility of negative externality (bonding SC) Attention also needs to be given to the dark side of SC (lack of bridging SC)
Kobe Earthquake 1995	1990~2008	District: 9 wards in Kobe city Proxy variables of SC: Number of established NPOs	Comparison between Mano district (high SC) and Mikura district (low SC) Nagata A, Fukushima B: Neighbourhood association is important SC made it possible to rebuild aggregate housing
Indian Ocean Tsunami 2004	2008	Quality data: 6 villages (case study) Volume data: 60 villages, 1600 people	SC is indispensable for disaster recovery Strong ties bring about the problem of excluding other members (lowest caste, women, elderly)
Hurricane Katrina 2005	2006	Unit: Zip code District 115 Proxy variable of SC: Voting rate of presidential election	SC is important for solving the NIMBY problem SC is the role of private insurance Multi-type SC provides resilience

Source: Aldrich, Daniel P. (2012), created from Chaps. 3 4, 5, 6, and 7
Note: SC in the table indicates social capital

The recovery level of the population after the Tokyo Earthquake of 1923 was greatly different for each district. In the elections of 1922 and 1933, districts with high voting rates and many demonstration marches showed resilience. The reconstruction from the Kobe Earthquake in 1995 shows that SC is important for the recovery of the population. Furthermore, the population growth rate of districts with a large number of NPOs established is much larger than those with few NPOs established. And in regions rich in SCs, they responded to fires with firefighting cooperation immediately after the earthquake. However, in the area where there is no cooperation, there was no joint activity of the residents at the site where neighbouring homes were destroyed by the fire.

In the Indian Ocean Tsunami in 2004, it was shown that villages with stronger bonding and linking were more resilient than villages without SC. In a village with residents' organisations, effective cooperation with NGOs and governments has ensured food, evacuation sites, support status, and so on. Regions without such an organisation were left behind on the map of recovery. However, a strong bond among certain members brings about the elimination of some major groups (Dalits, women, senior citizens). Standard disaster assistance procedures focus on repairing physical infrastructure damage, but SC is essential for disaster recovery.

The four cases differ from each other, but the areas rich in SC show that the recovery from the crisis has been realized efficiently and effectively through collaborative work and activities, and SC has shown the mechanism for providing resilience as follows.

(a) The deep bond of the SC functions as private insurance and promotes mutual support after the disaster.
(b) Deep social unity will support collective actions to solve the problem.
(c) Strong social ties strengthen the voices of survivors and reduce the possibility of leaving the district.

2.3.2 Human Contribution and Resilience

Reason (2008) talked about human involvement in both safety and resilience, stating that 'although most catastrophes are caused by unsafe human behaviour, on the other hand, it is also important that adaptations and compensations of human behaviour have brought the troubled system back from brink of disaster'. From the viewpoint of a human being who causes a lapse, he pointed out three points: a psychological mechanism in which human error and violating behaviour occur, a mechanism of occurrence of an organisational accident, and a change in viewpoint in accident investigation. From the viewpoint of a human being that saves the crisis, he pointed out two points: the case of surviving the crisis (military, aeronautical, medical, etc.) and the importance of looking at humans as 'a crisis saving hero'.

2.3.2.1 Personal Carefulness and Collective Carefulness

From the standpoint of recognizing humans as a potential danger, recognition and countermeasures of problems on the system are taken. System administrators believe that increasing the consistency of standard procedures, automation, and human behaviour and improving the consistency of system performance are solutions to undesirable variability, since it is important to make accident or incident reporting systems that work well.

However, it is also due to human flexibility (timely correction, fine adjustment, adaptation, etc.) that an incomplete system can be maintained in an unstable and fluctuating world. It is important to pay attention to the possibility of unforeseen events that might occur, find the possibility before finding accurate results, accurately grasp the possibility, and share the mental attitude necessary for recovery throughout the organisation; it is recognized as essential. In other words, it is shown that it is important to recognize that collective mindfulness and 'reporting culture' play an important role. The important elements of organisation resilience are in the group's carefulness, and it is said that maintaining intelligent wariness requires 'attentiveness' in individuals and groups.

2.3.2.2 Balance Between System Model and Person Model

Reason (2008) emphasizes the viewpoint of human beings able to save the crisis (to regard a human being as a hero) but also points out its adverse effects. For example, medical practice is 'manual work' and there are many possibilities for errors. In addition, solving problems on the spot poses a harmful effect; in some cases, the solution is not found in reporting the system's problems to those who should attempt to solve it, as this misses the opportunity to actually improve the system and can be seen as a sign of deterioration in the safety condition.

There are three problems in terms of the organisation: ① normalization of deviance, ② doing too much with too little, and ③ forgetting to be afraid. Restoration of a model that considers humans as a potential danger (system model) reduces fluctuations over models expecting a hero (person model) due to countermeasures focused on human errors (automation, check system, etc.). Although it cannot be set to zero defects, in order to increase resilience, it is necessary to restore the balance between the system model and person model and to build a system resistant to adverse effects.

2.3.2.3 Requirements for Highly Resilient and Secure Organisations

The job of the administrator is supposed to be to fix the system in the safety zone and make an amendment to offset the force to withdraw. Also, if proper correction fails, it will be out of the safety zone temporarily. Therefore, it is also necessary to simultaneously apply the same magnitude of correction to the external force in the opposite direction (simultaneity principle) and to make an appropriate correction in a timely manner. Furthermore, in order to make appropriate corrections, it is necessary to understand the ability to predict the occurrence of perturbation and factors that cause perturbation. Therefore, from the viewpoint of RE, the need for the following three abilities is mentioned:

(a) Anticipate: knowing what to expect
(b) Pay attention to: knowing what to search for
(c) Respond: knowing what to do

Risk prediction is the essence of resilience and is an inherent ability to enable an organisation to maintain or reacquire a dynamically stable state. As the avoidance of false decisions, resilience is the ability to adapt oneself to recognize and cope with unexpected disturbances. In addition, monitoring and managing the changing boundary conditions of the design basis event range is to understand how the system adapts to the disturbance in the environment. The characteristics of the system contributing to resilience are considered as follows:

(a) Buffer capacity: The size and type of confusion that can be absorbed/adapted without decisively damaging the structure.
(b) Flexibility and rigidity: Ability for the system to reconfigure itself in response to external changes and pressure.
(c) Margin: Degree to which the characteristic limit is close or unstable.
(d) Tolerance: If the system is near the boundary, will it be a graceful degradation with increasing stress or pressure or will it collapse rapidly if it exceeds adaptive capacity?

RE provides a supportive approach to the cognitive process that reconstructs an organisation's model of the issue of how to ensure safety before an accident occurs. Therefore, it is necessary to develop characteristics such as buffer, flexibility, instability, tolerance, and evaluation as indicators of factors contributing to resilience. In order to actively manage risks at the stage before actual results are obtained, it is necessary to know when to relax demand for productivity indicators and objectives related to efficiency, that is, when to make a trade-off type of decision.

Furthermore, Reason (2008) proposes the following method on the grounds that it should provide a method to adjust the balance between the short-term target set and the medium- to long-term target set.

First step: Develop tools that can monitor boundaries, namely, the competitive power (such as productivity) in the uncertain state that was considered in the design stage and the disturbance that is unlikely at the design stage, which is likely to move the system out of the design standard event.

Second step: If monitoring is able to recognize signs of unpredictable disturbances, such as consuming or diverting the resilient resources of the system, measures can be taken to reinforce the resilience of the system.

RE's challenge is to seek measures to maintain, improve, and re-establish resiliency in situations where buffers are degraded, safety margins have become unstable, processes have become rigid, and tightening has become severe. It may be said that this focuses on avoidance of control loss rather than recovery from control loss.

2.3.3 Building Resilience

Various methods are proposed for resilience building according to the object. In psychiatry, resilience is regarded as correspondence to trauma. Good self-esteem and social support are identified as factors promoting health and peace. Kato (2009) mentioned resilience factors that make it hard to receive PTSD and that contribute to recovery, such as optimism, altruism, sense of mission, social support with others, and receiving some kind of training. In addition, Aldrich (2012) focused on the resilience of communities in the midst of recovery from disaster and showed the results of analyses indicating that SC's role is important.

Reason (2008) views resilience as the ability to steer the organisational activity to navigate near the area where accidents can happen, always keeping it outside the dangerous area. That is, resilience is assumed to be a dynamic steering process, and the following capabilities are required:

(a) Sensitivity and high cognitive ability of the area where the organisation is in the danger zone
(b) Ability to respond promptly and effectively even if a signal of approach to a dangerous area or a danger of reality is detected, even if it is not predicted or unknown

It points out the need to develop characteristics such as buffer, flexibility, instability, tolerance, and evaluation index as factors contributing to resilience.

Zolli and Healy (2012) say that resilience requirements, such as resilience characteristics and necessary conditions, include avoiding dangerous circumstances, minimization of damage, and a short recovery period. This is similar to the three elements of RE (the ability to prevent bad things, the ability to prevent bad things from getting worse, and the ability to recover from bad things that have happened). Also, it is indispensable to avoid dangerous circumstances, to protect the damage, and to restore quickly from the damage. In summary, enhancing resilience means strengthening resistance so that it will not leave a favourable condition and adaptability (the ability to adapt to the change of situation while attaining self-goal) to unforeseen circumstances.

Therefore, building resilience means improving the ability of individuals and systems influenced by the environment to remain in the safety zone at all times and the ability to return to the safety zone by monitoring the approach to the grey zone. If you temporarily leave the safety zone, building resilience is to accumulate the ability to escape from the grey zone and danger zone and return to the safety zone (Fig. 2.3).

In order to remain in the safety zone during changes in the environment, we need to be adaptable, that is, to be less susceptible to changes and to increase resistance.

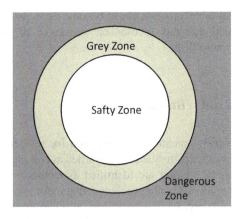

Fig. 2.3 Resilience and freedom from danger

For this, it is possible to respond by strengthening and utilizing the buffer function, absorbing the shock, expanding the tolerance, maintaining the function inherently, and adapting to the environment.

When approaching or leaving the grey zone, it is necessary to judge whether it is desirable to return to the safety zone or to seek a new equilibrium (reconstruction for function maintenance) instead. In this case, cognitive ability, predictability, and judgement power are necessary; in other words, it is possible to recognize and predict the influence from change by the extent of deviation from the safety zone, the degree of risk, etc., including the feasibility of whether it is better to return to the present state or move to a new equilibrium. Potential to predict and judge the situation including feasibility is required.

From the viewpoint of resilience against changes in the environment, the following three countermeasures are considered.

(a) Resistance: Enhancement of allowable capacity. Reduction of influence from change by utilizing buffer function.
(b) Adaptation: Absorb shock, respond to change, and maintain function inherently.
(c) Conversion: Rebuild the system so that the objective can be achieved and respond to the new environment.

Based on the above, the requirements of the mechanism to ensure resilience are as follows. In the case of individuals, both mind and body are balanced. In the case of an organisation, it is necessary to predict in advance the degree of the influence of the change on the environment, prepare plans such as countermeasures for minimizing the influence (disaster reduction), and exhibit recovery behaviour from the influence. In other words, current situation recognition and prior planning are important.

2.4 Conclusion

With regard to resilience, this chapter examined the transition of concepts and presented examples of what is necessary to increase resilience. Additionally, the chapter searched for hints on how to build resilience. After reviewing concepts in multiple areas of application, this chapter examined what individuals and organisations need to do to improve resilience. Resilience concepts are used in various fields but are based on the two aspects of original function continuity and recovery when facing environmental changes.

In the field of psychiatry, along with the risk factor of PTSD, the 'defence factor' became more noticeable, and resilience factors such as optimism, altruism, having social support with others, having a sense of mission, and receiving some kind of training were recognized. In modern medicine, it is pointed out that building resilience is an important point of treatment since there is no established treatment for PTSD at this time.

The examination of the result of the recovery process from the disaster showed that SC is the recovery engine. Regions rich in SC have achieved recovery from the given crisis efficiently and effectively through collaborative work and activities.

The concept of RE is becoming more sophisticated through its application to fields requiring improved measures for safety issues in areas such as air traffic control and medical safety. This chapter focused on the process, especially adaptability to change. RE provides a supportive approach to the cognitive process that reconstructs an organisation's model of the issue of how to create safety before an accident occurs. Therefore, it is necessary to develop characteristics such as buffer, flexibility, instability, tolerance, and evaluation as indicators of factors contributing to resilience. RE's challenge is to seek measures to build, maintain, improve, and re-establish resiliency in situations where buffers are degraded, safety margins become unstable, processes become rigid, and tightening becomes severe. It may be said that this focuses on avoidance of control loss, rather than recovery from control loss.

Building resilience means that individuals and systems influenced by the environment are gaining the ability to stay in the safety zone at all times, the ability to monitor the approach to the grey zone and return to the safety zone, or to temporarily leave the safety zone. It is the accumulation of the ability to escape from the grey zone and the danger zone and return to the safety zone. Based on the extent of the deviation from the safety zone, the degree of risk, etc., we will recognize and predict the influence from the change and predict the feasibility, including whether to return to the present situation or move to a new equilibrium. The ability to have sound judgement is required; it is necessary to predict in advance the degree of the influence on the change of the environment and to prepare plans such as countermeasures for minimizing the influence (reduction) and recovery behaviour from the influence.

References

Aldrich DP (2012) Building resilience: social capital in post-disaster recovery. University of Chicago Press, Chicago

Den R (2009) Resilience study in PTSD. In: Kato S (ed) Resilience new paradigm of modern psychiatry. Kanehara, pp 75–92 (in Japanese)

Folke C, Carpenter SR, Walker B, Scheffer M, Chapin T, Rockstrom J (2010) Resilience thinking: integrating resilience, adaptability, and transformability. Ecol Soc 15(4):20

Handoh IC, Kubota J (2012) Resilience conceptual theory. In: Kohsaka R (ed) Regional resilience. Shimizukobundo, pp 51–74 (in Japanese)

Holling CS (1973) Resilience and stability of ecological system. Annu Rev Ecol Syst 4:1–23

Hollnagel E, Woods DD, Leveson N (2006) Resilience engineering: concepts and precepts. CRC Press, Boca Raton

Kato S (2009) Significance of the concept of resilience in modern psychiatry. In: Kato S (ed) Resilience new paradigm of modern psychiatry. Kanehara, pp 1–23 (in Japanese)

Kato S (2012) Resilience culture creation. Kanehara (in Japanese)

Kawamoto H (2012) Expansion of possibility of experience and resilience. In: Kato S (ed) Resilience culture creation. Kanehara, pp 154–169 (in Japanese)

Kimura F (2016) Building resilience. *Tushinkyoikuburonsyu*, 18: 50–66 (in Japanese)

Kohsaka R (2012) Resilience from ecology to socio-economic field. In: Kohsaka R (ed) Regional resilience. Shimizukobundo, pp 16–33 (in Japanese)

Ohshima K, Abe Y (2009) History and present status of resilience concept – focusing on French area. In: Kato S (ed) Resilience new paradigm of modern psychiatry. Kanehara, pp 25–49 (in Japanese)

Otsuka K (2012) Aspects of culture and resilience. In: Kato S (ed) Resilience culture creation. Kanehara, pp 16–29 (in Japanese)

Putnum R (1995) Bowling alone: America's declining social capital. J Democr 6(1):65–78

Reason J (2008) The human contribution: unsafe acts, accidents, and heroic recoveries. CRC Press

Zolli A, Healy AM (2012) Resilience. Headline Publishing, London

Part II
Case Study and Issues

Chapter 3
Sustainable Activities for Rural Development

Shingo Yokoyama

Abstract In Japan which is heading straight to an ageing society with a declining birth rate, population decline is a serious issue. Many rural districts are advancing efforts which are different from tourism for attracting urban dwellers to rural areas. The focus of this paper is the examples of rural revitalisation through "exchange with a particular purpose".

The first case is support for rural districts by businesses. The important key for guaranteeing regional sustainability is in building a win-win business relationship, as rural communities and corporations work together to rediscover local resources and make full use of each other's forte, rather than a one-sided relationship where rural communities provide opportunities for farming to corporations as a service.

The second case is support for rural districts by young people from the cities. The key feature of the case example is that young people from cities not only come to the area to secure a place for enjoying mountain activity but are engaged to no small extent in the sustainability of the rural region.

Challenges such as the increase in disused farmlands and desolation of the forests caused by the ageing population, declining birth rate and depopulation can transform to appealing resources for city dwellers (workers).

For people living in cities and corporations, activities which let them feel the soil and commune with nature hold new hidden values such as the refreshment of the body and mind, formation of intercommunity and the joy of creating a place for shared enjoyment.

Keywords Rural revitalisation · Corporate Farm · Disused farmlands · Mountain activity · Maintain and Run

---

S. Yokoyama (✉)
Research Division, Institute for Areal Studies, Foundation, Sagamihara-City, Japan
e-mail: yokoyama@ias.or.jp

© Springer Nature Singapore Pte Ltd. 2019
C. Asahi (ed.), *Building Resilient Regions*, New Frontiers in Regional Science: Asian Perspectives 35, https://doi.org/10.1007/978-981-13-7619-1_3

3.1 Current State of Rural Districts

3.1.1 Future Population of Japan

According to the national census conducted in 2015, the population of Japan as of 1 October 2015 was 127,095,000, which was 962,000 less than in the previous survey in 2010. For comparison, it was the first time for it to have decreased since the national census began in 1920 (Statistic Bureau, Ministry of Internal Affairs and Communications 2015).

According to the estimates by the National Institute of Population and Social Security Research, the population of Japan is to continue to decrease, with the birth rate in the median case to be below 100,000,000 in 2053, and is expected to be 88,077,000 50 years later in 2065.

In a likewise manner, the changes in population by prefecture released by the National Institute of Population and Social Security Research in March 2013 indicate the total population of all prefectures in 2040 to be less than in 2010. The findings also show that the proportion of the entire population in Tokyo and the surrounding areas will be larger than the total population of the rest of Japan (National Institute of Population and Social Security Research 2017) (Fig. 3.1).

The trend in the future population by municipalities is even more remarkable.

In the national capital region, the Chukyo, the Kinki and major cities, there are relatively many districts where the population has levelled off or even decreased by about 20%. However, the population in some municipalities in places such as

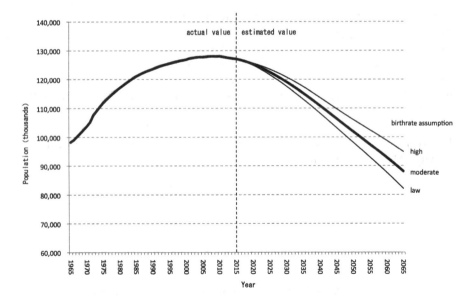

Fig. 3.1 Changes in the entire population of Japan. (Ref. National Institute of Population and Social Security Research 2017)

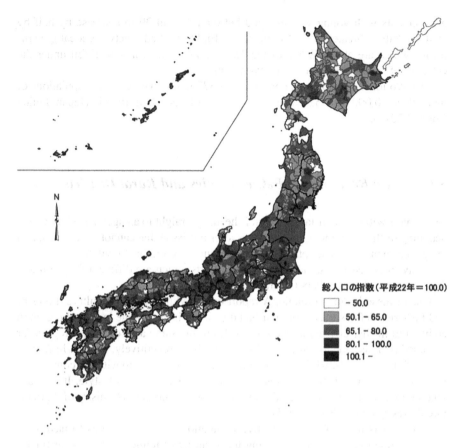

Fig. 3.2 Vital index of 2040 (with 2010 set as 100). Note: since future trends and changes in population by municipalities in Fukushima Prefecture are extremely hard to predict due to the Great East Japan Earthquake which occurred in March 2011, the future population estimate relates to the whole prefecture. (Ref. National Institute of Population and Social Security Research. 2013)

Hokkaido, Tohoku, Kii Peninsula and Shikoku is expected to be 50–60% of the population in 2010, and some are even below 50% (National Institute of Population and Social Security Research 2013) (Fig. 3.2).

3.1.2 Cities Threatened with Extinction

In 2014, a private research institute "Japan Policy Council" Population Meeting announced local governments which it expected to struggle with their operation, maintenance of social security and securing of employment due to a decline in population caused by the ever-declining birth rate. Specifically, it defined local governments with young women aged between 20 and 39 to decrease by half by 2040 as "cities threatened with extinction". Eight hundred ninety-six local governments, which are about 49.8% of the 1800 municipalities in Japan, fell under the category of "cities threatened with extinction".

The 896 local governments comprised of 373 municipalities with populations of more than 10,000 and 523 with populations of less than 10,000 (Japan Policy Council 2014).

3.1.3 New Relationship Between Cities and Rural Districts

As we have witnessed, in Japan which is heading straight to an ageing society with a declining birth rate, population decline is a serious issue that cannot be avoided, and the government is also adopting various measures for regional revitalisation.

Many rural districts are also advancing efforts which are different from tourism for attracting urban dwellers to rural areas.

One of these is dual domicile. A report by the Ministry of Agriculture, Forestry and Fisheries defines it as "For an urban dweller to have a home in a rural region in addition to his/her city home. He/she resides in the same area of a rural region for extended periods (one to three months), regularly or repetitively, to meet his/her or his/her family's needs, whilst maintaining a certain relationship with the community in question, as one of the measures to achieve his/her diverse lifestyle. It includes second homes but does not include summer or winter homes" (Ministry of Agriculture, Forestry and Fisheries 2005).

In fact, it is hard for the productive population working in cities to have dual domiciles due to constraints, including the securing of homes, expenses for travelling from the city centre, telework and stay-home work systems. However, there are cases of retired couples in dual domiciles living in farms with residences attached to them, such as the Kleingarten developed by local governments.

A concept called non-resident population appeared against the idea of the resident population, and the previously mentioned dual domicile is also a form of nonresident. Tourists are also treated as a sort of non-resident, but the style of tourism is changing from one that is for enjoying the scenery and shopping to one which focuses on a goal, such as experience and learning. Therefore, the conflicting ideas of the resident population and non-resident population do not fit in.

The focus of this paper is the examples of rural revitalisation through "exchange with a particular purpose". Tourism is transforming from an age where city consumers merely pass through rural districts to enjoy a holiday to a time where they engage in activities for finding the path to mutual progress as they become deeply involved with the local lifestyles, customs and creation of new businesses (Fig. 3.3).

This movement can be found not only in Japan but also abroad. For example, the city of Copenhagen declared the "end of tourism" in February 2016, to which the Ambassador of Denmark posted a comment on Facebook.

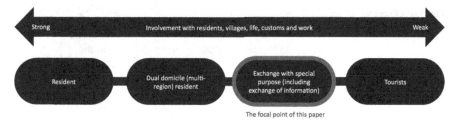

Fig. 3.3 Relationship between cities and farming communities and their forms

> **The New Tourism Strategy for Copenhagen Has Been Announced**
> Normally, governments and regions do a lot of PR to attract many tourists. However, the Copenhagen's new tourism strategy is titled "The End of Tourism".
>
> Until now, a vast number of consumers enjoyed tourism which was segmented into categories such as business and holiday, city and countryside and culture and cycling. The era of marketing tourism with beautiful photographs of attractive tourist sites has ended. The era for the government tourism bureau, our bureau, to suggest tourist sites in a condescending tone to consumers is also over.
>
> Tourism should be something that locals, businesses and tourists create together. Copenhagen will become a victim of tourists unless tourism improves the quality of the life of the people who live in the city. We cannot allow locals burdened by the waves of tourists that arrive due to mass media coverage and PR. Furthermore, treating tourists not as mere tourists but as temporary residents will make them a member of the local community and let them contribute to the community. If an experience on the street of Copenhagen could inspire tourists, it could potentially create a business which will grow from that experience.
>
> https://www.facebook.com/EmbassyDenmark/posts/1206014936101694

3.2 Businesses to Support Rural Districts

3.2.1 The Idea of Corporate Farm

In rural districts where depopulation is advancing, it is necessary to increase the non-resident population between cities and farming communities, in combination with the promotion of settlement, and city businesses count as one of the players.

The idea of farming communities and businesses working together to revitalise local communities is modelled on South Korea's "New Rural Community and New

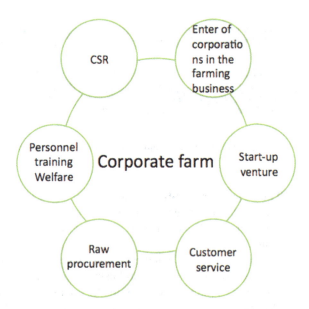

Fig. 3.4 Objectives of the Corporate Farm

Agricultural Cooperative Campaign", which was launched in 2004 as a national policy. In Japan, Shizuoka Prefecture began its "One Company, One Rural Village Shizuoka" in 2005.

Hokuto City in Yamanashi Prefecture, which will be introduced later, is promoting cooperative projects between farming communities and businesses, titled "Corporate Farm". Its objectives are to train corporate personnel, provide welfare, exercise CSR as well as procure raw materials, provide customer service, start-up ventures and have corporations enter the farming business (Fig. 3.4).

The significant difference between the Corporate Farm and hands-on farming experienced by tourists is that the former can ensure a certain number of visitors in the same period, every year. For rural districts that receive visitors, the income generated from tourists' spending on food and accommodation produces a positive effect on the local economy. Aside from that, corporate employees and clients would help with the work of cultivating land on abandoned farms as a cooperative project, and ideas from corporations can increase the potential for development of new products, i.e. produce and agricultural products. There is another advantage in that the Corporate Farm may provide a chance for the families and friends of corporate employees and clients to become repeat visitors to the farming communities.

For corporations, the advantages include the sense of unity that is fostered between employees through farming. The employees will come to understand one another's attributes and element through the division of farm work, and creativity will be nurtured through the stimulation of the five senses as they feel the soil instead of engaging in desk work.

3.2.2 Case Example of Hokuto City, Yamanashi

Hokuto City is at the northernmost tip of Yamanashi Prefecture with a population of 45,111 in 2015. The population estimated for 2040 is 32,880, and the city is one of the cities threatened with extinction.

It is about 120 km from Tokyo, which is about 2 h on the expressway.

From 2004, the local non-profit organisation "Egao Tsunagete" has been matchmaking corporate needs with the resources of its farming communities, and it has launched a project called "Corporate Farm" for which corporations and farming communities work together for the efficient utilisation of farm resources.

3.2.2.1 Resolving the Issue of Abandoned Farmlands, Rice Cultivation on Terraced Paddies, Sake-Making, and Commodification of Wood Thinned from Forests

Since 2008, the Mitsubishi Estate group of companies have been engaged in the "Sky and Earth Project" as part of their CSR activities, based in Masutomi Village, Hokuto City, Yamanashi Prefecture. Masutomi Village is a super-aged community with a population of 490, of which 66% are over 65. Fifty-two percent of farmlands are derelict (as of April 2016). From July 2008, the employees of the Mitsubishi Estate group of companies have been working to resolve the issue of abandoned fields and reclaim paddies (2800 m^2) and farm fields (1600 m^2) (as of March 2016).

From May 2010, the employees were joined by people working in the Marunouchi area to plant and harvest rice and developed a junmai sake made with rice they had harvested called "Marunouchi" in collaboration with a local sake brewery. The junmai sake "Marunouchi" they produce is sold in restaurants and shops in the Marunouchi area, of which 2150 were sold in 2011, the first year of production. Subsequently, 3000–4000 have been sold each year, which has contributed significantly to building the brand and expanding the market.

Since October 2008, the Mitsubishi Estate group of companies have been conducting forest thinning tours for its employees. They have also been giving forest thinning sessions and workshop for examining the utilisation of domestically produced timber for the forestry industry to share its challenges with the employees and consider how to use forest resources.

As part of the efforts, in August 2011, Yamanashi Prefecture, Mitsubishi Estate Company, Mitsubishi Estate Home and "Egao Tsunagete" concluded a partnership agreement for a sustainable and sound growth of the prefecture's forestry industry. They have agreed to increase the use of timber by working closely together to promote dissemination and education, coordinating production, supply and sales, boosting the strength of the Yamanashi timber brand and sending a message about its value.

As one of the tangible results of the partnership agreement, the FSC-certified (The Forest Stewardship Council's international certification for "eco-friendly products deriving from appropriately managed forests") construction materials made with thinned and undersized larch from Yamanashi are now accepted as standards for building two-storey homes by Mitsubishi Estate Home.

This is a good example where a local non-profit organisation and a corporation have worked together to reclaim and utilise local resources such as abandoned farmlands and timber from forest thinning which were not used efficiently. The tangible products and merchandise produced have expanded sales and created a brand.

Fig. 3.5a Terraced rice paddies before reclamation

Fig. 3.5b Terraced rice paddies after reclamation

3 Sustainable Activities for Rural Development 45

3.2.2.2 Cultivation of Native Variety Raw Material and Development of Company Products

There is a famous Yamanashi speciality called "Shingenmochi". "Kinseiken" in Hokuto City, Yamanashi, produces and sells them.

From 2012, Kinseiken began cultivating a local, native variety of green soybean, using a Corporate Farm by "Egao Tsunagete". Green soybean is the primary ingredient of roasted soy flour utilised in the previously mentioned Shingenmochi, and all Kinseiken's divisions including sales and marketing are working alternately in the field, besides the production unit which produces the confectionery, under the guidance of "Egao Tsunagete".

This attempt is significant in that every employee of the confectionery maker, not only those in production but sales and marketing, comes to love their company's product by physically getting involved in the process of making the primary ingredient of the company's product. It gives them the confidence to explain when selling to customers that "they had made the products themselves".

3.2.3 Summary

What the three case examples in this paper share is that they have produced significant advantages for the corporations, as they improved staff abilities and intercommunications and developed new products by the categories of business, even with cases which initially began as employee welfare or CSR.

The important key for guaranteeing regional sustainability is in building a win-win business relationship, as rural communities and corporations work together to rediscover local resources and make full use of each other's forte, rather than a one-sided relationship where rural communities provide opportunities for farming to corporations as a service.

3.3 Young People from the Cities to Support Rural Villages

3.3.1 Case Example of Efforts Made by Minami Alps City, Yamanashi Prefecture

Minami Alps City is in the western part of Yamanashi Prefecture with a population of 70,828 as of 2015. The population estimated for 2040 is 63,600. It is about 120 km from Tokyo, which is about the same distance as the previously mentioned Hokuto City. It is about 2 h on the expressway.

The west side of the city is mountainous with a series of 3000 m class mountains, including the second tallest mountain in Japan, Mt. Kitadake, and the 2052 m Mt.

Kushigata is on the east side of Minami Alps. Forests, fruit orchards and cities are to the east of the mountainous area.

The Minami Alps Mountain Bike Club launched as a private organisation in January 2016 which began its activities in 2013. It is a subsidiary organisation of an incorporated non-profit organisation "Minami Alps Sanroku Iyashi no Sato Zukuri", which tackles local issues with derelict farmlands, provides hands-on farming sessions and makes wine.

3.3.2 The Concept of "Maintain and Run"

Mountain biking was hugely popular in Japan in the 1980s and 1990s. Although there were many enthusiasts across Japan, there was friction with landowners and other mountain users, including hikers and nature conservation organisations, which resulted in many cases where biking in forests was restricted.

To dispel such senses of crisis and alienation, the Minami Alps Mountain Bike Club began the "Maintain and Run" initiative where they first maintained the MTB trails.

Minami Alps City had many old forest roads for transporting timber from forests, but the roads became desolated as time passed. "Maintain and Run" is an attempt at an efficient use of the forest resource by using the disused forest roads as MTB trails.

Fig. 3.6 Maintaining disused roads by The Minami Alps Mountain Bike Club

The Minami Alps Mountain Bike Club mainly consists of young people living in cities. They use their days off to visit Minami Alps City over 50 times a year, and the annual number of visitors is between 350 and 400.

The Minami Alps Mountain Bike Club is proactively engaged in maintaining disused roads and hiking trails, holding MTB events and tours for beginners on MTB trails, holding bike races for intermediate and advanced bikers, participating in local festivals and helping with farm work.

Their efforts are not based on "doing what they want and asserting their views" but on the idea to "take the lead in solving the problems in the community" so that they are trusted and needed by the community.

3.3.3 Participation in Village Events

The ageing of the population, extremely low birth rate and depopulation are rapidly progressing due to the rural exodus in many Japanese villages. They have caused an increase in the number of abandoned farmlands and have had a significant impact on the forestry industry, including the deterioration of the forests.

The decline in village population also causes problems in operating community efforts such as local cleaning activities, maintenance of water facilities and festivals.

The Minami Alps Mountain Bike Club sends over ten members each year to provide preparatory and operational support for village festivals, and some members are entrusted with the ceremonial dance performance during the celebrations. They are contributing significantly to the revival of the festivals which were on the precipice of extinction.

When a member of the club moved to a marginal village with only four households, and the Minami Alps Mountain Bike Club started to meet at the village, it generated communication in the community and made the area cheerful.

From 2017, the Minami Alps Mountain Bike Club will lease disused farmlands to cultivate and conserve the landscape. Now, they grow grapes for winemaking and spread the word about the region and the wines.

3.3.4 Effect of Measures Against Bird and Animal Damage

In recent years, damages to crops caused by wild birds and animals have become severe across Japan. The crop damage in 2014 was 19.134 billion JPY in Japan, of which 6.525 billion JPY was caused by deer, 5.478 billion JPY by wild boars, 1.732 billion by crows and 1.306 billion by monkeys.

Damages to crops caused by wild beasts have also increased in Minami Alps City, which was 3.480 billion JPY as of 2007.

Fig. 3.7 Operational support for village festivals

Fig. 3.8 Harvesting work

One of the factors for the increase in the damages in agricultural and forestry lands is the decrease in economic activities in the mountains, i.e. the decline of the forestry industry and the reduction in the use of fuelwood in agriculture.

As mentioned above, the Minami Alps Mountain Bike Club in Minami Alps are leading to restore disused forest roads as MTB trails.

Using the mountains differently from the old ways of agriculture and forestry creates a buffer between the mountains, forests and villages, and it works as a deterrent against wild beasts from entering the villages.

Fig. 3.9 Sensor camera locations

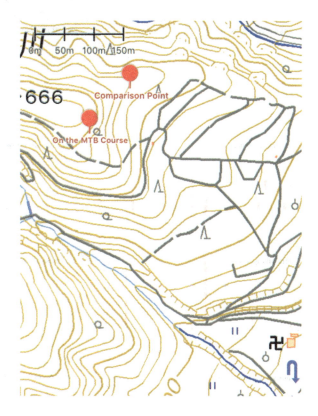

Between June and October 2016, the club installed two sensor cameras, one on the MTB course which they had developed in a forest in Minami Alps and one on a ridgeway (comparison point) with similar terrains. They conducted a demonstration experiment to see the effect the use of the MTB trail has on the sighting of wild beasts (Figs. 3.9 and 3.10).

The following traits were found:

(a) Many sightings of deer on the MTB course and comparison point as of June 2016 when the course was not fully in use. There were also many sightings of monkeys in the comparison point.
(b) In July 2016, sightings of wild beasts dramatically decreased (though monkeys were sighted) due to the increase in the use of the course.
(c) In August 2016, there was almost no sighting of deer and monkeys, except squirrels, Japanese martens and meles, as the course was frequently used.
(d) In October 2016, there was no sighting of deer or monkeys as hunters and hounds used the old roads, in addition to the MTB course.
(e) It has become clear that whilst the use of the old roads by the MTB Club, hunters, hikers and forestry workers controls the sighting of deer and monkeys up to a point, the sighting increased when they did not use the roads for prolonged periods.

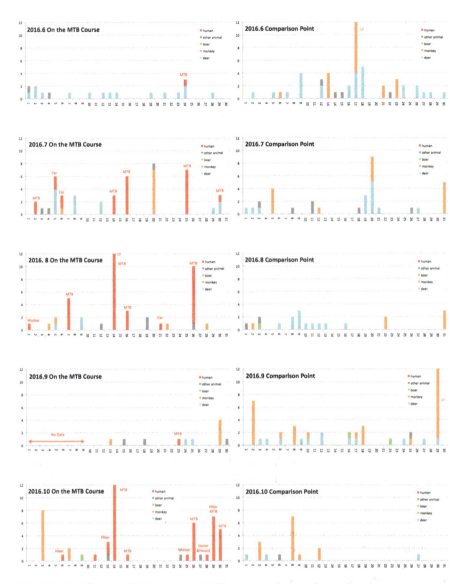

Fig. 3.10 Sightings of wild beasts on the MTB course and comparison point

3.3.5 Summary

The key feature of the case example of Minami Alps City is that young people from cities not only come to the area to secure a place for enjoying mountain biking but are engaged to no small extent in the sustainability of the rural region. They maintain deserted forest roads and participate in the festivals and events of the fading village.

3 Sustainable Activities for Rural Development

Also, it is also worthy to note that their use of the mountain as their MTB trail course may provide a possibility for alleviating the measures against bird and animal damage the villages have suffered in recent years.

For a city dweller, a rich natural environment about 2 h by car or train is very appealing, but some locals live there. To merely use nature, ignoring the villagers, would only cause objections and friction. There are advantages for both sides when visitors provide as much cooperation as possible and become trusted by the locals to deal with the various challenges posed by the ageing of the population, declining birth rate and depopulation in rural regions. It would also lead to revitalising the rural areas.

3.4 To Change a Crisis into Opportunity

3.4.1 Change the Way We See Regional Resources

The first challenges of Japan's rural villages are the ageing of the population, declining birth rate and depopulation. Many local governments aim to increase I-U-turn visitor population to tackle these problems, but that is hard to achieve straightforwardly in reality.

On the other hand, challenges such as the increase in disused farmlands and desolation of the forests caused by the ageing population, declining birth rate and depopulation can transform to appealing resources for city dwellers (workers), once they change the way they see things slightly.

Abandoned farmlands do not generate any income for farmers but rather foment damages caused by animals. However, for people living in cities and corporations, activities which let them feel the soil and commune with nature hold new hidden values such as the refreshment of the body and mind, formation of intercommunity and the joy of creating a place for shared enjoyment.

3.4.2 Boost Values by Increasing Participants

In this way, there are many rural villages with unfavourable resources that come to possess significant values for their residents once they alter their perception. It is necessary to increase the number of participants in the activities to discover and enhance their values.

Measures to increase tourists conventionally are not bad ideas. However, as in the case of corporate employees and clients, and the Minami Alps Mountain Bike Club, for participants visiting a region with a purpose, regional resources of a village are not mere materials for consumption but are something that can extend the life of their function. That is why they have the potential to become proactive participants which do not use the resources more than necessary but take full advantage of them in a sustainable manner.

Non-profit organisations play a significant role in both Hokuto and Minami Alps cities, with rural villages, city corporations and residents as key participants.

Nowadays, we often hear the term DMO as part of policies for attracting tourism. DMO is short for Destination Marketing Organisation or Destination Management Organisation. It is also important to position it as organisations responsible for the marketing and management of entire rural districts for rediscovering the local resources, revitalising rural regions and promoting the germination of new businesses, and not from the perspective of tourism policies.

References

Japan Policy Council (2014) Estimated population of municipalities based on population reproduction power. Available at: http://www.policycouncil.jp/pdf/prop03/prop03_1.pdf. Accessed 25 July 2017

Ministry of Agriculture, Forestry and Fisheries (2005) Survey on possibility of support for nature-rich residential area by semi-settling population

National Institute of Population and Social Security Research (2013) Future estimated population of region

National Institute of Population and Social Security Research (2017) Future estimated population of Japan

Statistic Bureau, Ministry of Internal Affairs and Communications (2015) National census

Chapter 4
Small Activities to Transmit Environmental and Cultural Resources: The Case of the Takasegawa River in Kyoto

Noriko Horie

Abstract Although Shimokiyamachi area is adjacent to the Kyoto downtown, it has maintained a peaceful atmosphere and environment with waterfowl on the Takasegawa River, which is an environmental and cultural resource. The residents that have led the area for many years are ageing, and regional participation by new residents has been insufficient. Therefore, volunteers formed an executive committee, recorded the memories of the important history that residents maintained about local environmental and cultural resources, and issued a small newspaper to share these memories. In addition, the committee developed riverbeds to increase enjoyment of the river environment and to promote interaction among new and old residents and visitors. This chapter presents the case of a small human network aimed at regional revitalization using a small newspaper to transmit regional memories and promote river resources for interaction while experiencing the river environment. Activities by volunteers' human networks for regional tasks are difficult to sustain because funds and systems are unreliable. However, because of population decline and ageing, the residents cannot support the region alone, and participation from outside the region is indispensable. To transmit the environmental and cultural resources of the region, it is necessary to continue to revitalize the area using the human network that includes residents and visitors.

Keywords Takasegawa River · Regional revitalization · Cultural transmission · Historical transmission · Riverbed events

4.1 Introduction

The Shimokiyamachi area is adjacent to Shijo Kawaramachi, the biggest downtown area of Kyoto City. Although Simokiyamachi is an area where tourism has recently increased, it maintains a peaceful environment of townhouses along the Takasegawa

---

N. Horie (✉)
Department of Public Policy, Faculty of Sociology, Bukkyo University, Kyoto, Japan
e-mail: horie@bukkyo-u.ac.jp

© Springer Nature Singapore Pte Ltd. 2019
C. Asahi (ed.), *Building Resilient Regions*, New Frontiers in Regional Science: Asian Perspectives 35, https://doi.org/10.1007/978-981-13-7619-1_4

River with a calm atmosphere and rich environment with waterfowl. However, the population that has been economically driving the area for many years is ageing, and although the community participation of new residents living in the condominiums is increasing remarkably, it is not always sufficient. Memories of relationships with the Takasegawa River, which is a precious environmental and cultural resource of the region, and the history of overcoming the landfill crisis through residents' opposition are not being transmitted. There are concerns about maintaining the environment, which has been well preserved to date (Fig. 4.1).

To respond to these issues and to revitalize the region, volunteers inside and outside the region formed an executive committee. First, the executive committee discovered and recorded the history of the Shimokiyamachi area and disseminated it through newspapers, aiming to preserve and transmit it. Second, the executive committee developed riverbeds in the Takasegawa River, planned events, and managed events for the new and established residents and visitors to interact, connect with the Takasegawa River, and share the value of the elegant local environment. The riverbed site is at the Takasegawa River in front of Bukkoji Park, which is the only small park in the area (Fig. 4.2).

Many research reports have considered regional revitalization using environmental and cultural resources, and many of them investigated the use of urban rivers and parks (e.g. Japan River Association 2016; Parks and Open Space Association of Japan 2012). There also are reports on regional revitalization in downtown areas (e. g. Sugiyama and Ito 2010) and on regional management of parks (e.g. Horie 2013). However, most of these studies are based on existing organizations and

Fig. 4.1 Shimokiyamachi area (small townhouses lined up along Takasegawa River)

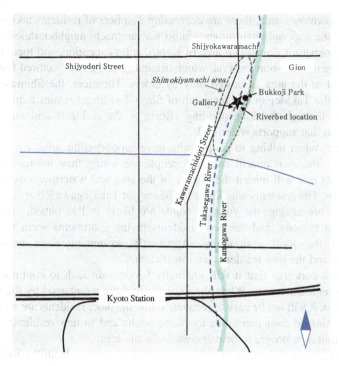

Fig. 4.2 Location of Shimokiyamachi area and Takasegawa River

administrators. An exception is Tajima et al. (2013), who focused on small-scale art projects, used a bottom-up approach and autonomous entrance structure by 'strangers' as a regional activation method, and assessed the relationship between the sustainability of activities and the communication structure. Small projects are effective for improving a region's appeal, and this type of effort is expected to increase in the future, although it is not easy to sustain. This paper presents the case of a small human network aimed at regional revitalization based on regional issues in an area adjacent to the biggest downtown area of Kyoto. In the balance of the paper, some evaluations are examined after the description of the details of the study.

4.2 Regional Issues and the Need for Countermeasures

In the past, the Takasegawa River supported the prosperity of Kyoto as the artery in the centre of Kyoto and the Fushimi port responsible for water transport, connecting Kyoto to Osaka via the Yodogawa River. After the transport function was lost, the river became and currently is a valuable environmental and cultural resource in the downtown area.

In the downtown area, there are decreasing numbers of residents taking responsibility for the regional environment. Shijo Kawaramachi neighbourhood, which is the most prosperous downtown area of Kyoto, is no exception, and there are some towns where the Jizo-bon Festival, which originally was a child-centred festival and major event in the area, is hosted only by elders. Therefore, the Shimokiyamachi area along the Takasegawa River south of Shijo-dori Street retains a quiet historic appearance through the long-standing efforts of the residents and maintains an environment that supports waterfowl.

However, when talking to people who have supported the area, we heard that, even in the Shimokiyamachi area, the people are losing their influence over the young adults that will inherit the history of the area and waterfowl environmental preservation. The residents who know the history of Takasegawa River and preserve the scenery are ageing, the younger adults are likely to live outside the area for employment reasons, and the new residents in the apartments seem to have no interest in the local community. Apparently, communications between the established and the new residents are insufficient.

There are concerns that it will gradually become difficult to continue hosting traditional regional events. When the local atmosphere maintained by the residents has been lost, it will not be easy to recover. While the older residents are with us, it is urgent to transmit their memories to young adults and to new residents, and it is urgent to find new people to be responsible for the area.

The Takasegawa River has a history of overcoming three landfill crises through residents' oppositions. The interviews with people who were active in the area suggested that the enjoyable memories and rich experiences of playing in the Takasegawa River and the Kamogawa River encouraged them to act on behalf of the local environment and engage in town-planning activities.

The Takasegawa River, which was once a familiar playground for loach and fishing for children, has now become a sightseeing river. Although it is clean, beautiful, and elegant to look at, there are concerns that this regional environment cannot continue to be protected because, unlike the established residents, new residents have little experience playing in the Takasegawa River. To maintain the environment of the Takasegawa River, it is necessary for younger people and new residents to have fun, rich, and dense relationships with the Takasegawa River.

In response to this regional problem, the executive committee is trying a unique approach. Kyoto is not only an ancient city visited by many tourists; it also is an international exchange city, academic research city, and a cultural and artistic city where researchers, foreign students, and artists stay. Various visitors stroll around and they are a part of the landscape of the Shimokiyamachi area. There are numerous talented people in the area, including residents and people from outside the area who could support the area. We believe that the active participation of experts, students, and volunteers inside and outside the region would effectively and indispensably support the areas where residential leadership is decreasing.

Therefore, we are planning to transmit the area's environmental and cultural resources by recording the memories of the people of the area and disseminating them inside and outside of the area through a small newspaper. In addition, we also have developed a part of the riverbed where people can enjoy the Takasegawa River. On the riverbed, established and new residents of all ages can gather with visitors, artists, researchers, and students to share the peaceful and rich regional environment.

4.3 Content of Initiatives

Between March 2015 and March 2017, the *Takasegawa Kikimiru Shimbun* (hear and see newspaper) was established, the riverbed area Takasegawa Kikimizu Garden was established and began operations, information was transmitted using Internet social networking sites, and a human network was formed.

4.3.1 Takasegawa Kikimiru Shimbun (Fig. 4.3)

After the prelaunch issue of March 2015, *Takasegawa Kikimiru Shimbun* was irregularly issued seven times until March 2017, printing about 5000–10,000

Fig. 4.3 *Takasegawa Kikimiru Shimbun*

Table 4.1 Main contents of *Takasegawa Kikimiru Shimbun*

Issue	Issue date	Retro interview	Main content
Prelaunch issue	Mar 2015		Announcement of project start, event guidance, and retro interview notice
1	Jun 2015	Mr Seiji Inoue, Chairman of the Nagamatsu Autonomous Federation	Request for ideas for riverbed events, history of Takasegawa River, and Shinko festival (part of Gion Festival)
2	Aug 2015	Mr Akira Kaneko, President of Takasegawa River Hossyokai	Introduced the purpose and guidance of the riverbed event, Jizo of Shimokiyamachi
3	Oct 2015	Mr Hiroshi Tanaka, Chairman of the Kiyamachikai	Report on riverbed event and rewards, questionnaire results, Takasegawa music festival, riverbed rental information, and world archaeology conference
4	Mar 2016	Mr Masakazu Ymamamoto, Vice-Director of Kyoto City Archaeological Museum	Information on riverbed tea ceremonies, world archaeology conference information, and other event information
5	Aug 2016	Hanaougi Tayu, the highest rank traditional entertainer in Shimabara	Summer riverbed event, information on the world archaeology conference satellite venue event, and other events
6	Dec 2016	Mr Takuzo Murata, Head of the Nagamatsu fire department	Questionnaire results of summer riverbed event, Takasegawa Music Festival, Takasegawa Sculpture Exhibition, World Archaeological Congress, and so on
7	Mar 2017	Mr Goro Suminokura, descendant of a great man regarding the Takasegawa River	Exhibition report, questionnaire results, and event guide

copies per issue. The newspaper is printed on double-sided A3 paper, in colour, and folded in half. The main contents of the publications are shown in Fig. 4.3 and Table 4.1.

Members of the executive committee review the contents of the newspaper, and the person responsible for design and layout organizes the page on the computer for the printing company. Regarding distribution, the newspaper has been distributed by incorporating it with the *Kyoto Shimbun* in the area and by distributing it through local shops, stakeholders, relevant groups, and so on. *Takasegawa Kikimiru* is positioned as a tool for recording and transmitting the memories of the area. Specifically, we interviewed the residents about their associations with the Takasegawa River and how they have lived, and, under the title 'Retro Interview', we recorded their memories with illustrations and narratives. In addition, old photographs and other materials have been used to share the memories of the area, which has attracted interest.

4.3.2 Establish and Operate the Riverbed Takasegawa Kikimizu Garden

4.3.2.1 Location

The riverbed installation of *Takasegawa Kikimizu Garden* is at the Takasegawa River in front of Bukkoji Park, which is the only small park in the area. Bukkoji Park is on 957 square metres between the Kamogawa River and the Takasegawa River. Therefore, the executive committee arranged riverbed so that people can access it from a stairway in front of Bukkoji Park and the Takasegawa River–Four Seasons Art Gallery, which owner is a member of the executive committee. The location is proximate to the Bukkoji Bridge, so that people can watch the events from the bridge. To instal the *Takasegawa Kikimizu Garden* in the Takasegawa River, the executive committee applied for permission from Kyoto City, which administers the Takasegawa River.

4.3.2.2 Creation and Installation on the Riverbed

Creation of the riverbed installation relied on donations. Kitayama cedar was provided by the Keihoku Town Forestry Association, prepared by Keihoku Precut, and assembled and installed on the riverbed by Fuji Home Co., Ltd. Fuji Home Co., Ltd. was the construction company responsible for renovating the gallery. The cooperation of Keihoku Town Forestry Association and Keihoku Precut was obtained through Fuji Home Co., Ltd.

4.3.2.3 Event Management

During the summer of 2015, the riverbed events occurred from the 7th to the 22nd of September. The executive committee and some local groups arranged daily workshops and exhibitions of artistic collaborations. In the spring of 2016, the riverbed events spanned on March 18 to April 10 to take advantage of the cherry blossom season. In the summer of 2016, it was available from August 25 to September 10. The gallery and the riverbed installation were positioned as satellite venues of the 8th World Archaeological Congress (August 27 to September 2). Some archaeology workshops and student planning events were held there, providing an opportunity for interaction with local communities and visitors such as researchers and artists. The main events are listed in Table 4.2 and depicted in Figs. 4.4 and 4.5.

4.3.2.4 Transmission of Information Using Social Networking Sites

Since the executive committee started working, members have occasionally been provided with information via Facebook or other social networking sites on the Internet. In addition, events have been announced on the Kyoto Tourism official site.

Table 4.2 Main events

Dates	Examples of main events
Sep 7–Sep 22, 2015	Ice column excavation experience
	The supreme tea ceremony
	Kyoto top spinning on the water!
	Art bazaar
	Yukata photo gallery
	International workshop
	Book café
	Kendama performance
Mar 18–Apr 10, 2016	Bamboo craft workshop
	Street picture story show
	Tea ceremony in Kotatsu
	Tea ceremony and photo session
	Erhu concert
	Meditation and café
	Magic show
	Harmony in Spring by Ms. Jennifer
Aug 25–Sep 10, 2016	Let's make excuse by melting ice!
	Make summer fireworks!!
	Let's tea party!
	Lantern banquet
	Chopsticks making
	Discovery! Takasegawa River
	Make diagrams using *Maco*
	Everywhere with field notes

4.3.2.5 Formation of a Human Network

Members of the executive committee have worked on various activities, but there are limits to what they can do. Therefore, in each case, we asked for cooperation from new people we met through our activities and have developed activities. For example, one event was realized by introducing both a Romanian researcher and a traditional townhouse owner from Hanaougi Tayu who was interviewed in the fifth issue of *Takasegawa Kikimiru Shimbun*. It was a lecture about Shimabara, which is the oldest licenced quarter in Kyoto and Tayu, who are highly ranked traditional entertainer, presented in a beautiful townhouse and given in Japanese and English.

4.4 Organization and Financing

The members of the executive committee are a painter (representative), a university teacher (deputy representative), a gallery manager (manager), a real estate agent (resident), an inventor (new resident), a satirical cartoonist, and a sculptor. We

4 Small Activities to Transmit Environmental and Cultural Resources... 61

Fig. 4.4 Types of riverside use

Fig. 4.5 Example of riverside use by local children and foreign tourists enjoying an event arranged by a student group

obtained cooperation from organizations that had been active for many years, such as Takasegawa River Hosyokai (a local environmental preservation group) and Kiyamachi Kai (a restaurant owners' group). To gain permission to use the Takasegawa River, the activity was required to be local and not a commercial project. Therefore, the executive committee and the president of Takasegawa River Hosyokai visited the head of Shimogyo Ward and the Kyoto City River Management Division in Kyoto City to explain the project, and then, the executive committee was granted permission. In other words, because of the cooperation of people who had worked for a long time on the environmental conservation activities of the Takasegawa River, despite being almost an outsiders' executive committee, it obtained permission to set up a riverbed installation.

After funds were raised, the executive committee received a program designation subsidy to solicit donations widely through Kyoto Foundation for Positive Social Change. It was necessary to demonstrate the executive committee's organizational stability and reliability to be certified. Most of the members of the executive committee became members of the Kyoto Arts Council (its chairman is the member of the executive committee who is a sculptor), which had already obtained social recognition, to avoid complicated administrative procedures and to position the executive committee as activities of the committee. This made it possible to solicit for donations over the Internet through Kyoto Foundation for Positive Social Change. In addition to announcing the need for donations in *Takasegawa Kikimiru Shimbun* and Facebook, we employed a donation box during the riverbed installation establishment period. The executive committee also received a subsidy (grant) from Kyoto Prefecture.

The riverbed installation was as described above. Regarding how to keep riverbed parts, Kojyuku (a tutoring school for learning and career support) agreed with its purpose and underwrote it without charge. However, it was impossible to fund the entire project with donations and subsidies; therefore, the executive committee sought paid advertisements in the *Takasegawa Kikimiru Shimbun* and asked for participation fee at the riverbed installation events. Other financial needs were filled by the members. Furthermore, although it was not financial aid, the Kyoto City International Association sponsored me. Public accreditation and subsidies are not directly related to funding, but they were effective for explaining that the activity was not a commercial endeavour.

4.5 Evaluation of Activities

4.5.1 The Questionnaire Survey

4.5.1.1 Outline of the Survey

A questionnaire survey was conducted on visitors who attended the riverbed events. The purpose of the survey was to learn about the characteristics, impressions, opinions, and evaluations of the visitors to the events and to explore improvement

4 Small Activities to Transmit Environmental and Cultural Resources. . .

Table 4.3 Outline of questionnaire survey

Date	Summer 2015	Spring 2016	Summer 2016
Number of responses	Total = 327	Japanese = 51	Japanese = 77
		English = 17	English = 52
		(Total = 68)	(Total = 129)
Item	Cognition	Cognition	
	Use frequency	Information medium	
	Evaluation	Purpose of visit	
	Knowledge of the Takase	Evaluation	
	River	Knowledge of the Takase River	
	Free opinion	Free opinion	
	Characteristics	Characteristics (age, gender, place of residence, employment location)	
	Age, gender, place of residence, employment location	In the English language questionnaire, instead of knowledge on the information medium, Takase River, place of visit, number of Tokyo visits, companions, and nationality were asked	

measures and the direction of development. Horie Seminar, Department of Public Policy, Faculty of Sociology, Bukkyo University, fielded the survey. In the summer of 2015, a questionnaire in Japanese was used, but Japanese and English questionnaires were fielded in the spring and summer of 2016. The results of the survey were published in *Takasegawa Kikimiru Shimbun* and reported to relevant organizations. Table 4.3 shows the numbers of responses to the surveys and their main items.

4.5.1.2 Evaluation Results from the Surveys

The questionnaire asked the respondents to evaluate the *Takasegawa Kikimizu Garden* on five levels for each of the following items:

(a) (This project is) good for enjoying the Takasegawa River.
(b) (This project is) good for bringing residents and visitors together.
(c) (This project is) good for activating this area.
(d) (This project is) good for children's play.
(e) (This project is) good for enjoying art and culture.
(f) (This project is) good for learning about the environment of this area.
(g) (This project) prompts me to make the Takasegawa River an important resource.
(h) (This project) prompts my interest in this area.
(i) (This project) improves the impression of this area or Kyoto.
(j) I'd like to come again, if possible.

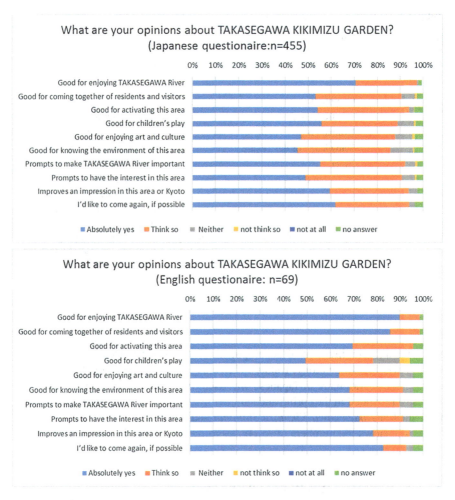

Fig. 4.6 Evaluation results

More than 80% of the items were answered 'absolutely yes' or 'I think so', which are considered high evaluations. In addition, in the open-ended items, many favourable impressions and opinions were given, there were comments about lack of public relations, and there were ideas for improvement. However, the survey was limited to visitors during the riverbed event period, and we did not obtain opinions from other people. Figure 4.6 describe the evaluation results on the *Takasegawa Kikimizu Garden*.

And main comments provided in the open-ended portion of the questionnaire were as follows:

- Please increase the number of events for children.
- Since I have no opportunity to play freely in the river, it was a pleasant experience for my kids.

4 Small Activities to Transmit Environmental and Cultural Resources...   65

- The river is very beautiful and comfortable.
- Everyone could feel free to join and feel favourable.
- More PR [public relations] should be done.
- A good surprise.
- Great idea!! Beautiful site!
- Please go on and do more!
- Really fun and welcoming. So good to sit on the wooden benches with the feet in the water. Thanks a lot.
- Very nice atmosphere!!!
- Very creative idea.

4.5.2 Evaluation by Media

In the summer of 2015, when the riverbed was introduced, major newspapers, such as *The Kyoto Shimbun*, *The Mainichi*, *The Asahi Shimbun*, and *Yomiuri Shimbun*, and Internet media reported on it in July and August after the press release was issued. Since then, activities have been favourably reported in articles, including magazine articles.

4.5.3 Regional Reputation

Although issued irregularly, *Takasegawa Kikimiru Shimbun* records and communicates memories of the area in interviews and is becoming established as an effective medium. It also was possible to confirm the significance of the riverbed installation events as opportunities for rich and fun experiences in the Takasegawa River and as a place where established residents, new residents, and visitors could interact. However, there was a different response when the executive committee talked with residents.

There were positive comments, such as 'children want to experience the river' and 'no one will throw garbage into the river where the children are playing'. However, there were also negative reactions. As background for the negative reactions, it is believed that population ageing in this area is considerably advanced and that opportunities to watch children play on a daily basis are few. Some people placed importance on risks, such as water-related risks, and they expressed worry about injuries from glass fragments on the river bottom (riverbed), rather than the value of children freely playing in the river. In addition, there were several negative reactions from local residents, such as noise caused by the visitors, discomfort due to strangers stagnating, and misunderstandings caused by inadequate communication of the purpose of the events. It is thought that efforts to share the purpose with the residents and promote participation in the event were not enough.

4.6 Possibilities and Issues

In using parks and rivers, which are public apaces, what the administrator emphasizes is to ensure fairness, safety, and nonprofitability. When various actors try to exploit these environmental and cultural resources to revitalize a region, we aim for flexible responses while maintaining a balance with public opinions. The execution of relevant activities should make an area activate.

Since the activities of spring 2015, we have been planning and managing riverbed events and other activities that share the importance of the local communities and consideration for the environment by publishing *Takasegawa Kikimiru Shimbun*, among other things. Although the significance of the series of activities was confirmed, fundraising is not easy. Publishing a newspaper entails production costs and printing fees, and installation costs and removal costs are necessary for the events. Whether we can continue in the future is not certain. For the newspaper, it is necessary to review the current A3 duplex printing methods and to consider tools that are cost-effective. Regarding the editing personnel, it is desirable to consider transferring the newspaper staff positions on to younger and newer residents, including new residents and young mothers who participated in the riverbed events.

Despite expectations for future riverbed events, there are many difficulties to accomplishing that, such as durability problems of the riverbed's installation, compensation to victims of accidents, complaint handling, and so on. Continuity is always pointed out as a problem for projects aimed at regional revitalization; however, the purpose of this project is not to reproduce itself but to revitalize the region. Even if new activities were to emerge and disappear one after another, the important thing for revitalization of the region would be to continue collecting various human resources motivated to make the region activate.

In principle, regional responsibility rests with the local people and landowners. However, in this area, the population is ageing, the population has decreased, and the number of new residents that do not know the history or culture of the community is increasing. Moreover, in areas with many visitors, such as tourists, residents and visitors need to behave with respect towards the environment to maintain it. While keeping local talent at the centre of the human network, it is necessary that residents and visitors participate in the area in various ways.

Acknowledgements This work was supported by JSPS KAKENHI Grant Number 16K01203.

References

Horie N (2013) A study on functions as bases for region described in the management policy of National Government Parks. Park administration & Management Research No. 7, pp 51–56

Japan River Association (2016) Features: "Riverside and Town vitalization" for production of prosperity of areas centering river and city planning, Kasen (River), No. 840

Parks and Open Space Association (2012) Theme for this issue; The collection of examples on parks and open spaces, Parks and Open Space, 72(5)

Sugiyama K, Ito T (2010) A study of local activation to hold an event at multi place in the central area of the city. AIJ Tokai Chapter Architectural Research Meeting, No. 48, pp 553–556

Tajima Y, Onishi M, Ogawa K (2013) The variables of continuity in art projects by analyzing communication: changes from a "separate & role-style" communication to "voluntary & share-style" communication. J Jpn Inf Culturol Soc 20(2):27–34

Chapter 5
Management of Depopulated Areas Viewed as Concept of GES Environment: The Case of Kumogahata in Kyoto

Yoshinori Ida and Kiyoko Hagihara

Abstract The aim of this study is to consider depopulation from the viewpoint of managing the environment. This study focuses on Kumogahata in Kyoto and regards the depopulation as an environmental problem. By approaching the issue from the viewpoint of environmental management, depopulation is regarded as one aspect of the diversity of the region. In the management of the environment, it is necessary to focus on the social background of environmental issues. Thus, the social background was understood by considering some activities and the purposes of the various associations in Kumogahata. As a result, it was found that there are various associations having a variety of purposes in the depopulated areas. Consequently, we propose to add the new step of "forming a residential type of exchange population" to the existing plan.

Keywords Depopulation · GES environment · Management of the environment · Exchange population · Various associations in Kumogahata

5.1 Introduction

This study is an attempt to consider depopulation from the viewpoint of environmental management. The declining birth rate, the aging population, and the excess concentration of population in the Tokyo metropolitan area as demographic trends are central issues facing modern Japan. According to "Population Projections for Japan" released by the National Institute of Population and Social Security Research, the total population will decrease by 40 million people from 2010 to 2060 based on the projection of medium fertility and medium mortality. As to the demographic

---

Y. Ida (✉)
Parks and Recreation Foundation, Tokyo, Japan

K. Hagihara
Tokyo Metropolitan University, Tokyo, Japan
e-mail: khagi@tb3.so-net.ne.jp

© Springer Nature Singapore Pte Ltd. 2019
C. Asahi (ed.), *Building Resilient Regions*, New Frontiers in Regional Science: Asian Perspectives 35, https://doi.org/10.1007/978-981-13-7619-1_5

composition, the young population is expected to decrease by 4% and the productive-age population by 12.9%, while the elderly population is expected to increase by 16.9%. The proportion of the population in the Southern Kanto Region block comprising Saitama, Chiba, Tokyo, and Kanagawa among the total population is estimated to increase from 27.8% in 2010 to 30.1% in 2040.

Debates surrounding depopulation have changed over time. The term *kaso* (depopulation) first appeared publicly in the "Interim Report by the Economic Council, Regional Committee" released in 1966 to describe the "state where it has become difficult to maintain a certain level of living due to a decline in the population" (see Hagihara and Hagihara 1991). This definition will be applied in this study as well. Back then, the cause of the problem was "social decrease," which means an outflow of the population to urban areas. However, with the advent of the population-declining era from the mid- to late-2000s, the influence of "natural decrease," which means the number of deaths exceeds the number of births, became stronger, while there has been no end to the excess concentration of population in the Tokyo metropolitan area, further accelerating the process of depopulation in rural communities. As a result, "extinction" of local communities have been talked about as a real possibility, as represented by concepts such as "marginal village" and "cities at risk of disappearing," which has deepened the sense of crisis toward the status of depopulation.

As a national measure against depopulation, Act on Emergency Measures for the Development of Depopulated Areas was established in 1970 as a temporary statute with a 10-year term limit, which has been extended repeatedly up to the present. The act designates municipalities that meet certain population and financial requirements as "underpopulated areas," to which preferential treatment has been given, for example, issuing of depopulation bonds. As a measure against the declining population in the entire Japan, Act on Overcoming Population Decline and Vitalizing Local Economy in Japan was introduced in 2014, which portrays medium- to long-term vision for sustaining the population of about 100 million people in 2060 through "comprehensive strategies for overcoming population decline and vitalizing local economy" in the national government, prefectures, and municipalities. In May of the same year, the Japan Policy Council's Paper Group on Depopulation released a report called "Strategy to put a stop to Japan's low fertility and revitalized local communities for the growing twenty-first century" (commonly called "Masuda Report"). The objective here is to form regional urban centers in wide-area blocks under the philosophy of "selection and concentration" and realize the "desired fertility rate" of 1.8%, by stopping the flow of people into Tokyo (Masuda 2014).

This study approaches the issue of depopulation from the viewpoint of environmental management in local communities by positioning depopulation as one of the environmental problems that have occurred among many intertwined elements. In specific terms, we will describe various purposes that exist in a certain region and those who pursue them, as well as relationships among them, and reveal the existence of various purposes in line with the theoretical concepts of the region. We will then discuss how gaining an understanding of the situation where various purposes exist and are related with each other can be useful for the purpose of addressing depopulation (Ida 2017).

Section 5.2 places depopulation among environmental issues and describes the viewpoint of environmental management. Section 5.3 applies that framework to an area called Kumogahata in Kyoto City Kita Ward and identifies various associations associated with this region and their purposes as the social background. By making reference to "community-building vision for three school districts in Kitayama" as the current way of management in Kumogahata, Sect. 5.4 describes the challenges surrounding the measures against depopulation and possible measures from the standpoint of environmental management bearing in mind the various purposes found in the region.

5.2 Management of the Environment

5.2.1 Depopulation as an Environmental Issue

There are three relevant environmental systems (Fig. 5.1; see also Chap. 1): the geo-environment where the law of geophysics governs, for example, climate change and natural disasters such as earthquakes, floods, droughts, and typhoons; the eco-environment where the law of ecology governs, for example, ecosystem functions and services; and the socio-environment where rules of society govern, for example, human well-being (Hagihara et al. 1995, 1998; Hagihara 2008a, b). If the geological space where the geo-environment exists is the entire earth, the

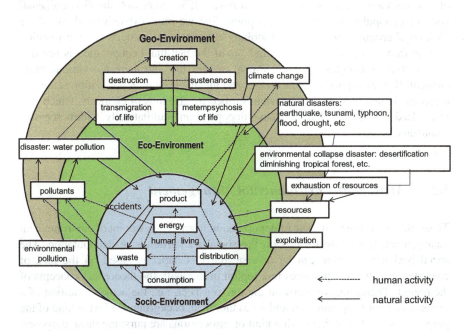

Fig. 5.1 GES (geo-, eco-, and socio-environment)

eco-environment cannot exist without the geo-environment, and the socio-environment cannot exist without the geo- and eco-environments. Humans are members of the geo-, eco-, and socio-environments.

System here means "(1) system that consists of parts and elements comprising the whole and plays a certain function as a whole, while those parts and elements interact with each other; (2) system that defines the whole and has a boundary that separates outside (environment) and inside; and (3) parts and elements themselves are often systems that have the features described in 1 and 2 (sub-system, low-order system). Such nested structure is called hierarchical structure." Based on this definition, the environment for a person consists of every single thing that exists around him or her and is the sum with a hierarchical structure formed by those things that are related with each other. If depopulation is placed in this concept, depopulation is "one aspect of the environment that is a demographic element of a certain society" and is "a sub-system of the environment as the sum formed by all the elements of the society relating with each other." If depopulation is causing some sort of defects to the environment as the sum of a certain society, then depopulation can be regarded as an environmental problem.

With GES environment in mind, Hagihara (2008a, b) proposes "environmental management from the viewpoint of *seikatsusha* (the people)" as "what *seikatsusha* do not just by taking an interest in the environment right in front of their eyes but also by thinking about what kind of backgrounds, i.e., what kind of historical, cultural, political, living, and technological social backgrounds are causing the environmental issues they are faced with, how many possible measures they can take, and what kind of impacts those measures are going to have." If we approach the environmental issue of depopulation from this viewpoint, first we must extensively think of the social backgrounds, instead of just looking at the population decrease, the situation right in front of our eyes. This reminds us of the fact that depopulation is just one element that constitutes the environment as the sum and there are various other elements that are related with each other and that the state of depopulation is not just a certain element but also a subsystem formed by all kinds of elements, which as a result leads us to the idea of seeing depopulation multilaterally within regional management.

5.2.2 Method of Environmental Management

To see the environmental issue of depopulation from the viewpoint of environmental management, this study focuses on the social backgrounds of depopulation. The social backgrounds here can be diverse, but this paper is based on the idea of coexistence of diverse purposes in a region in line with the theoretical concepts of the region. Therefore, we focus on the micro aspect, i.e., the actual condition of a region faced with depopulation and set as the social backgrounds of what kind of the purposes can be found there, what kind of associations are pursuing those purposes, and how they are related with each other. The purposes of a region here mean "purposes that exist in a region," and we regard the purposes of all the subjects who engage in activities in the region irrespective of where they live as "purposes of the region." However, it is not easy to list every single purpose of all the individuals that exist in the region, we focus on various associations operating in the region and list their purposes as a certain level of collective opinions of the people.

The entire picture of the region from the perspective of various associations and their purposes will be overviewed, instead of focusing particularly on the status of depopulation as the social background.

We introduce Kumogahata in Kyoto City Kita Ward as a region faced with depopulation, classify the associations operating there according to their purposes and sectors that they belong to, and describe what kind of purposes the relationships among the associations contribute to. As Kumogahata is not an administrative district, it is not therefore a legally depopulated area. But in terms of its population and structure by age groups, Kumogahata meets the depopulation requirement of a designated depopulated area under the Act on Special Measures for the Regional Development of Depopulated Areas established in 1980 (see Chap. 3 in Hagihara and Asahi 2016). The region is actually under the state of depopulation, considering the fact that schools and transportation services have been abolished in recent years.

5.3 Social Backgrounds of Depopulation in Kumogahata

5.3.1 Overview of Kumogahata

Kumogahata is located 12 km north of the central area of Kyoto City (see Fig. 5.2). It is about 30 min car ride from the central area, but it is isolated from the outside world as a hamlet, and it takes about an hour and a half on a steep slope from the nearest hamlet Nishikamo on foot. The total area is 19.33 km^2, which accounts for about 20% of Kita Ward (94.92 km^2). Of the total area, the forest covers an area of 17.95 km^2, which accounts for 93% of the area. It is said that the area was developed as a lumbering area during the construction of Heiankyo (ancient Kyoto). During the medieval period, the area supplied fuelwood and firewood to the Imperial Court (Kyoto City 1993), and the lumber business has been the center of its industry since the modern times as well. It is also a land associated with the royal family, for example, Imperial Prince Koretaka lived a secluded life there in his later years, and it was an imperial hunting ground during the modern age. It is also the headwaters area of Kamo-gawa River, which is the symbolic representation of "a city of Sanshisuimei, or scenic beauty, Kyoto."

In 2003, a simple water supply system fed by underground water was established in the area, but before that the area took water from the valley. When Kyoto City came up with a "plan to eliminate areas without broadband access in Kyoto City" in 2009, Kumogahata was listed as one of the areas without broadband access and had to wait until 2013 before access became available. In terms of the Kumogahata

Fig. 5.2 Location of Kumogahata in Kyoto City

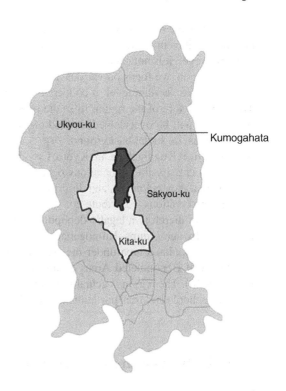

elementary and junior high school, the junior high school was closed in the academic year 2011 and the elementary school in 2012. Since then, the children of the area go to schools in other areas on a school bus. In terms of the transportation, the bus, which was the only public transportation system connecting the region and the urban area, was abolished in March 2012. From April of the same year onward, a route taxi called "Mokumoku-go" is operated twice a day by Kumogahata Self-government Promotion Association (hereinafter, Self-government Promotion Association). As a store where people can purchase commodities, there is a space for purchase within the Kumogahata branch office of the Forest Cooperative (hereinafter, Forest Cooperative). In terms of medical care, a physician comes to the Kumogahata branch office of Kita Ward once a week.

While the population has leveled off and the number of households keeps increasing in Kyoto City and Kita Ward, both the population and the number of households have kept decreasing in Kumogahata after peaking in 1960. As of 2010, the number of households was 68 and the population was 175. If we look at the fluctuations in the proportions of each age group, we can see that there have been a marked decrease in the proportions of those under the age of 15 and increase in the proportions of those aged 65 or older, particularly since 1990 (see Table 5.1). In terms of the employment status, 40 people, who accounted for 31.7% of the employed workers in the area, were engaged in forestry as of 1995, but the number decreased to 11 in 2010, which accounted for 11.3%. In terms of the business scale

Table 5.1 Demographic data of Kyoto City, Kita Ward, and Kumogahata according to national census

		1960	1970	1980	1990	2000	2010
Kyoto City	Number of households	316,567	420,768	523,708	552,325	620,327	681,581
	Total population	1,284,789	1,419,165	1,473,065	1,461,103	1,467,785	1,474,015
	Percentage of population under 15 years old	24.0	20.3	21.0	15.8	12.7	11.6
	Percentage of population over 65 years old	5.7	7.5	10.4	12.7	17.2	22.4
Kita-ku	Number of households	31,890	42,304	52,307	51,075	55,514	56,315
	Total population	123,230	135,681	136,181	127.348	126,125	122,037
	Percentage of population under 15 years old	23.3	19.3	18.8	14.0	11.9	11.0
	Percentage of population over 65 years old	6.0	8.1	11.3	14.1	18.6	23.4
Kumogahata	Number of households	100	91	81	79	73	68
	Total population	501	428	336	298	244	175
	Percentage of population under 15 years old	31.5	22.9	20.8	16.8	14.3	4.0
	Percentage of population over 65 years old	8.8	11.7	12.8	19.1	30.3	38.9

according to the number of employees, lodging, food, and beverage service industry is the largest with 16 people working (Kyoto City 1993, 2010).

5.3.2 Purposes of the Associations and Their Activities

The associations that have continuously carried out activities in Kumogahata or are involved in Kumogahata can be divided into public associations ("Kita Ward," "Kumogahata Council of Social Welfare," "Kumogahata Association for the Promotion of Physical Education," "Kumogahata Chojukai (longevity association)," "Kumogahata Unit of Kita Fire Fighting Team," and "Kumogahata Self-government Promotion Association") and private associations ("Yamanushi-kai (association for mountain owners)," "Sugi Yoshitaro," "Forest Cultural Festival Executive Committee," "Kumo Club for Kumogahata People, Mountains and Living," "JA Kyoto-chuo City, Ichiharano Branch, Female Division, Kumogahata Branch (hereinafter, Female Division)," and "Wakanaka-kai"). Below, these associations are sorted according to their purposes: (a) interregional exchange, (b) maintenance of community living, (c) extraordinary experience, (d) conservation of nature, and (e) moneymaking.

(a) Interregional exchange

"Yamanushi-kai": This is an association for forest owners established in 2003, acting as an acceptance mechanism of an outsider forest volunteer organization "Sugi Yoshitaro" (Shimada 2005).

"Regional Revitalization Committee" was set up in 2009 within the Self-government Promotion Association to hold various events to attract people from outside.

"Forest Cultural Festival Executive Committee": Established in 2005; the festival attracts many people as the largest event of the area.

"Kumo Club for Kumogahata People, Mountains and Living": Established in 2013; this is a small-scale club but serves as a place where members within and outside the area can interact with each other.

"Kita Ward": The ward established a "Community-building Proposal and Assistance Program for the People of Kita Ward" in 2012 to support voluntary and spontaneous community-building activities by the people of the ward and offers subsidies to projects supporting exchange among people in the northern mountain area (see Table 5.2).

(b) Maintenance of community living

Kumogahata has associations that are similar to the ones established in other districts (or school districts) in Kyoto City, such as "Kumogahata Council of Social Welfare," "Kumogahata Association for the Promotion of Physical Education," "Kumogahata Chojukai," "Kumogahata Unit of Kita Fire Fighting Team," and "Kumogahata Self-government Promotion Association," all of which are run to maintain community living in each field.

Table 5.2 Projects covered by "community-building proposal and assistance program for the people of Kita Ward" in Kumogahata

Fiscal year	Number of subsidized projects in Kita Ward	Projects covered by the program in Kumogahata	Project implementing bodies
2012	20	10th Forest cultural festival in Kumogahata	Kumogahata Forest Cultural Festival Executive Committee
		Project for appealing the new attractiveness of Kita Ward	Group for making Kita Ward enjoyable
2013	22	11th Forest cultural festival in Kumogahata	Kumogahata Forest Cultural Festival Executive Committee
		Mokumoku Project (1st to 5th)	EN lab.
		Regional revitalization project in Kumogahata (firefly viewing/event to enjoy autumn in Kumogahata)	Kumogahata Self-government Promotion Association, regional revitalization committee
2014	22	Mokumoku Project (6th to 9th)	EM lab.
		Kumogahata Moving Art	Kumogahata Moving Art executive committee
		Regional revitalization project in Kumogahata (event to enjoy spring in Kumogahata/Christmas party in Kumogahata)	Kumogahata Self-government Promotion Association, regional revitalization committee
2015	19	Forestry experience for parents and children "Let's get familiar with the living in Kumogahata"	Kyoto City juvenile guidance committee, Hiragino Branch
2016	29	Circle of mountain work experience connecting with the town	Mountain work circle Sugi Yoshitaro

"Kumogahata Self-government Promotion Association (hereinafter, Self-government Promotion Association)": This association aims to promote friendship among the members, foster the notion of self-governing community, and improve the welfare of the community; the committees' setup within the association engages in activities related to infrastructure, welfare, health, public relations, etc.

"Self-government Promotion Association": The association operates "Mokumoku-go" as a means of transportation; about 50% of the cost is funded by the free bus pass system for senior citizens, which covers the cost burden of those aged 70 or older living in Kyoto City, to "Mokumoku-go," and about 20% of the cost is funded by a national program to "assist regional feeder systems" established to "secure and maintain a living and transportation network appropriate for the regional characteristics and the actual conditions."

"JA Kyoto-chuo City, Ichiharano Branch, Female Division, Kumogahata Branch (hereinafter, Female Division)": Purchase of commodities; the division contributes to the area through the process of making arrangements for group purchases and delivering the goods four times a year.

"Kumogahata Council of Social Welfare": Medical welfare; The council holds "Hata-sukoyaka Circle" once a month (from 2010 onward); Exercise, lectures, etc. are provided for senior citizens of the area to prevent them from becoming dependent on nursing care.

"Kumogahata Association for the Promotion of Physical Education": The association holds ball games and sports festivals in the area to promote exchange among the residents.

"Kumogahata Chojukai": The association is run on a membership system for residents aged 60 or older. Meals and trips are arranged for the members. The Female Division takes care of the members of Keirokai, which is a group for the elderly aged 70 or older living in the area.

"Wakanaka-kai": Inheritance of local culture, a traditional event called "Matsuage," which is a fire ceremony displaying fire characters in the night sky, is carried out every summer by men aged between 16 and 35 living in the area.

Disaster control measures: Kumogahata Unit of Kita Fire Fighting Team engages in activities such as fire drills and disaster drills.

(c) Extraordinary experience

"Sugi Yoshitaro": This group carries out activities as a group of people who want to do mountain work mainly forestry work (volunteer) in Kumogahata in Kyoto City Kita Ward.

"Ideal Forest Project": An offspring of "Sugi Yoshitaro"; the project creates opportunities where various people can experience the fun of mountain work.

"Forest Cultural Festival": Members of "Sugi Yoshitaro" are the main members of the executive committee; the festival provides an opportunity for people to enjoy and get to know the forest and the cultural of the mountain village by enjoying food cooked with fuelwood and experiencing activities related to mountains.

"Kumogahata Ashitani Association for People and Nature": This is an association for "appreciating the relationship between nature and people; carrying out activities to enjoy, understand, learn about, and protect nature; and valuing the network and harmony of people through these activities"; the association holds "spring gathering" once a year for the general public to enjoy mountain walking in Kumogahata.

"EN lab.": This is an education-based voluntary organization for "deepening an understanding of the environment and various matters surrounding human beings; the organization holds "Mokumoku Project," a workshop for elementary school children in Kumogahata elementary and junior high school, which has been closed.

"Kyoto City Kita Ward Juvenile Guidance Committee, Hiragino Branch": This is a group in Hiragino, a motogakku (school district system unique to Kyoto City) adjacent to Kumogahata; the branch holds a camp every summer in Kumogahata elementary and junior high school for children in the 4th, 5th, and 6th grades within the school district; the branch also carried out a forestry experience event (2015).

"Shiraume Sports Club (commercial organization)": Field archery range; the club offers sports utilizing the natural landscapes and the climate.

5 Management of Depopulated Areas Viewed as Concept of GES Environment:...

(d) Conservation of nature

"Environmental conservation committee within Self-government Promotion Association": The committee monitors industrial waste disposal facilities of the area and illegal dumping.

"Female group of Self-government Promotion Association": The group makes soups from waste oil, which began out of considerations for the water quality of Kamo-gawa River; this has been carried out for 25 years since 1990.

"Kumogahata Commons, Yui-no Ringyo Kumiai" is an organization established by three mountain owners of the area; the organization undertakes the mountain work to "rejuvenate the forest."

"Ideal Forest Project": The project became an independent project after the dissolution of "Shinku Tanku Kyoto" established to expand the use of forest biomass. The project is based on the proposal of a recycling society using the forest in Kumogahata as a field where forest biomass is produced and consumed there.

"Kumogahata Ashitani Association for People and Nature": This is a conservation group of Paeonia obovata Maxim, which is an endangered species of flora; its activity field Ashitani is designated as "natural habitat protection area."

Kyoto Prefecture designates rare species, such as *Andrias japonicus* and Paeonia obovata Maxim, as endangered species in Kyoto Prefecture Red Data Book;

The Kamo-gawa River Ordinance introduced in 2007 designates the area within Kumogahata, the most upstream of Kamo-gawa River, which used to be excluded from the river conservation zone, as the "area of Kamo-gawa River for the preservation of the environment" and puts a restriction on the development in the area.

(e) Moneymaking

"Hataka" and "Rakuunso": Restaurants; "Rakuunso" is also an accommodation facility.

"Self-government Promotion Association": The association operates "Mokumoku-go"; it is necessary to obtain a fare revenue of about 1.48 million yen in addition to subsidies provided by Kyoto City and the national government; because the deficit is covered by the Self-government Promotion Association, the association needs to work on securing revenues by increasing the number of "Mokumoku-go" users.

5.3.3 Relationships Among Various Associations

Hereinafter, we will cast a spotlight on what kind of purposes the interrelationships among the associations contribute to as a result.

The following are the relationships associated with interregional exchange and extraordinary experience.

"Sugi Yoshitaro" is given a field in Kumogahata through negotiation and coordination with "Yamanushi-kai" and carries out activities while receiving guidance from the Forestry Cooperative.

"Regional Revitalization Committee" receives cooperation from "Sugi Yoshitaro," "Kumogahata Ashitani Association for People and Nature," and others when holding various events, such as "firefly viewing."

"Forest Cultural Festival Executive Committee" hosts the "Forest Cultural Festival," but associations such as "Sugi Yoshitaro," "Ideal Forest Project," and "Kumogahata Ashitani Association for People and Nature" as well as Self-government Promotion Association and Forest Cooperative also participate in the festival and offer cooperation.

"Kita Ward Juvenile Guidance Committee, Hiragino Branch" holds summer camps and forestry experience programs for elementary school students with support from the Self-government Promotion Association.

As described above, the associations cooperate with each other, and their relationships themselves become interregional exchange. If activities implemented this way invite the general public to participate, then there will also be another type of interregional exchange and extraordinary experience within them. Kita Ward's "Community-building Proposal and Assistance Program for the People of Kita Ward" provides subsidies to such initiatives, but because there is a limit to the number of subsidies that can be provided to the same or similar projects, it is difficult to build a continuous relationship.

Relationships associated with the maintenance of community living are primarily through subsidies and entrustment of business activities from Kyoto City to various associations. But there are also relationships among the associations, for example, the "Female Division" is entrusted by "Kumogahata Council of Social Welfare" and Self-government Promotion Association with the activities of Keirokai or shares places of activities with the Forest Cooperative. In addition, after the public transportation was abolished, the only means of transportation "Mokumoku-go" is run by Yasaka Jidosha Company with funds provided by the Self-government Promotion Association, Kyoto City, and the national government. In terms of the traditional event of the area "Matsuage," members of "Sugi Yoshitaro" offer help due to shortage of staff of "Wakanaka" who are the local residents in charge of the event.

In terms of the relationships associated with conservation of nature, Kyoto City designated "Kumogahata/Ashitani Association for People and Nature" as a conservation group of Paeonia obovata Maxim in 2012 and its activity field as "natural habitat protection area" in 2014, thus supporting more flexible and viable conservation activities of the association. Currently, operations of industrial waste disposal companies in the Kumogahata area have been restricted due to designation of the "area of Kamo-gawa River for the preservation of the environment" under Kyoto Prefecture's Kamo-gawa Ordinance. They are now monitored by the Self-government Promotion Association. The compensations for the activities by the "Kumogahata Commons, Yui-no Ringyo Kumiai" and its purchase of equipment are subsidized by the national government, while waste oil collection activities and waste oil soap-making activities of "Female Division" are subsidized by Kyoto City and the Self-government Promotion Association.

In terms of the relationships associated with moneymaking, the revenue of Yasaka Jidosha Company is secured by the subsidies granted by the national government and Kyoto City for the operation of "Mokumoku-go." Because the deficits resulting from the operation of "Mokumoku-go" are covered by the Self-government Promotion Association, we believe that an increase or decrease of the number of users is not a big problem for Yasaka Jidosha Company for the time being.

5.4 Environmental Management in Kumogahata

5.4.1 Community-Building Vision for Three School Districts in Kitayama

The objective of the "community-building vision for three school districts (Kumogahata, Onogo, and Nakagawa) in Kitayama" (Kita-ku 2014) developed in 2014 is to achieve an appropriate population, i.e., maintain and increase the settled population in the areas faced with depopulation. The intermediate objective is to increase the exchange population, i.e., "tourists and individuals or associations coming to the area and engaging in various activities" in accordance with Step 1 to Step 4 of the seven steps of the "community-building flow" included in this vision (see Table 5.3). As methods to increase the settled population, the vision lists "(1) a method to establish a system or a mechanism directly encouraging "settlement," such as subsidies to support settlement or a vacant house bank system, and "(2) a method to increase the exchange population through various events and encourage a portion of the people who came to like the area toward 'settlement'". Judging from the steps stipulated, the vision is created with the latter in mind. In accordance with these, Kumogahata is expected to proceed with various efforts in four focus areas: (1) bond within the community, (2) creation of industries, (3) settlement and transportation, and (4) exchange activities.

There are two major issues with the scheme of first increasing the exchange population and then turning it into an increase of the settled population.

The first issue is how the residents of Kumogahata would see private associations formed primarily by outsiders. The exchange population is regarded in the vision as "those who interact with the area, those who engage in community-building activities together, and those who wish to settle down in the area in the future." The workshop called "Let's Talk about Kumogahata" officially launched in 2015 is an event where those who have some sort of connections to the residents of Kumogahata or to the area and those interested in Kumogahata gather. Upon its launch, the local residents expressed that "they feel a heavy burden toward the event,

Table 5.3 Overview of the "community-building flow" in community-building vision for three school districts in Kitayama

Step 1	Going back to the vision (future image)	Proceeding with various community-building activities by always checking whether the activities are in line with the vision
Step 2	Enjoying the community-building activities	If people involved in community-building activities are enjoying the activities, they become spirited. This is also "revitalization" and contributes to community-building
Step 3	Connecting the activities	Activities can be enriched if individuals, associations, and businesses can exchange information and cooperate with each other and become connected with each other
Step 4	Sending out information	There will be peers within and outside the area, and people outside the area will be interested in the area if we send out information on our community-building activities to outside world so that people can "get to know" the area
Step 5	The exchange population increases	If we send out information, more people will come to the area and become fans of the area. Thus, the exchange population, including those who support the area and participate in community-building activities together, will increase
Step 6	The settled population increases	A portion of the exchange population will express a desire to settle down in the area. If the exchange population from outside increases and the area becomes vibrant, those who are from the area may come back
Step 7	Achieving "vibrancy" and "tranquility" in the area	If the population increases in an appropriate manner, two good things, vibrancy and tranquility, of the area can be achieved

and as regional residents, they cannot offer cooperation to programs proposed by outsiders" while showing an attitude to welcome outsiders using Kumogahata as the field of their activities as voluntary support groups.

In addition, even though the area is an aging society with a declining birth rate, new opportunities where the residents and outsiders can interact with each other have been continuously created, which is a point worthy of attention in line with the direction that the "community-building flow" is aiming for (Ida 2017). Given the fact that most of the opportunities that have been continuously provided as of 2015 are offered by outside private associations, it is obvious that outside private associations play a significant role in obtaining the exchange population. However, the purposes of these private associations, which play a central role there, are mainly extraordinary experience and conservation of nature, not necessarily interregional exchange or settlement to the area. The private associations may provide opportunities for interregional exchange out of gratitude for the area or due to relationships with other associations, but it is logical to assume that they leave the area eventually if their original purposes cannot be achieved. Therefore, to retain the exchange population, it is necessary to acknowledge that the original purposes of the private associations must be respected first.

The second issue is the gap between an increase of the exchange population and an increase of the settled population. It is necessary to realize that there is a significant hurdle between an increase of the exchange population and an increase of the settled population, i.e., the question of "how to turn the increased exchange population into the settled population." Judging from the dialogues exchanged during the 6th community-building conference for the people of Kita Ward held in June 2014 among the members, the organizer, and the ward mayor, in the three school districts of Kitayama, which are urbanization control areas, there is a conflict between the fact that not being able to build a new house has become an obstacle to those who wish to move to the areas and the desire of the community to demand conservation of nature. This shows that they have no choice but to compromise by appealing to the outside world through the use of vacant houses and an increase of the exchange population. But according to the vice-chairman of the Kumogahata Self-government Promotion Association, although there were 17 vacant houses in Kumogahata as of 2014, the owners were reluctant to rent out or sell their houses to others because "they want to go there every once in a while and have a relaxed time" or out of feelings for their ancestors and for the area. In addition, since the launch of the three school districts of Kitayama website, no information has been posted regarding the vacant houses in Kumogahata, which indicates that it is not easy to increase the settled population through the use of vacant houses.

5.4.2 Measures Against Depopulation Seen from Environmental Management

Bearing in mind that there exist two major issues in the current management system in Kumogahata, i.e., "respecting of the purposes of outside private associations" and the "gap between the exchange population and the settled population," here we discuss the measures against depopulation in this area. According to the seven steps of the "community-building flow," Kumogahata is now at the Step 4 and Step 5, which are the stages for sending out information and increasing the exchange population. What has happened so far mostly basically fulfils the expectations mainly thanks to the active engagements by the private associations, as described above. However, the roles of these private associates are not necessarily consistent with their original purposes. It is also not easy to establish an acceptance structure even though some people from the exchange population wanted to move to and settle down in the area.

As a method to address depopulation under these circumstances, a new step of "forming a residential type of exchange population" should be added after Step 5, the stage of "increasing the exchange population." Currently in Kumogahata, there are interactions among various associations and individuals but most of such interactions are single-day relationships during the events or activities conducted in the area. We believe that allowing the exchange population to stay for a certain length of time not only increases the variety of tourism but also serves as an opportunity for people to actually feel what it is like to live in the area, which will be meaningful to encourage settlement. It is also important to consider this type of staying experience in association with the purposes of the private associations engaging in activities in the area. For example, if a single-day stay can offer an opportunity to experience forestry work under the original purpose of "extraordinary experience," then staying for a few days can offer an opportunity to experience a taste of what it is like to live in the mountains in addition to the experience of forestry work. If the community can enrich the elements that may contribute to the purposes of the private associations, it will probably result in attracting and retaining the exchange population. The use of vacant houses can be reconsidered during this stage of "forming a residential type of exchange population." The difficulty of the use of vacant houses has been mentioned earlier, but letting migrators from outside live in vacant houses may result in the disconnection of ties between the vacant house owners and the community and does not necessarily have a positive effect on the area. Bearing these in mind, we believe that it is less difficult to allow outsiders to use the vacant houses during the allotted time period than to provide those houses to migrators as their residence. If the exchange population stays longer in the area, a closer relationship will be established with the community, which should lower the hurdle in the provision of vacant houses.

Either way, if increase of the exchange population is regarded only as a way of increasing the settled population in the future, various initiatives implemented for that purpose will be denied of their values unless they can contribute to the maintenance and increase of the settled population and may even be discontinued. However, the "proposal on the future measures for rural communities including underpopulated areas" released in March 2015 by the Paper Group on the Depopulation Problem operating under the Ministry of Internal Affairs and Communications proposes to deal with the problems that underpopulated areas cannot address on their own through the "scheme of rural community network zone" led by organizations of each community and points out that it is of importance to collaborate with various bodies within and outside the rural community network zone to carry out the scheme and turning the local communities into organizations open to the outside world. This is an example that shows that the exchange population itself is valuable whether the visitors turn into residents or not. Thus, one idea for tackling the issues found in the current management system as pointed out from the viewpoint of environmental management is to improve the quality of the exchange population, rather than to try and increase the exchange population and turn it directly to an increase of the settled population. In Kumogahata, the first farmer *minshuku* (guest house) called "Zemon" opened in August 2016. This is not just an addition of an accommodation facility in the area, but it is of an extremely significance as the gateway to the formation of a residential type of exchange population, as the couple running the place has relationships with all kinds of associations and projects, including "Ideal Forest Project" and "Sugi Yoshitaro."

We can say that there is a power within Kumogahata to attract and accept outside associations as various outside voluntary organizations gather in Kumogahata and carry out activities. It is a different kind of vitality of Kumogahata, while no such vitality is found in terms of population and activities by the residents. How Kumogahata is going to utilize this, what it provides and gains within the relationships with various outside bodies that gather, and what it aims for under such circumstances will be very insightful and useful as a way of managing an underpopulated area.

5.5 Concluding Remarks

We approached the issue of depopulation from the viewpoint of environmental management and discussed regional management using the cases of Kumogahata as an example.

We showed that there were various associations with a variety of purposes in Kumogahata, and outside private associations are the ones playing a significant role in achieving the objective of interregional exchange envisioned in the current management system of Kumogahata. However, this is not what those private associations come to the area for. Their purpose is, for example, to gain extraordinary experience. Thus, if they cannot adequately achieve their purposes, then they may leave the area. In addition, there are obstacles such as the issue of vacant houses in order to turn an increase of the exchange population into the settled population. We therefore proposed to add the new step of "forming a residential type of exchange population" as a specific measure against these situations.

We described the problems found in the current management system and measures against them based on the findings obtained from the viewpoint of environmental management, but "an increase of settled population" is not an absolute path from the stance of coexistence of diverse purposes. For example, from the viewpoint of dual habitation promoted by the Ministry of Land, Infrastructure, Transport, and Tourism, the step of "forming a residential type of exchange population" may become tied to the directions of the area other than "increase of the settled population." Examination into these different options is an issue to be addressed in the future.

Acknowledgments We would like to express our deepest gratitude to those who live in Kumogahata and those who are associated with Kumogahata for offering support for our writing of this paper and providing various information and documents.

References

Hagihara K (ed) (2008a) Environmental management from the viewpoint of 'Seikatusha'. Showa-do, Kyoto (in Japanese)

Hagihara Y (2008b) Adaptive system planning methodology for environment risk management. Kyoto University Press, Kyoto (in Japanese)

Hagihara K, Asahi C (eds) (2016) Coping with regional vulnerability: preventing and mitigating damages from environmental disasters. Springer, Tokyo

Hagihara K, Hagihara Y (1991) The role of intergovernmental grants in underpopulated regions. Reg Stud 25(2):163–172

Hagihara Y, Takahashi K, Hagihara K (1995) A methodology of spatial planning for waterside area. Pap Reg Sci 25(2):19–45

Hagihara Y, Hagihara K, Takahashi K (1998) Urban environment and waterside planning. Keiso Shobo, Tokyo (in Japanese)

Ida Y (2017) Management of depopulated areas viewed as environmental problem: the case of Kumogahata in Kyoto. Stud Reg Sci (forthcoming) (in Japanese)

Kyoto City (ed) (1993) Shiryo Kyoto no rekishi: Dai rokkan [Historical sources: History of Kyoto, Vol. 6], Heibonsha (in Japanese)

Kyoto City (1997 [2010]) Kyoto-shi chiiki tokei yoran [Kyoto City Area Statistical Directory]. Kyoto City (in Japanese)

Kyoto City, Kita Ward Office (2014) Community-building vision for three school districts in Kitayama compiled by Onogo Community Association, Nakagawa Self-government Council, Kumogahata Self-government Promotion Association and Kyoto City, Kita Ward Office, Regional Power Improvement Section of Kyoto City Kita Ward Office (in Japanese)

Masuda H (2014) Chiho shometsu: Tokyo ikkyoku-shuchu ga maneku jinko kyugen [Disappearing local communities: drastic decrease of population caused by the excess concentration of population in the Tokyo Metropolitan area]. Chuo Koron sha (in Japanese)

Shimada S (2005) Shinrin boranthia to sanson jumin tono kankeisei ni kansuru kenkyu: kinki chiho no shinrin boranthia dantai eno anketo chosakekka wo chushin ni [A paper on the relationships between forest volunteers and residents of the mountain villages: with a focus on the results of the questionnaire survey conducted with forest volunteer groups in Kinki Region]. J For Econ 51(3):29–37 (in Japanese)

Chapter 6
Resident's Awareness About Inheritance of Greenery in Gardens

Shogo Mizukami

Abstract Housing land space is a high proportion of land use in urban areas. Therefore, vegetation of individual gardens contributes to greening of the metropolis and amenity. In this chapter, I surveyed resident's conscious about greenery for private gardens in a detached houses area. Gardens may be lost through house renovations or ownership changes. Preservation of gardens leads to an increase in greenery in the urban area. I examined resident's awareness of the inheritance of greenery in a private garden and searched for unfavorable conditions of gardens such as trimming trees. As a result, the transfer side and receiving side had different consciousness. Consciousness for inheritance of greenery is affected by the regional community and social awareness. It is important to initiate an interest in greenery and teach the greenery of a garden contributes to the urban environment. It is also necessary to consider how to maintain the greenery, for example, tree trimming and cleaning, in the community.

Keywords Private garden · Greenery · Regional environment · Resident's consciousness · Urban area

6.1 Research Background

The gardens at residential house buildings in cities are a secondary form of land use that accompanies these buildings' purpose as dwellings, and the greenery in each of individual garden is quite small scale when considering the green environmental policies for cities. However, residential land comprises a lot of the land use found in cities, so it is possible that the accumulation of greenery found in gardens could make a contribution to the green environment of a city. Greenery is currently starting to be thought of as an important environmental factor in cities, and several examples

---

S. Mizukami (✉)
Department of Public Policy, Faculty of Sociology, Bukkyo University, Kyoto, Japan
e-mail: mizukami@bukkyo-u.ac.jp

© Springer Nature Singapore Pte Ltd. 2019   87
C. Asahi (ed.), *Building Resilient Regions*, New Frontiers in Regional Science: Asian Perspectives 35, https://doi.org/10.1007/978-981-13-7619-1_6

of studies that have been done in other countries on this subject are Smardon's (1988) study that shows the roles of garden plants in urban environments and Burgess et al.'s (1988) study that demonstrated the value of urban green spaces. There have been many studies that have been done on assessing the amount of greenery in cities, and such studies include Shinji's (1975) study that calculated the level of satisfaction that was caused by the amount of greenery using psychological evaluations related to the ratio of land that is covered in greenery. However, according to the study done by Tokyo Metropolitan government (2006), the land use in Japan's main metropolis of Tokyo has a high ratio of building lots and a low ratio of open space compared with other metropolises around the world. According to another study done by the Tokyo Metropolitan government (1999), 56.0% of the land use for the districts located in Tokyo was comprised of building lots. The breakdown of the land use for these building lots by building type was as follows: 55.9% of the land in these areas was used for residential purposes, 16.5% was used for commercial districts, 15.4% was used for public services, 12.1% was used for industry, and 0.1% was used for agriculture.

The main factor that determines the amount of greenery in the residential environments in cities is the growth of trees and shrubs over time, and Mizukami and Hagihara (2011) reported that there are continuing trends for greenery to increase after residential districts are developed. However, it is also possible that the greenery in gardens will be lost when a residence is rebuilt. It is anticipated that the amount of greenery in a city will increase due to the growth of greenery if greenery in gardens continues to be maintained even if the owners change or houses are rebuilt. In recent years, there have been attempts to have the trees and shrubs taken over within the premises of apartment building complexes that are being rebuilt (Kogiso 1998), but there have not been advances in policies related to greenery being passed on house residences. However, Kida et al. (2006) reported that residents are aware that the greenery in private residences contributes to the entire region. It has been pointed out that greenery has the advantage of creating tranquility but is also accompanied by the burdens of maintenance (Tsutsumi et al. 2005), and because of this, it is necessary to investigate the challenges and possibilities of having greenery be inherited in residential houses.

When considering the preservation of greenery in modern local communities, it is essential to investigate the concept of the "publicness" of the locality. Takahashi (1982) stated that the creation of public parks is an important task for people's living environment. However, Kubo et al. (1986) pointed out that while recognition has been given to the importance of public greenery, residents are not actively cooperating to make public greenery. Kwun et al. (1994) noted that the public nature of the preservation of green spaces has an impact on citizens' awareness, and based on this, it seems important to investigate the publicness of greenery based on people's way of interacting with greenery.

The inheriting of greenery has the significance of having an individual's possession being taken over by other people or future generations, and in this sense, it shows that greenery is shared by many people. This seems to have the implication of greenery being public according to differences in a shared time line.

6 Resident's Awareness About Inheritance of Greenery in Gardens

So how do citizens feel about the inheritance of the greenery of gardens? For example, if a person moves from their dwelling, would they want the person who is living there after them to take over the greenery of the garden they had cultivated? Also, would they want to take over the greenery of the garden where they are moving to?

The present study investigates people's thoughts about the greenery of private citizens' gardens by looking at residential environments in urban areas based on the abovementioned awareness of the issues. It also examines the question of what sorts of attributes and thoughts make people desire the inheritance of greenery. Moreover, it looks the challenges facing the inheritance of greenery by investigating the burdens of maintenance, management, and care for greenery and the idea that garden greenery is not desirable.

6.2 Research Methods

6.2.1 The Selection of the Areas Targeted by the Study

The survey targeted residential districts of houses in Machida city in the Tokyo Metropolitan area as an urban residential environment. The rate of building lots in the land use in Machida city in the areas zoned for urbanization was 45.5%, and residential land use comprised 71.6% of these building lots. Since the period of rapid growth, Machida city has developed as a suburb, and it is an area where a lot of development of residential districts has taken place. Because a great number of residential districts have developed here over the course of a few decades, it is also an area where it is possible to compare a great number of residential districts that were developed during different years. A difference has been observed in the amount of greenery in people's homes due to the growth of trees and shrubs that is consequent upon the amount of time that has passed since the development of these districts, so it is necessary to consider several different target areas that were developed at different times to properly consider the differences in the environmental conditions of the greenery.

Thus, this area was considered to be appropriate as a target site for the survey, and 43 residential districts were selected that had 50 or more buildings from residential districts in Machida that were developed from 1944 to 2004.

6.2.2 Questionnaire Survey

A questionnaire survey was conducted to investigate resident's consciousness about greenery in their gardens. A thousand questionnaires were distributed to 43 residential districts. There were a total of 5018 buildings developed in the residential

Table 6.1 An outline of the questionnaire survey methods

Targets of survey area	Machida city in the Tokyo metropolitan area 43 residential districts
Number of surveys distributed	1000
Method for investigation	Posting distribution, collect by mail
Period	2010/7/29–8/31

Table 6.2 The collection results for the questionnaires

Number of surveys distributed (A)	Number of surveys (B)	Response rate (B/A)
1000	517	51.7%

districts that were targeted by the survey, and a questionnaire survey was distributed to 1000 of these houses. A total of 1000 questionnaires were distributed, and considerations were made for the differences in the time periods when the residential districts were developed. Because there were few houses in residential districts that were developed before 1960, 100 questionnaires were distributed to such districts; 180 questionnaires were distributed to the residential districts developed in each of the following time periods 1960s, 1970s, 1980s, 1990s, and 2000s. The number of questionnaires that were distributed for each time periods was determined, and each of the residential districts was distributed their proportion of questionnaires depending on the number of buildings that were developed. An outline of the examination methods is shown in Table 6.1. The number of collected questionnaires was 517 (reference Table 6.2). The sex ratio of the respondents was 43.0% male and 57.0% female, and the age range that was most prevalent in the respondents was people in their 60s. The respondents tending to in a high age range is a limiting condition on the results of this survey, and this could potentially have been impacted by the sampling method for targeting residents living in houses.

6.2.3 Analytic Methods

First, the study examines question of what sorts of attributes residents have that are associated with them desiring the inheritance of garden greenery. It also clarifies if differences in sex, basic attributes like age, people's way of interacting with greenery, and community activities or awareness of making a contribution to society have an impact. The residents' awareness is also clarified by investigating the relationship between the question items based on the responses obtained from the questionnaire. The analytic methods employed were a correlation analysis, a cross analysis, and multiple classification analysis. Then, the study clarifies what types of people provide care for greenery and if they feel a burden from doing so. A factor analysis was performed with regard to the care burden, and the behaviors involved with care

6 Resident's Awareness About Inheritance of Greenery in Gardens

were organized based on the relationship between several specific items on the work done to care for the greenery. Then, the study examines the question of what types of care became a burden. The significance level in this manuscript and the tables summarizing the statistics are indicated by $**P < .01$ and $*P < .05$. The numerical value V is Cramer's V coefficient that expresses the strength of the relationship found in the Chi square test.

6.3 Results of the Analysis

6.3.1 Factors that Determine the Intention to Take Over Greenery

What types of personal attributes and thoughts do people who want garden greenery to be passed down have? It seems like the desire for greenery to be passed down is impacted not only by personal attributes like an individual's age, sex, or interest in nature but also by the state of greenery in their homes and their way of interacting with it. Additionally, the inheritance of greenery transfers the possession of the greenery to the person who lives in that location next, and it also allows for the possibility of the greenery to be taken over by future generations. In this sense, it shows that greenery is shared by many people. Accordingly, people's way of interacting with their residential area and their sense of making contributions to society might also influence their thoughts about the inheritance of greenery.

To test the above hypothesis, the present study examines the factors that regulate the awareness of the inheritance of garden greenery. It seems like this sort of inheritance works in two different directions. This is the difference between the awareness of "wanting someone to take over the greenery of one's own garden" and "wanting to take over the garden greenery from the previous resident." Each of these things was inquired about in questions in the questionnaire, and responses were received to the following two questions: "If you were to move, do you think you would want leave your garden greenery behind and have the person who lived there next to take it over?" and "If you were to move, do you think you would want to take over the garden greenery from the person who lived there before you?" The following were multiple-choice responses to both of these questions: The choices for the first question were "(1) I would want them to take it over," "(2) I can't say either way," or "(3) I don't think I would want them to take it over." The choices for the second question were "1. I want to take it over," "2. I can't say either way," or "3. I don't want to take it over."

The present study examines the impact of the four concepts of (a) "personal attributes," (b) "interactions with gardens," (c) "interactions with the area," and (d) "sense of making a contribution to society" as factors that regulate people's awareness about this sort of bi-directional inheritance.

6.3.1.1 The Relationship Between Variables

There were various items that indicated these four concepts. The subordinate variables for the analysis of the residents' (a) "personal attributes" were *sex*, *age*, and *interest in nature*. The subordinate variables for the analysis of the residents' (b) "interactions with gardens" were *amount of garden greenery*, the *level of care for greenery* in the garden, and *attachment to garden greenery*. The subordinate variables for the analysis of the residents' (c) "interactions with the area" were *interaction with one's neighbors*, the *sense of permanent residency*, and *attachment to area*. The subordinate variables for the analysis of the residents (d) were *interest in volunteer activities* and *the way of thinking about social benefits*.

The questions and choices for responses for the subordinate variables in the questionnaire are shown in Table 6.3.

The interactions between the abovementioned 11 subordinate variables and the items on the two types of awareness about the inheritance of greenery of "wanting someone to take over the greenery of one's own garden" and "wanting to take over the garden greenery from the previous resident" were examined using a correlation analysis. This analysis resulted in finding a correlation between many of the variables (reference Table 6.3). While there was an interaction seen between variables

Table 6.3 Each concept and subordinate variable

Concepts	The subordinate variables	Correlation coefficient between in heritance	
		"Wanting to take over one's own garden greenery"	"Wanting to take over the garden greenery from the previous resident"
(a) Personal attributes	"Sex"	n.s.	n.s.
	"Age"	n.s.	n.s.
	"Interest in nature"	$R = .270**$	$R = .258**$
(b) Interactions with gardens	"Amount of garden greenery"	$R = .140**$	n.s.
	"The level of care for greenery in the garden"	$R = .186**$	$R = .161**$
	"Attachment to garden greenery"	$R = .286**$	$R = .248**$
(c) Interactions with the area	"Attachment to area"	$R = .269**$	$R = .267**$
	"Interaction with one's neighbors"	n.s.	$R = .139**$
	"The sense of permanent residency"	$R = .151**$	$R = .125**$
(d) Sense of making a contribution to society	"Interest in volunteer activities"	$R = .107*$	$R = .180**$
	"The way of thinking about social benefits"	$R = .109*$	$R = .182**$

6 Resident's Awareness About Inheritance of Greenery in Gardens 93

for many pairs, it is also possible that there was a spurious correlation whereby the variables were impacted via other variables. Therefore, a multiple classification analysis was performed to examine any such impacts by simultaneously inserting the subordinate variables for each of the concepts.

Additionally, the subordinate variables where a correlation was observed with the awareness about such inheritance will be shown, and the directionality with regard to awareness about such inheritance will be written out briefly. A trend was observed where people desired greenery to be inherited when they had a higher *interest in nature* and a larger *amount of greenery*, provided a higher *level of care for the greenery*, felt more *attachment to garden greenery*, tended to feel more *attachment to the area*, were more active in their *interactions with their neighbors*, tended to feel like they wanted to continue living at their current address as a *permanent residence*, had a stronger *interest in volunteer activities*, and tended to think about prioritizing the benefits of everyone in the nation in their *way of thinking about social benefits*.

6.3.1.2 Examination of Multistage Factors

To examine the factors that regulate people's awareness about the inheritance of garden greenery, a multiple classification analysis was performed by setting the subordinate variables of the following four concepts as the independent variables (a) "personal attributes," (b) "interactions with gardens," (c) "interactions with the area," and (d) "sense of making a contribution to society." Upon investigating the correlations between the independent variables that were inserted, there were strong mutual relationships between the subordinate variables that were for the same one of each of the concepts. Therefore, the variable adopted for each of the concepts was limited a single variable, and these variables were simultaneously inserted. The variables inserted for the correlation analysis in section (1) took the variable with the highest correlation coefficient for each of the concepts.

First, three models were examined for the factors that regulate the awareness of "wanting someone to take over one's own garden greenery." Model 1 inserted (a) "personal attributes" and (b)"interactions with gardens" as the independent variables. Model 2 added the concept of (c) "interactions with the area," and model 3 added the concept of (d) "sense of making a contribution to society."

One reason for examining three models that inserted these four concepts was that the models were asking about thoughts concerning the specific target of personally owned greenery, so this allowed for the investigation of (a) "personal attributes." Additionally, because people are attached to their personally owned greenery, considerations were made for (b) "interactions with gardens." Then, because it seems like the existence and effects of garden greenery make a contribution not only to the individual who owns them but also to the local environment, (c) "interactions with the area" was added into the model. Furthermore, it seems like the inheritance of greenery carries with it significance to the public, as was described in 3.1, so (d) "a sense of making a contribution to society" was also investigated. Concepts (a)–(d) range from narrow individual thinking about the

Table 6.4 The relationship between the subordinate variables and the idea of "wanting someone to take over one's own garden greenery"

Concepts	The subordinate variables	Model1 partial correlation ratioβ	Model2 partial correlation ratioβ	Model3 partial correlation ratioβ
(a) Personal attributes	"Interest in nature"	0.193**	0.181**	0.174**
(b) Interactions with gardens	"Attachment to garden greenery"	0.211**	0.158*	0.154*
(c) Interactions with the area	"Attachment to area"	–	0.197**	0.197**
(d) Sense of making a contribution to society	"The way of thinking about social benefits"	–	–	n.s.
Multiple correlation coefficient:		0.335**	0.384**	0.391**

F-test: **$P < 0.01$, *$P < 0.05$, *n.s.* not significant, − not available

greenery that one personally owns to broad thinking regarding the entire region or society. They show the trends of an expanded range, so this analysis added variables in an order that would broaden this range.

The results of the analysis showed that (a) "personal attributes," (b) "interactions with gardens," and (c) "interactions with the area" had a correlation with the awareness of "wanting someone to take over one's own garden greenery." People with strong interests in nature, strong attachments to gardens, and strong attachments to the area tended to want others to take over their gardens (reference Table 6.4).

There was not impact observed for people's *way of thinking about social benefits* that was inserted in model 6.3. The line of thinking of wanting someone else to take over the greenery that is in one's possessions was not due to thinking about the effects of greenery on the public, and it can be seen as a desire caused by attachment or love for one's own personal property.

At the same time, the three models were investigated with regard to the factors that regulated the other direction of thinking regarding the inheritance of greenery whereby a person was "wanting to take over the garden greenery from the previous resident."

This analysis resulted in the subordinate variable of *attachment to garden greenery* that had been significant in models 1 and 2 losing its determinacy in model 3 (reference Table 6.5). Thus, attachment to garden greenery is not directly connected to wanting to take over someone else's greenery, and it seems like it could have shown a spurious connection due to a connection with another thought.

Additionally, the impact of thinking about social benefits was acknowledged, and a trend was demonstrated where people who thought more about prioritizing the benefits of everyone in the nation had stronger desires to want to take over greenery. Accordingly, it seems like an awareness of making a contribution to society had an impact on people's awareness about inheriting greenery, and this was in separate from the impacts of their interactions with gardens or the area.

6 Resident's Awareness About Inheritance of Greenery in Gardens

Table 6.5 The relationship between the subordinate variables and the idea of "wanting to take over the garden greenery from the previous resident"

Concepts	The subordinate variables	Model1 partial correlation ratioβ	Model2 partial correlation ratioβ	Model3 partial correlation ratioβ
(a) Personal attributes	"Interest in nature"	0.178**	0.155**	0.133*
(b) Interactions with gardens	"Attachment to garden greenery"	0.191**	0.140*	n.s.
(c) Interactions with the area	"Attachment to area"	–	0.197**	0.200**
(d) Sense of making a contribution to society	"The way of thinking about social benefits"	–	–	0.144**
Multiple correlation coefficient:		0.307**	0.359**	0.385**

F-test: **$P < 0.01$, *$P < 0.05$, *n.s.* not significant, – not available

The above showed that there are some differences in the ways of thinking between people with the awareness of "wanting someone to take over the greenery of their own garden" and those with the awareness of "wanting to take over the garden greenery from another person." It was demonstrated that the idea of wanting to take over greenery was impacted by thoughts that prioritize the benefits of the whole society over the individual, and this seems to be connected to thoughts about making a contribution to society.

6.3.2 The Influence that the Burden of Managing Greenery Has on the Inheritance of Greenery

In order to have greenery be inherited, it is essential to consider the undesirable things that are caused by the existence of greenery and the burden of its care, maintenance, and management. Next, the present study will get an understanding of the situation regarding these negative aspects.

6.3.2.1 Care for Greenery

The perceived *burden of care* for garden greenery was measured using the responses to the question "do you or your family feel a burden for the management or care of the garden greenery?" that was asked in the questionnaire (reference Fig. 6.1). The aggregate results for the *level of care for greenery* in one's home and the variables used in the analysis done in Sect. 6.3.1 are shown in Fig. 6.2.

The total percentage of people who felt that the burden of care was "difficult" or "somewhat difficult" was 64.8%, and more than half of the respondents felt a burden.

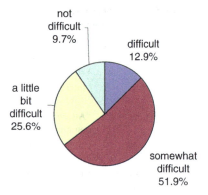

Fig. 6.1 Perceived burden of caring for the garden greenery

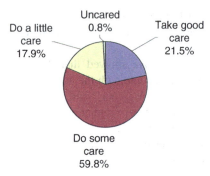

Fig. 6.2 Level of care for home greenery

Additionally, the total percentage of responses for the level of care where people tended to "take good care" and "do some care" was 81.3%, and this can be interpreted as many residents taking care of the garden greenery in their own homes.

A cross analysis was performed on people's awareness of the above two items associated with care and the awareness about the inheritance of greenery. Cramer's V coefficient that was derived from the results of the analysis is shown. There was no significant difference observed between the perceived burdens of care and thinking along the lines of either "wanting someone to take over the greenery of one's own garden" or "wanting to take over the garden greenery from the previous resident." Additionally, a significant difference was found for level of care for greenery (one's own garden, $V = .157^{**}$; the garden of a previous resident, $V = .122^{*}$). People who feel that they take good care of their own gardens had a stronger awareness that desired greenery to be taken over, but there was no interaction observed between whether or not a person felt a burden of care and their awareness about taking over greenery.

The results of a cross analysis between level of care and perceived burden showed a significant difference between the two ($V = .238^{**}$). There was a trend that was seen where the more a person took good care of their greenery the less they felt a burden of care. It was anticipated that taking good care of greenery would proportionally have a large burden, but it is also possible to assume that because the people did not feel a burden, they were able take good care of the greenery. To get an

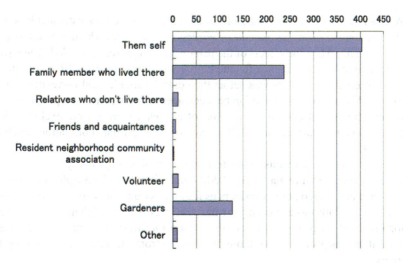

Fig. 6.3 The people who mainly provide care for the greenery in their home garden

understanding of the burden and level of care and the interaction with the residents' awareness, it is necessary to examine a means of ascertaining these things using more objective indicators.

Next, the study obtained responses using a multiple-choice format (multiple selections were permitted) for questions about who mainly does the care of the garden greenery in people's homes (reference Fig. 6.3). The most frequent responses about people who mainly took care of garden greenery were the respondent them self (81.1%) or a family member who lived there (47.7%), and the percentage of responses that indicated that a gardener took care of the greenery was 25.6%.

To investigate what type of state the gardens of the people who hired gardeners were in, a cross analysis was performed on its relationship with *perceived burden of care* for greenery and the *amount of garden greenery*. The results showed a trend where the larger the *amount of greenery* was, the more people had gardeners ($V = -.166**$), and these results also showed a trend where the more people felt that the *perceived burden of care* was difficult, the more they hired gardeners ($V = -.142**$).

Additionally, a significant difference was found in the cross analysis between the responses for the respondents' age and their hiring gardener to take care of their greenery ($V = .237**$). There was a significant difference observed in relation to the respondents' age and years of residency ($V = .413**$). In other words, there was a higher percentage of people who were older who hired gardeners, and the older people were, the more years they tended to reside at their home.

Both the amount of greenery and the respondents' age were observed as having an interaction with whether or not people hired gardeners, but if it is assumed that older people have gardens with more greenery, it is not clear which variable, age or amount of garden greenery, has an impact on hiring a gardener. Therefore, a partial correlation analysis was performed to study the factors that influence hiring a gardener.

Age was set as the control variable, and correlations were investigated based on the interaction between the *amount of garden greenery* and whether or not people hired a gardener when the effects of the respondents' age were excluded. The results showed a significant difference for the partial correlation analysis ($R = -.166**$). *Amount of garden greenery* was set as the control variable, and correlations were investigated based on the interaction between ages and whether or not people hired a gardener when the effects of the *amount of garden greenery* were excluded. The results showed a significant difference for the partial correlation analysis ($R = -.191**$).

Based on the above results, it seems that the amount of greenery is a factor that encourages people to hire gardeners. Additionally, it seems like people in higher age ranges have often lived at their residences for more years, and so it is likely that they have a garden with more greenery. It has also been supposed that age might be a factor involved for hiring gardeners that is separate from the amount of greenery because it causes people to feel more of a burden from the exhaustion of caring for greenery.

6.3.2.2 Perceived Burden of Work Done to Care for Gardens

What specific types of work make the residents feel a burden in the management of their garden greenery? In general, the literature that was reviewed brought up eight items that are jobs associated with caring for garden greenery, and these items were brought up, and the perceived burden associated with them was inquired about (reference Fig. 6.4).

The tasks for which the respondents had the highest rates of feeling a burden and choosing the answers "1. It is a burden" or "2. It is somewhat of a burden" were "b) mowing or weeding," and this was followed by "a) pruning and cutting trees and shrubs." On the other hand, the job that people felt the least burden for was "f) spreading fertilizer."

A factor analysis (principal component method, varimax rotation) was preformed, and the results were organized to examine how people perceive the abovementioned jobs necessary for caring for garden greenery (reference Table 6.6).

The results of the analysis could be interpreted as showing the primary factor for burden is related to "maintenance and management of greenery" that has grown, and this is based on the high amount of burden associated with items like pruning, weeding, or cleaning associated with these tasks. They could also be interpreted as showing that the secondary factor for burden is related to "cultivating greenery," and this is based on the high amount of burden associated with tasks like spreading fertilizer, transplanting, and watering.

The content of the work that is done can be broadly divided into two types of work: jobs done with the purpose of cultivating plants and jobs done with the purpose of maintaining the cultivated plants or managing them like cleaning. The rate that these two factors contribute to burdens is roughly the same at 29.7% and 29.6%, and this can be interpreted as people considering the tasks related to

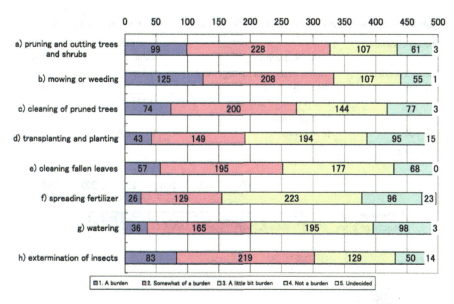

Fig. 6.4 The burdens of care and management of garden greenery

Table 6.6 The results of the factor analysis on the burden of jobs done to care for greenery

Care for greenery	Factor1	Factor2
c) Cleaning of pruned trees	**0.712**	0.321
a) Pruning and cutting trees and shrubs	**0.675**	0.320
b) Mowing or weeding	**0.671**	0.365
e) Cleaning fallen leaves	**0.603**	0.497
f) Spreading fertilizer	0.324	**0.868**
d) Transplanting and planting	0.427	**0.618**
g) Watering	0.340	**0.611**
h) Extermination of insects	0.445	**0.526**
Contributing rate (%)	29.7	29.6
Cumulative contributing ratio (%)	29.7	59.4

cultivating plants and the tasks related to their maintenance and management as being perceived in an identical manner as the main work for taking care of a garden.

Next, a multiple regression analysis was performed by setting the two factors that were obtained through this factor analysis as the independent variables and setting the *perceived burden of care* for greenery as the dependent variable (reference Table 6.7). The results found a significant difference based on the coefficient of determination being $R^2 = 0.557$, and this can be explained as them being factors related to the *perceived burden of care*. When the interpretability of each of the factors is looked at according to the standard partial regression coefficients, "maintenance and management of greenery" had a coefficient of 0.606, and this was high when compared with the coefficient value of 0.325 that was obtained for the "cultivation of greenery."

Table 6.7 Multiple regression model to explain the perceived burden of care for greenery

The dependent variable	Care for greenery	Coefficient value	t-value	F-test
The independent variables	Maintenance and management of greenery	0.606	18.687	**
	Cultivation of greenery	0.325	10.015	**
	Constant number		89.757	
n = 444	R = 0.746	$R^2 = 0.557$		**

**$P < 0.01$

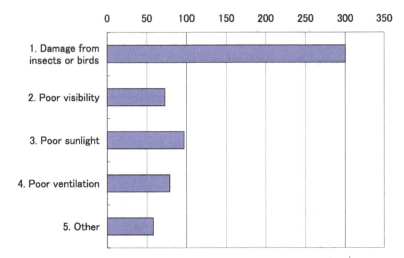

Fig. 6.5 Points that are not desirable for garden greenery

The above results indicated that when dealing with the care for greenery, people feel a greater burden from pruning and the maintenance and management that accompanies it such as cleaning compared with the tasks that accompany the cultivation of greenery. Of course, the cultivation of greenery is mainly work that is done during the initial period when plants are being put into the garden, and after a certain amount of growth has taken place, maintenance and management become the primary tasks. Thus, there is a difference in the times when these tasks take place, and it seems like the frequency of work and the differences in the time periods when the gardens are created could affect perceived burden.

6.3.2.3 Things Those Are Undesirable for Garden Greenery

Some events that are generally mentioned as being undesirable for garden greenery are insect damage, damage from birds, and poor ventilation, visibility, and sunlight. To grasp the residents' awareness of their greenery, multiple responses were obtained about "undesirable things that are applicable" (reference Fig. 6.5).

Upon totaling the results, the most frequent selection was "1. The occurrence of damage from insects or birds," and this response were given by 60.4% of respondents. A cross analysis was performed in relation to the *amount of garden greenery* to investigate if these undesirable events had an impact on the differences in amounts of garden greenery. These results did not indicate a significant difference. The things that were no desirable for the greenery were not caused by the amount of greenery; rather, it seems like the arrangement of the greenery might have had an impact on if undesirable situations arose. However, there was a significant difference demonstrated when a cross analysis was performed between years of residency and the responses that indicated that the "sunlight became poor" ($V = .169**$). It seems like the longer people have resided in their homes, the more the trees and shrubs have grown and become tall, and this could potentially obstruct the sunlight. Additionally, it is possible that people take care to do things like pruning and trimming to adjust the greenery so that it doesn't fall into a state where there are undesirable obstructions to airflow, sunlight, and visibility. However, insect and bird damage can hurt the greenery regardless of whether people put care into their gardens.

6.3.2.4 Greenery in the Future

Figure 6.6 shows the results of the responses to the multiple response questions asking about "where would you like to see greenery increased in the future?" The percentage of people who answered the greenery by their own homes or in the neighborhood was 27.2% and 11.7%, respectively, and these were not very prevalent responses compared with other answers. There were many responses about public places such as park (61.4%), schools (48.1%), and roadside trees (57.7%).

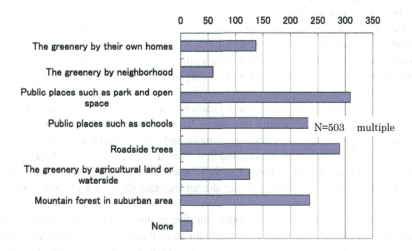

Fig. 6.6 Greenery that we want to increase in the future

Additionally, there were many responses (46.7%) for places where there has always been a certain level of greenery such as mountain forests and rivers, but this was a low percentage compared with places that are close to residential districts like parks, schools, or roadside trees.

A significant difference was found with people's "home garden greenery" when a cross analysis was done between the selection of each of these responses and their relationship with awareness about the inheritance of greenery. The Cramer coefficient for "wanting someone to take over the greenery of one's own garden" was $V = .195**$, and it was $V = .210**$ for "wanting to take over the garden greenery from the previous resident." A trend was observed where people who chose the response that they wanted to increase the greenery in their own home garden tended to have more awareness about the inheritance of greenery. The results did not indicate a significant difference between the selections of any of the other responses.

6.4 Discussion

There are two different directions in which people can think about the inheritance of greenery. One of these directions is the desire for the next resident to take over the greenery that one owns, and the other direction is the desire to take over someone else's greenery. There were differences observed in the factors that determine each of the types of awareness.

The line of thinking of desiring greenery to be inherited by wanting to have others to take over one's own greenery tended to be seen in people who had more attachments to their own gardens. However, it became clear that the line of thinking where a person wanted to take over greenery from others was not impacted by the level of attachment to gardens but was impacted by a person's awareness about making contributions to society.

The inheritance of greenery signifies that the effects brought about by greenery will affect the region and future generations. Accordingly, when people are thinking about making contributions to other people, the region, or the general environment rather than just about their own benefits, they seem like they might have different desires about such inheritance.

It is possible that residential garden greenery will be lost when a house is rebuilt. Because the cycle of rebuilding houses in Japan is fairly short and spans several decades, the promotion of inheriting greenery and prevention of such losses would benefit from an improved understanding that, even if greenery is personal property, it is useful for the region and whole of society. Additionally, in order to have greenery be inherited, it is essential to consider the undesirable things for greenery and the burden of caring for it.

There is a high percentage of people who live in houses who feel a burden from caring for greenery, cultivating it, or maintaining or managing it, and the percentage of people who hire gardeners increases in houses where there is a larger amount of greenery and a higher age range.

Tall trees contribute to increasing the amount of greenery, but on the other hand, they can bring about undesirable situations like being located in a way that causes less sunlight. However, it has been supposed that the pruning and cutting down of tall trees are tasks that create a large burden for elderly people. These sorts of burdens of care drive people to not want greenery to be inherited, and they could potentially be reasons that people don't want to increase the greenery in their home gardens in the future.

Based on the above results, it seems like some things that are important for the inheritance of greenery are PR done to increase people's interest in nature and encouraging people to have interactions with greenery. Additionally, an improved understanding of the contributions that individual small privately owned gardens make to the local environment also seems quite important. Gardens function as a location for greenery in residential environments, but whether or not they have a full quantity of greenery depends on the owners' preferences. The growth of trees and shrubs requires a long time, and the understanding of individual greenery's contributions to the environment is improving, so it can be anticipated that there will be community-wide improvements that include the maintenance and management of caring for green environments.

While the questionnaire survey used in the analysis of this paper ascertained the respondent's age and sex as basic attributes, it did not ascertain their academic backgrounds, occupations, or income. It has been assumed that a high income will be associated with spacious residential areas or large lots for people's homes, and the size of a lot seems like it will have an impact on the amount of greenery and the area of the garden. Additionally, it is possible that people's awareness about volunteering and their ways of thinking about benefits could differ depending on their academic backgrounds or occupations. It is also possible that there could be changes in people's way of interacting with their regions or attachments depending on their occupations.

However, it was not possible to clarify these points due to the limitations of the survey items that were used in this study. However, the result of having extremely few items that were related to personal attributes that could have potentially made people feel resistance about answering was that a high response rate was secured. One future challenge that should be tackled is a deep investigation of the residents' awareness and the precise impacts that personal attributes have on it.

References

Burgess J, Harrison CM, Limb M (1988) People, parks and the urban green: a study of popular meanings and values for open spaces in the city. Urban Stud 25:455–473

Kida Y, Urayama Mo, Matsuura K (2006) A study on the local habitants consciousness to greenery landscape in housing lots: in case of 5 residential areas in Nagoya City. Summaries of technical papers of annual meeting Architectural Institute of Japan, F-1, pp 389–390

Kogiso Y (1998) An attempt to inherit greenery and community upon public housing rebuilding: community landscape and greenery of housing. J Jpn Inst Landsc Archit 62(1):33–35

Kubo T, Nakase I, Abe D, Masuda N, Shimomura Y (1986) Attitudes by residents towards the private and public greens in their neighborhood. Jpn Inst Landsc Archit 49(5):209–214

Kwun K, Abe D, Masuda N, Shimomura Y, Yamamoto S (1994) Study on the various effects of conserved forest in Newtown on residents through the questionnaire survey. Jpn Inst Landsc Archit 57(5):187–192

Mizukami S, Hagihara K (2011) Recovery of greenery in a suburban detached housing area: aspects of greenery landscapes. Jpn Sect Reg Sci Assoc Int 41(1):15–28

Shinji I (1975) Study of limit of natural surfaces in our living environment. Jpn Inst Landsc Archit 38(4):16–31

Smardon RC (1988) Perception and aesthetics of the urban environment: review of the role of vegetation. Landsc Urban Plan 15(1–2):85–106

Takahashi R (1982) Structure and style of green spaces as an essential element in human environment. Jpn Inst Landsc Archit 46(2):140–146

Tokyo Metropolitan Government Bureau of City Planning (1999) Land Use in Tokyo: Overview of Land Use Survey. Tokyo Metropolitan Government

Tokyo Metropolitan Government Bureau of Environment (2006) Annual Report on the Environment in Tokyo. Tokyo Metropolitan Government, p 12

Tsutsumi D, Amano K, Ameda S (2005) Study on plants environment of detached house yard from view of Resident conscious. Summaries of technical papers of annual meeting Architectural Institute of Japan, F-1, pp 1125–1126

Part III
Design and Policy for a Resilient Regional System

Chapter 7
Types of Social Enterprises and Various Social Problems

Fumiko Kimura, Kiyoko Hagihara, Noriko Horie, and Chisato Asahi

Abstract This chapter surveys the performance of social enterprises and examines how they solve various social problems. Social enterprises can be regarded as a new model of modern non-profit organisations (NPOs). They are working to challenge and untangle the various social obstacles we face today, such as issues relating to the environment and well-being, the inequality of educational opportunities, and the disparity in income distribution.

Although prompt action must be taken to overcome these challenges, governments alone cannot find an answer to them in a satisfactory manner, so social enterprises have recently stepped in and are shifting the boundaries. From the viewpoint of sustainability, to accomplish their various targets, they need to earn money by generating their own business. They also need to receive contributions or investments to continue their activities. Many start-up social enterprises are struggling to obtain resources such as manpower, contributions, and grants. The success stories of social enterprises impact various fields. Through tough experiences, some of them obtain business know-how. Afterwards, they can support other NPOs. This movement suggests that the community supports social enterprise, such as business incubators.

The Ministry of Economy, Trade and Industry (METI) reported 27 cases in the Social Business Casebook (Ministry of Economy, Trade and Industry, Social

---

F. Kimura (✉)
Division of Correspondence Education, SOKA University, Tokyo, Japan
e-mail: fkimura@soka.ac.jp

K. Hagihara
Tokyo Metropolitan University, Tokyo, Japan
e-mail: khagi@tb3.so-net.ne.jp

N. Horie
Department of Public Policy, Faculty of Sociology, Bukkyo University, Kyoto, Japan
e-mail: horie@bukkyo-u.ac.jp

C. Asahi
Department of Urban Science and Policy, Faculty of Urban Environmental Sciences, Tokyo Metropolitan University, Hachioji, Tokyo, Japan
e-mail: asahi@tmu.ac.jp

© Springer Nature Singapore Pte Ltd. 2019
C. Asahi (ed.), *Building Resilient Regions*, New Frontiers in Regional Science: Asian Perspectives 35, https://doi.org/10.1007/978-981-13-7619-1_7

Business Casebook (Earthquake Disaster Recovery Version) – social business for reconstruction of disaster area). http://www.meti.go.jp/press/2011/01/20120113002/20120113002.html (2013/9/11) (in Japanese) 2012) regarding the recovery process after the Great East Japan Earthquake. We examine various cases and demonstrate how society-oriented corporations and business-oriented non-profits deal with numerous tasks, with a focus on short-term problems such as the basic services of daily life. The actors involved include seven non-profits and three for-profit organisations. A higher number of for-profit groups deal with medium-term or long-term challenges such as business risk.

Keywords Social enterprises · Public goods · Third-sector non-profit organisation

7.1 Introduction

In response to social issues such as securing safety nets, the environment, welfare, medical care, and education, the government has provided public goods and responded to problems in the past. However, due to reductions in the fiscal budget, government activities alone cannot adequately respond to social challenges. In recent years, efforts by the third sector – which includes non-profit organisations (NPOs) and non-governmental organisations (NGOs) – to address social problems have received attention (Borzaga and Defourny 2001; Crutchfield and Grant 2008; Drucker 1990; Noya 2009). Social enterprises are attracting attention as business entities involved in solving today's social and economic problems by utilising business to make a profit, rather than for charitable activities or volunteering. In addition, we mentioned the role of corporate social responsibility (CSR) and socially responsible investment (SRI), in social, economic, and environmental problems (Kimura et al. 2013, 2015). Various initiatives were launched in the private sector in order to help with the recovery process following the Great East Japan Earthquake on 11 March 2011. There are also movements such as individual volunteer activities and fundraising (Japan Fundraising Association (ed.) 2015; Saga 2011).

Social enterprises procure funds and human resources (volunteers, expertise, and specialised skills) and handle the issues encountered by various entities. Furthermore, it is recognised that not only do they solve social problems but they also involve the community in the process of solving problems and change society through their problem-solving proposals. A representative example of such a social enterprise is Grameen Bank, founded by Muhammad Yunus (2007). In 2006, the bank and its founder were jointly awarded the Nobel Peace Prize. Today, under the guidance of the World Bank, projects are being implemented in over 40 countries based on the Grameen Bank's model.

Concepts and structures such as organisational missions, business opportunities, public goods, and the supply of services are arranged based on conditions such as activity fields, available resources (people, goods, money, information), and behavioural principles. Section 7.2 defines social enterprises, explains the present circumstances (based on previous research and an overview of how social enterprises have emerged), and outlines the literature. Section 7.3 explores the optimal form of an organisation for solving problems and the role it plays. Section 7.4 portrays cases of commercial organisations and NPOs.

7.2 Outline and Definition of Social Enterprises

7.2.1 The Rise of Social Enterprises

Various researchers have looked at the socialisation of commercial organisations, the commercialisation of NPOs, and the emergence of the third sector and new public concepts, such as the recession of the welfare state and active CSR activities (Borzaga, Edwards et al., Evers, Lipietz, Tsukamoto). The literature contains examples of issues being addressed by neighbourhood associations, self-governing associations, municipalities, and volunteer groups. For-profit organisations operate through market exchanges, while governments collect taxes and provide public goods and services based on taxpayer consensus. NPOs emphasise the outcomes of solving social challenges and deal with matters such as market exchanges and charity acts, which do not attract due to attention in the market. The presence of social enterprises as a third sector is increasing, comprising organisations that cannot be defined by market mechanisms and charity frameworks (Fig. 7.1).

Tanimoto (2006) points out that it is not only NPOs who are making efforts to find answers to social problems but commercial organisations as well. Furthermore, Tsukamoto (2011) indicates that the boundary between the for-profit and non-profit sectors is 'ambiguous' regarding the rise of social enterprises. For-profit entities are 'socialised', while NPOs are 'commercialised'. In other words, CSR-driven companies seek to gain not only economic value but also social value, and companies are

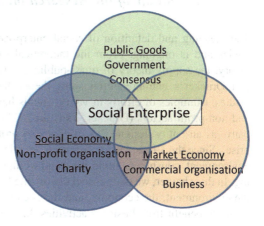

Fig. 7.1 The rise of social enterprises. (Source: Created by the author)

increasing their added value as they improve their social conditions. On the other hand, NPOs rely on donations and public subsidies less and less and now actively earn revenue. In the USA and the UK, the background to the 'commercialisation' of NPOs is the government's austerity measures.

Tanimoto (2006) and Tsukamoto and Yamagishi (2008) examine how social enterprises have emerged. In the USA, after the Reagan administration, the size and functions of the Federal Government shrank; the same phenomenon occurred in the UK after 2000, when the Blair administration decided to eliminate social exclusion and promote social enterprises from the viewpoint of reforming public services.

The flow of social enterprises in Japan is an extension of community and social businesses, which has been advanced by the Ministry of Economy, Trade and Industry (METI) since the time of former Prime Minister Junichiro Koizumi. These efforts have been promoted to create jobs and revitalise regions (METI 2008). These players are collectively called the third sector. They not only play roles as government subcontractors but also act to solve social problems. To that end, it is necessary to improve the legal and economic environment for social enterprises, including legal, tax, social finance, and support systems (Tanimoto, Tsukamoto).

In Europe, the role of the third sector and the private sector has led to the creation of a concept called the 'new public', which is the entity responsible for administering public goods and services that governments formerly provided (Borzaga, Edwards et al. 2013; Evers, Lipietz 2001). Tsukamoto (2011) shows that social enterprises face the following difficulties in solving issues through business methods: (1) It is difficult for the beneficiary to bear the cost; (2) in terms of public assistance, it is difficult to become a party to public subsidies or contracts; (3) groups that cannot pay service fees are eliminated; (4) there is indifference in the face of strengthening social capital; and (5) they are susceptible to becoming institutionalised.

7.2.2 An Outline of the Research on Social Enterprises

The meaning and definition of social enterprise has been discussed from various angles and is ongoing. From the theoretical side, aspects such as organisational theory, the supply theory of quasi-public goods, Schumpeter's innovation theory, and Drucker's entrepreneurial spirit theory have been studied. Regarding case studies, examples of efforts in various fields have been explored in both the profit and non-profit sectors (Drucker, Tsuyuki 2011). Tanimoto (2006) defined a 'company' as an entity designed to solve social problems as a 'society-oriented enterprise'. Since the 1980s, the idea of fixing social problems (affecting areas such as the environment, consumers, minorities, and welfare) through business has been emerging. In this chapter, we define 'socially oriented attitude' as an attitude that considers the environment, the economy, and the society. This outlook does not include the desire to benefit from business activities. In contrast, the 'market-oriented attitude' assigns priority to profit. Regarding companies' contributions to society, these efforts are defined as companies doing their best to help society; these efforts relate to broad concepts that include the corporate citizen's support for arts and culture (the French term *mécénat*, roughly translated as *patronage*) and philanthropic activities carried out by companies.

In terms of social enterprise theory, there are two different views in the USA and Europe. Differences in the definition of CSR are reflected in the way that social enterprises are arranged. In the USA, CSR is the foundation of corporate citizenry, which means that a company contributes to the community (e.g. by letting local residents use the company's facilities) and conducts charitable activities (such as making donations) (Kimura et al.). Recently, the notion of philanthropic capitalism (social contribution capitalism) has been seen in efforts by Google and is also drawing attention (Tsuyuki). In contrast, the government plays a larger role in European CSR.

Social enterprises in the USA consider business revenue to be the main source of income and regard donations and membership fees as unstable financial resources. They argue that independence and sustainability cannot be maintained as long as enterprises depend on individuals, subsidies, and grants from the government (Dees). Discussions on social enterprises began with a reduction in the government budget, the commercialisation of NPOs due to a drop in private contributions, and corporatisation. However, the focus of the discourse is gradually shifting towards social entrepreneurship. A good social entrepreneur needs to possess the following qualities: (1) business profitability (not for volunteering); (2) innovation and new structures; and (3) sociality (the ability to create new orders and norms concerning social missions, outcomes, and issues). Furthermore, by adding the new added values of 'social contributions' and 'social orientations', social entrepreneurship falls in line with market expansion strategies via general commercial enterprises; social enterprise theory has developed by including these notions (Suda 2010). On the other hand, in Europe, social enterprises recognise that people face challenges such as poverty, disabilities, and long-term unemployment. These people are excluded from the labour market and the community. They suffer from 'social exclusion' and are reintroduced into society. Given that 'social inclusion' is a common policy within the European Union (EU), EU governments support companies that work on issues of social exclusion and inclusion (Borzaga and Defourny, Evers).

Kerlin (2006) presents a comparative study of social enterprise theory between the USA and Europe. Social enterprises in the USA focus on commercialisation to generate profit, and business entities (i.e. in terms of socially oriented activities by for-profit corporations with social missions) are paying attention. Since the 1980s, the rise of small governments has become a factor in creating businesslike NPOs. Dees (1998) describes the hybrid organisation, which has changed the fundraising environment in that it promotes the commercialisation of NPOs; social enterprises are seen as hybrid organisations that combine social objectives and business methods. Hybrid groups thus belong in a mixed sector that lies between philanthropy and business.

Table 7.1 A comparison of social enterprise theory in the USA and Europe

Item		USA	Europe
Kerlin	Priority activities	Increased income	Social benefits
	General organisation	NPO $(501(c)(3))^{(1)}$	Cooperative
	Main subjects	Non-profit activities in general	Personal services
	Types of social enterprises	Many	A few
	Beneficiary participation	Limited	Common
	Main support	Private funds	Government/EU
	Field of study	Management, social sciences	Social sciences
	Related fields	Market economy	Socioeconomics
	Framework of law	Insufficient	Improving due to various ideas
Evers	Principle of profit distribution	Excluding cooperatives and mutual aid associations, shifting to a position centred on profit and non-distribution constraints	In a position restricting the private acquisition of profit; cooperatives and mutual aid associations are included

Source: Created from Evers and Laville (2004) and Kerlin (2006)
Note: Donation organisation deduction group (NPO), certified as an organisation in Article 501 (c) (3), prescribed by the US Internal Revenue Service

Meanwhile, European social enterprises have developed while coping with the problem of 'social exclusion'. They respect the public interest, whereby the ratio of public funds (such as donations, subsidies, and grants) is high in comparison to the USA (Noya). Table 7.1 compares the USA and Europe (Evers, Kerlin).

In Japan, METI calls social enterprises 'social businesses', as shown in Fig. 7.2, which introduces the notion based on the two axes of 'sociality' and 'profitability' (2008). However, as there is no agreement on the definition, basic data (the number of social enterprises in each country, the number of employees, market size, etc.) are not well-developed (Borzaga and Defourny, Yamauchi).

7.2.3 The Definition of Social Enterprises

Enterprises are classified into private and public. Private enterprises are based on the investments and management of civilians, accumulating profit and paying dividends to shareholders. Public companies, on the other hand, are owned and operated by national and local public entities, such as water supply and the minting of currency. The

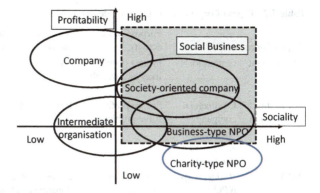

Fig. 7.2 Social business as indicated by the Ministry of Economy, Trade and Industry. (Source: Ministry of Economy, Trade and Industry (2008), 'Social Business Study Group Report' p.3)

concept of a social enterprise does not fit within the traditional framework of private enterprises and has come to be known as the 'third sector'. In the late 1980s and 1990s, policy changes relating to concepts such as 'small government' and the 'third way' were promoted in Europe and the USA following reviews of welfare state policy (Noya). Under these circumstances, the third sector became an entity engaged with NPOs and non-governmental organisations (NGOs) to advance solutions to social problems. In other words, social enterprises are entities that seek to resolve various social problems in a wide range of fields such as medical care, welfare, education, the environment, and culture (Borzaga and Defourny, Evers, Noya, Yunus).

In this chapter, with reference to the above definitions, we regard social enterprises as entities that gather society's resources to tackle challenges by solving social problems. Social enterprises are defined broadly as follows: (1) They aim to solve social problems; (2) they gather resources from society to find answers to social challenges. Socially responsible investment (SRI) is a type of investment based on social (nonfiscal information) evaluation as a criterion when deciding where to place investments. We believe that it is worth supporting companies that aim to achieve or improve CSR.

7.3 Types of Organisations and the Functions of Social Enterprises

7.3.1 Types of Organisations

Social enterprises can take various forms, such as cooperation with the government, commercial organisations, and NPOs. They provide goods and services, support other entities, and offer specialised functions. The main types of NPOs based on the Japanese legal system are (1) foundations or incorporated organisations, which were created by the new system of public interest corporations; (2) NPOs; (3) school corporations; (4) social welfare corporations; (5) religious groups; (6) rehabilitation protection NPOs; and (7) medical corporations (Yamauchi). Based on the above

Table 7.2 Types of organisations that provide goods and services

Type of organisation		Purpose of the activity	Sources of funding for business activities	Activity
Government	Central/local	Protect people's lives and wealth	Tax	Supply public goods and services
For-profit organisation	Commercial company	Secure profit, solve problems	Revenues, loans, investment funds	Supply private goods and services
	Society-oriented company			
NPO	*Business-type NPO*	Accomplish a mission	Business revenues, donations, subsidies, etc.	Solve social issues
	Charity-type NPO		Donations, subsidies, etc.	

Source: Created by the author

definitions, we consider the providers of goods and services from the angle of government policies and business opportunities, as well as organisations that intend to solve social problems. In other words, an organisation is considered a social enterprise if its priority is to resolve social challenges, even if it is a for-profit entity that is a 'society-oriented company'. 'Business-type NPOs' are included among social enterprises since they generate revenue and find answers to issues by using diversified sources and resources, such as dues and donations. However, 'charitable NPOs' are excluded from the definition of social enterprises based on the category of 'company' as explained in the previous section. Charitable NPOs try to solve problems by using subsidies, membership fees, donations, etc. as the main source of funding; this type of NPO has a small proportion of business revenue (Table 7.2).

In this chapter, we focus on 'society-oriented enterprises' and 'business-type NPOs', which are among the organisations shown in Table 7.2. We define them as social enterprises in a narrow sense. The establishment and operation of social enterprises require support for various resources and the provision of information. However, requests from social enterprises and the goods provided by resource holders (potential resource providers) are diverse. Therefore, support from intermediary organisations is necessary to match resource holders with social enterprises. Intermediate support organisations have become important in ensuring that social enterprises' activities are sustainable. Although there are various definitions of intermediate support organisations, Yamauchi et al. (2013) consider their main role in Japan to consist of the following: (1) mediating management resources (human resources, funds, information) and (2) promoting networking between NPOs. Social enterprises utilise society's various resources to solve problems by cooperating with different entities, for instance, through partnerships with supporters (Fig. 7.3).

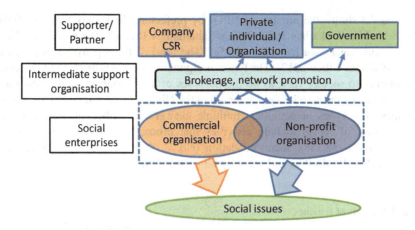

Fig. 7.3 Social enterprises and supporters. (Source: Created by the author)

Table 7.3 Number of NPOs by prefecture

Prefecture	Number of NPOs	%
Tokyo	9280	19.3
Osaka	1652	3.4
Saitama	1573	3.3
Chiba	1559	3.2
Kanagawa	1367	2.8
Subtotal (the above 5 prefectures)	15,431	32.2
Other prefectures	32,542	67.8
Total	47,973	100.0

Source: https://www.npo-homepage.go.jp/portalsite/bunyabetsu_ninshou.html
Note: This data was current as of 1 July 2013

According to the Cabinet Office's website (https://www.npo-homepage.go.jp/), there were 47,973 NPOs as of the end of July 2013 and 264 certified NPOs as of the end of June 2013 (Table 7.3). When a corporation is certified as an NPO, donation tax credits can be deducted based on the new contribution tax system of 2010 and the revision of the NPO Act. The merits of certified NPOs are recognised in statements like 'donations have become easy to collect' (76.1%) and the increase in 'social credit or gains in awareness' (66.6%) (Cabinet Office 2012). However, since the current criteria necessary to acquire certification are high, 45% of the corporations are not prepared to apply. Furthermore, among the eight certification requirements, the most difficult one to satisfy for 67.8% of NPOs was the Public Support Test (PST) ($n = 546$). The PST stipulates that the proportion of donations to current revenue amount be more than a certain ratio (1/5). In the amendment, the possibility of acquiring certification has improved since two standards were added. PST now requires that 'an average of 100 or more people per year donate 3000 yen or more' (Cabinet Office 2011a, b, Japan NPO Center).

116 F. Kimura et al.

Table 7.3 shows the number of NPOs by prefecture. In Tokyo, there are 9280 (19.3%), while Osaka has 1652 (3.4%). Saitama has 1573 (3.3%), Chiba has 1559 (3.2%), and Kanagawa has 1367 (2.8%). The total of the top five prefectures is 32.2% (Cabinet Office 2012). The types of organisations that provide various goods and services to society vary, as do the purposes of and resources for the activities. Table 7.4 shows the activity field and ratio of the NPOs as an example of the types of activities. The types of activities (multiple answers) described in the articles of incorporation of NPOs include activities that promote health, medical care, or welfare (No. 1, 58.1%), social education (No. 2, 46.9%), and advisory and aid functions (No. 19, 46.0%) and are shown in Table 7.4.

Table 7.4 Fields of activities of NPOs

No.	Type of activity	Number of corporations (multiple answers)	%
No. 1	Activities to promote health, medical care, or welfare	27,600	58.1
No. 2	Activities to promote social education	22,301	46.9
No. 3	Activities to promote town planning	20,369	42.8
No. 4	Activities to promote tourism	565	1.2
No. 5	Activities to promote agricultural mountain fishing villages or middle mountain areas	508	1.1
No. 6	Activities to foster academics, culture, arts, or sports	16,308	34.3
No. 7	Activities to preserve the environment	13,516	28.4
No. 8	Disaster relief activities	3734	7.9
No. 9	Regional safety activities	5425	11.4
No. 10	Activities to promote human rights or peace	7864	16.5
No. 11	Activities to promote international cooperation	9139	19.2
No. 12	Activities to promote the formation of a gender-equal society	4171	8.8
No. 13	Activities aimed at children's health	20,338	42.8
No. 14	Activities to promote the development of an information society	5412	11.4
No. 15	Activities to advance science and technology	2614	5.5
No. 16	Activities to stimulate the economy	8048	16.9
No. 17	Activities to support the development of vocational abilities or the expansion of employment opportunities	10,954	23.0
No. 18	Activities to protect consumers	2993	6.3
No. 19	Advice or assistance activities, including contacts of the management or organisations conducting the activities listed in the preceding items	21,875	46.0
No. 20	Activities similar to those listed in each of the preceding items or activities specified by ordinance in designated city	66	0.1

Source: https://www.npo-homepage.go.jp/portalsite/bunyabetsu_ninshou.html

7.3.2 Procedure for Carrying Out Tasks and the Functions of Social Enterprises

7.3.2.1 Procedure for Solving Problems

The main procedure for finding answers to social challenges unfolds as follows: (1) discovering problems; (2) preparing solutions; (3) implementing solutions; and (4) evaluating the execution of the solution. Upon discovering an issue, some sort of information is disseminated. For example, the matter is discussed in terms of the subject facing challenges (consultations, complaints, petitions, etc.); meanwhile, it is important that the problem be perceived in a sensitive way. If we can recognise a problem and define it, we can shift to the planning stage to solve it. At this stage, it is necessary to clarify the following: the reaching objectives, maintenance and confirmation of necessary resource estimates (human resources, funds, materials, etc.), process charts, role-sharing, and communication systems. The ability to procure resources and implement actions plays a major role at the time of execution, but when comparing reality and the draft of a plan, it is imperative to review the plan as necessary. To assess the results, an evaluation indicator is used as a criterion to judge whether the initial purpose can be achieved.

7.3.2.2 Functions of Social Enterprises

In solving problems through the above four steps, there are uncertain factors, and trial and error is necessary at each stage. The Japanese government imposes many restrictions, such as single-year budgets and the fiscal year time period; if a plan is certain, it can be adopted, but plans with trial and error tend to struggle for support. Furthermore, in the case of a commercial enterprise, tolerance levels for trial and error are low. Social enterprises that solve problems well are 'society-oriented' ones with innovative power and social missions, as well as 'business-type NPOs' that try to solve problems by utilising diverse resources. In other words, we think that social enterprises are capable of proposing and disseminating problem-solving methods, such as model presentation (typing), information sharing (case collection), and so on. Presenting problem-solving techniques can be considered a new business model because they contain innovation, leading to business opportunities. Social enterprises show how to solve challenges during each stage of trying to fix them (Fig. 7.4).

7.4 Characteristics of Organisations

Social enterprises tackle difficult tasks using business methods. In this chapter, we focus on business-type NPOs and society-oriented enterprises (commercial organisations), as shown in Table 7.2. For society-oriented enterprises, we expect social

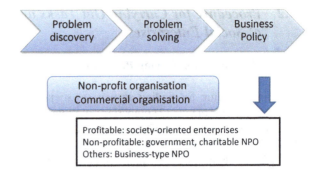

Fig. 7.4 Functions of social enterprises. (Source: Created by the author)

contributions to occur through the core business. Meanwhile, business-type NPOs tend to organise missions, present challenges based on the cognition and definition of tasks, and are included in case studies. The Regional Economy and Industry Group of METI (2012) published the 'Social Business Casebook (Earthquake Disaster Recovery Version)' in January 2012 as an example of activities for the reconstruction of areas affected by the Great East Japan Earthquake. This report covers 27 cases and 31 enterprises (14 organisations, 12 limited companies (Ltd. Cos.), and 5 other corporations). In the activity field (multiple answers), 'regional activity or town planning' consisted of 67.7%, while 'social business support' accounted for 54.8% (Table 7.5).

The report includes examples of NPOs and commercial organisations, so this chapter will take this casebook as a concrete example. During the Great East Japan Earthquake, local government offices were affected, and they could not carry out their normal functions. The primary, short-term task was to provide support for victims' daily needs and to rescue evacuees. However, regarding the medium and long term, concepts such as 'town planning' and 'social business support' are essential to developing future players of regional reconstruction and revitalisation. During post-earthquake disaster reconstruction, both short- and long-term emergency measures are required. Table 7.6 summarises the necessary support for each period.

In the case of for-profit organisations that can solve problems and earn money at the same time, it is necessary to grasp what the needs are in a niche market (e.g. mobile food trucks) while recognising and defining the task at hand. Ways to implement solutions and generate profit by constructing a new business model occur through innovation. Business opportunities and CSR activities are also revealed in the process. A new movement known as 'creating shared value' (CSV) aims to solve social challenges through business methods whereby companies acquire new opportunities by combining economic and social value (Porter 1980). Regarding NPOs, it is difficult to expect them to earn much profit, but if it is possible to earn business revenue (for covering expenses), this allows for business to continue. NPOs can continue to act to fulfil administrative functions and accept volunteers and donations.

7 Types of Social Enterprises and Various Social Problems

Table 7.5 Social enterprises' fields of activities

Activity area	Total No.	(%)	Ltd. Co. No.	(%)	NPO No.	(%)
Environment · new energy	4	12.9	1	4.0	2	6.5
Local activity · town development	21	67.7	9	36.0	11	35.5
Education · child-rearing	1	3.2			1	3.2
Social business support	17	54.8	8	32.0	8	25.8
Human resource development/independence support	5	16.1	2	8.0	3	9.7
Agriculture	6	19.4	3	12.0	3	9.7
IT/informationisation	2	6.5	1	4.0	1	3.2
Welfare · insurance · medical	4	12.9	1	4.0	2	6.5

Source: Ministry of Economy, Trade and Industry (2012)

Table 7.6 Assistance needed by disaster victims

Time period	Daily goods (clothing, food, etc.)	Residence	Maintaining health	Funds
Short term	Food, clothing, daily necessities (stockpiles, supporting goods, etc.)	Shelter	Medical dispatch	Living funds (solatium, financial donations, etc.)
Medium term	Daily living support (daily necessities, work, health maintenance, etc.)	Temporary housing	Temporary clinic	Living reconstruction funds (income, insurance claims, financing)
Long term	Living reconstruction support (industrial infrastructure and infrastructure development)	Reconstructed houses	Clinic	Entrepreneurial funds, working capital (funds, finance)

Source: Created by the author

The casebook is divided into three parts: (1) identifying the types of task and solving consumer needs; (2) creating entrepreneurs and employment; and (3) creating new financing mechanisms. Then, two time-based categories are created (short term and medium to long term), and the management entity is divided between NPOs and other types of corporations and for-profit organisations. These are shown in Table 7.7 (METI 2012).

In the short term, there are seven cases of NPOs and three cases of for-profit organisations. Regarding the medium and long term, there are eight and nine cases of for-profit and non-profit organisations, respectively. In emergencies such as providing living support at evacuation centres, NPOs are initially dispatched, and emergency responses are carried out to take advantage of mobility. Afterwards, in the event that business services are necessary during recovery or reconstruction, and profitability can be expected, a for-profit organisation will function as a business entity, which includes personnel training and corporate support.

120 F. Kimura et al.

Table 7.7 List by issue or subject

		(A) Settlement of consumer needs	(B) Entrepreneurship and job creation	(C) Creation of new financing mechanisms
Short term	Non-profit	A 'bio-toilet' that does not use water	Misanga on the beach, 'making a ring (Tamaki)' support to ensure self-reliance by creating jobs in temporary housing	Support for expanding the sales channels of farmers who suffer from insufficient information – support by finding funds
		Utilise camping trailers for simple, temporary housing		
		Employ 'lightweight truck market' during disasters		
		Donate wood assembly kits ('fixed assembly') to affected areas to ensure privacy at the shelters		Donations and support for disaster areas via social investment
	For-profit	On-demand movement using community taxes[a] + lifestyle support services	Food supply and reconstruction support, reconstruction of affected areas + mobilisation of the region outside the affected zones	
			Harvesting 'reconstruction tomatoes' by developing a soil conditioner that counteracts salt	
Medium and long term	Non-profit	Practising at-home medical care for elderly people in affected areas	Revitalising local industry in the form of regional tourism + youth entrepreneurship support	Finding citizens willing to provide funds, which continue to support reconstruction
			Establishing an antenna shop, planning and holding property events in the metropolitan area, training the next generation of leaders	
			Practical business school 'Tohoku Marche'	
			Regeneration of agriculture by nurturing new farmers	
			Start selling products on the Internet in affected areas to maintain jobs for those who	

(continued)

7 Types of Social Enterprises and Various Social Problems

121

Table 7.7 (continued)

		(A) Settlement of consumer needs	(B) Entrepreneurship and job creation	(C) Creation of new financing mechanisms
			work in agriculture, forestry, and fishing	
			Creating 'opportunities' for motivated women	
	For-profit	Implementation of health promotion services for temporary housing residents	Promoting the creation of new towns by establishing new companies and utilising natural energy	Assistance to affected areas by giving small amounts of funding
			The sixth industrialisation[b] of agriculture and the creation of new employment	
			Restructuring food and beverage companies using mobile food trucks and construction of the first stage, 'movement by mobile food trucks', and the second stage, 'food villages'	
		A long-established supermarket[c] launched its store on the Internet	Supporting disaster-affected companies through internships	
			Job creation for females in temporary housing	
			The sixth industrialisation[b] of Sanriku Coast's fishing industry	

Source: Ministry of Economy, Trade and Industry (2012)

[a]Mobility service operated according to the users' needs (provided by bus or taxi)

[b]Sixth industrialisation is to promote the integration of agriculture, forestry and fishery production, processing and sales, and the creation of new industries utilising regional resources

[c]Matsubaya Co., Ltd., which started a business as a daily goods general store in Namie Town, Fukushima Prefecture, in 1927

Regarding the types of activity, there are 8 cases (5 NPOs, 3 for-profits) associated with the settlement of consumer needs, 15 instances of entrepreneurship and job creation (7 NPOs, 8 for-profits), and 5 cases (4 NPOs, 1 for-profit) associated with financing mechanisms. In terms of solving consumer needs and the creation of financing mechanisms, securing business is a problem. For entrepreneurship and job creation, some attention can be given to ensuring business performance using the know-how and innovation of for-profit organisations.

No matter whether the project entity is an NPO or for-profit, social enterprises are thought to 'connect' affected areas in various ways. Medium- and long-term support measures for regional job creation include producing foodstuff (agricultural, forestry, and fishery products) and creating handicrafts and local specialty products. In the case of for-profit organisations, if it is possible to solve challenges and generate revenue, it is possible to grow profit, create employment, and fix problems at the same time. Forms of creating wealth consist of ventures such as social, small, and community businesses; the base of the economic pyramid; and CSR activities. In order to smoothly support and consider activities (such as business start-ups, launching activities, and sustaining business), it is necessary to organise the functions and roles of intermediate support organisations, as shown in Fig. 7.3.

7.5 Conclusion

In this chapter, we examine the characteristics of 'socially oriented enterprises' (for-profit organisations) and 'business-type NPOs' (non-profit organisations), thereby clarifying social issues and the differences between organisations. The relationship between them is demonstrated, along with their features. As by-products of social enterprises that solve challenges, functions are revealed such as recognising issues and raising questions, the innovation of solutions, and the presentation of new business models. METI's 'Social Business Casebook (Earthquake Disaster Recovery Version)' was used as a guide, and an outline was prepared for the activities of NPOs and commercial organisations.

In the short term, there are many examples of NPOs. In the medium and long term, in addition to NPOs, there are many examples of commercial organisations. In an emergency, NPOs are initially dispatched and take emergency measures such as providing living support at evacuation centres through utilising mobility. Afterwards, during the recovery or reconstruction period, if profit can be expected, the business entities involved include human resource development and corporate support. In particular, there is a possibility of generating business through the sixth industrialisation, which 'connects' new jobs with new business, supports disaster-affected companies with funds, and 'connects production and consumption areas'. It is important that these social enterprises and their support organisations collaborate while complementing each other's functions and that they explore directions of support. The main actors are NPOs (these include those supporting social enterprises, financial NPOs, and pro bono initiatives, in Latin pro bono publico (Saga), providing skills and knowledge cultivated through occupations via volunteer activities, NPO support centres, intermediate support organisations, and social welfare councils); for-profit organisations (venture capital, incubators, SRI, enterprises, CSR departments, management consultants); and governments (METI, MLIT, local governments). For that reason, it is necessary to organise the functions and roles of intermediate support organisations.

In addition, social enterprises are required to have the ability to mobilise resources in society and solve problems. We think that the idea of social capital can be used to explain the difference in the mobilising power of various resources.

References

Borzaga C, Defourny J (eds) (2001) The emergence of social enterprise. Routledge, London

Cabinet Office (2011a) Survey on actual condition of specified non-profit organisation in 2010 and usage status of specified non-profit corporation system. https://www.npo-homepage.go.jp/data/report29.html (2011/12/20) (in Japanese)

Cabinet Office (2011b) Internet questionnaire survey report on accounting of specified nonprofit corporation, https://www.npo-homepage.go.jp/data/report20.html (2012/8/28) (in Japanese)

Cabinet Office (2012) Survey report on actual condition of specified non-profit organization in Heisei 20th and usage status of certified specified nonprofit corporation system, https://www.npo-homepage.go.jp/pdf/h23_npo_nintei_chousa_all.pdf (2013/9/18) (in Japanese)

Crutchfield LR, Grant MH (2008) Forces for good: the six practices of high-impact nonprofits. Wiley & Suns

Dees JG (1998) Enterprising nonprofits. Harv Bus Rev 76(1):55–68

Drucker, P. F. (1990). Managing the nonprofit organization. Harper

Edwards R, Smith G, Buchs M (2013) Environmental management systems and the third sector: exploring weak adoption in the UK. Environ Plann C Gov Policy 31:119–133

Evers A, Laville JL (eds) (2004) The third sector in Europe. Elgar

Japan Fundraising Association (ed) (2015) Giving Japan 2015. Japan Fundraising Association (in Japanese)

Japan NPO Center. http://www.jnpoc.ne.jp/ (2012/9/6) (in Japanese)

Kerlin JA (2006) Social Enterprise in the United States and Europe: understanding and learning from the differences. Voluntas 17(3):246–263

Kimura F, Hagihara K, Asahi C, Horie N (2013) How social enterprises solve their problems. Stud Reg Sci 43(3):341–356. in Japanese

Kimura F, Hagihara K, Asahi C, Horie N (2015) Types of social enterprise and various social problems. Stud Reg Sci 45(1):87–100. in Japanese

Lipietz A (2001) Pour le tiers secteur. La Decouverte

Ministry of Economy, Trade and Industry (2008) Social business study group report. http://www.meti.go.jp/press/20080403005/03_SB_kenkyukai.pdf (2011/9/1) (in Japanese)

Ministry of Economy, Trade and Industry (2012). Social business casebook (Earthquake disaster recovery version) – social business for reconstruction of disaster area-, http://www.meti.go.jp/press/2011/01/20120113002/20120113002.html (2013/9/11) (in Japanese)

Noya A (ed) (2009) The changing boundaries of social enterprises. OECD, Paris

Porter ME (1980) Competitive strategy: techniques for analyzing industries and competitors. Free Press

Saga I (2011) Probono – new social contribution, new way of working. Keisoshobo (in Japanese)

Suda Y (2010) Social enterprise in US – towards post-social entrepreneurs. World Labor 60 (10):36–43. (in Japanese)

Tanimoto K (2006) Social enterprise – the rise of social enterprises. Cyuoukeizaisha (in Japanese)

Tsukamoto I (2011) Social enterprise as an alternative model of the nonprofit sector. Plann Adm 34 (3):25–30. (in Japanese)

Tsukamoto I, Yamagishi H (2008) Social enterprise–make social contribution businesslike. Maruzen (in Japanese)

Tsuyuki M (2011) Diffusion process of social innovation and the role of social entrepreneurs. Plann Adm 34(3):45–50. (in Japanese)

Yamauchi N, Tanaka T, Okuyama N (2013) The Japanese nonprofit almanac. Center for Nonprofit Research & Information (in Japanese)

Yunus M (2007) Creating a world without poverty. Public Affairs

Chapter 8
Overviews of Waste Management Policies in Japan

Shigeru Fujioka

Abstract In Japan, household waste management is the responsibility of municipalities, while industrial waste management is the responsibility of the waste-generating businesses. Because most companies do not have their own waste treatment facilities, it is common for them to contract with licensed companies that have waste treatment facilities. Contracting fees and highly recycling or environmentally friendly facilities are very costly. The problem is that waste disposal companies do not have any incentive to engage a good contractor.

With the progress of decentralisation in 2000, local governments were able to introduce their own local taxes. In 2002, an industrial waste tax was introduced in Mie Prefecture to fund the disposal of industrial waste. However, if a disposal company enters into an agreement with a contractor that has a good facility certified by the prefecture, the tax is not assessed. In Mie Prefecture, a comparison of the amount contracted to taxable facilities to that of tax exempt facilities before and after the introduction of tax showed those who owned tax exempt facilities tended to have a higher rate of increase. It is possible that the introduction of the tax contributed to better waste disposal. By 2016, 27 of 47 prefectures had introduced industrial waste taxes.

Keywords Industrial waste · Local government · Tax · Incentive

8.1 Waste Administration in Japan

Let us first present an outline of the laws and administration associated with waste in Japan.

In Japan, as a general law on waste, the Waste Management and Public Cleansing Act (hereinafter referred to as the "Waste Management Law") has been established.

S. Fujioka (✉)
Tokyo Metoropolitan Government, Tokyo, Japan
e-mail: RXE21054@nifty.ne.jp

© Springer Nature Singapore Pte Ltd. 2019
C. Asahi (ed.), *Building Resilient Regions*, New Frontiers in Regional Science: Asian Perspectives 35, https://doi.org/10.1007/978-981-13-7619-1_8

The Waste Management Law defines waste as "garbage, oversized garbage, cinder, sludge, faeces and urine, waste oil, waste acid, waste alkali, animal carcasses, and other filth or unwanted matter, both solid or liquid". Among those wastes, those other than industrial waste are defined as non-industrial waste. The Waste Management Law defines industrial waste as "cinder, sludge, waste oil, waste acid, waste alkali, waste plastic, and other waste determined by government ordinance that are generated during business activities". Business activities refer to a wide concept that includes schools, hospitals, and government without limitation to commercial businesses.

Based on the definition—"waste other than industrial waste"—waste generated in domestic life is considered non-industrial waste, including kitchen refuse and oversized garbage. Industrial waste refers to waste associated with business activities that are limited and enumerated by law. Some waste associated with business activities are classified as non-industrial waste. These are called business-related non-industrial waste, which includes paper and kitchen refuse similar to domestic garbage.

The antonym of "waste" is "valuables". Even if it becomes useless to someone, as long as it can be sold to someone else, it is considered "valuable". If it cannot be sold, and has to be collected with or without fee, it is considered "waste". Recycled resources that can be 100% reused will be considered "waste" if they are collected by a recycling processor for a fee. Depending on the changes in the market, metal scraps and used paper, and used cars and electronics, can be "wastes" or "valuables" for reasons such as technological progress and rarity; thus, it is difficult to physically and objectively define "waste".

The Waste Management Law stipulates that non-industrial waste management is the responsibility of municipalities, while industrial waste management is the responsibility of the waste-generating businesses. Non-industrial waste is collected and transported by municipalities or contractors commissioned by municipalities and processed by public cleaning facilities operated either by a single municipality or jointly by multiple municipalities. Because non-industrial waste is processed as a government service under government responsibility, improper processing following collection is relatively rare.

On the other hand, the regulation states that industrial waste must be processed by waste-generating businesses as their own responsibility; thus, it is rare for municipality (cities, towns, villages, and prefectures), where such businesses are located, to process industrial waste as a part of government service. Waste-generating businesses either process waste by themselves according to the standard stipulated by the law or contract licensed private companies. Most businesses do not own treatment facilities, excluding large-scale manufacturers, and even if businesses own treatment facilities, the majority of these facilities are limited to intermediate processing: there is hardly any case where a business is able to treat their waste from emission to final disposal. The contracting of processing companies is an issue waste-generating businesses cannot avoid (Table 8.1).

8 Overviews of Waste Management Policies in Japan

Table 8.1 Classification of industrial waste

	Accompanying all business activities	
1	Cinder	Coal waste, incinerator residual ash, furnace cleaning residues, other incineration waste
2	Sludge	Mud remaining after treatment of factory wastewater, etc. and mud that occur in the manufacturing process of various manufacturing industries (sludge after treatment by activated sludge method, building pit sludge, carbide dross, bentonite sludge, car wash site sludge, etc.), excluding manure
3	Waste oil	Mineral oil, animal and vegetable oil, lubricating oil, insulating oil, cleaning oil, cutting oil, solvent, tar pitch, etc.
4	Waste acid	Photographic fixing waste liquid, waste sulfuric acid, waste hydrochloric acid, various organic waste acids, all acid waste liquid, etc.
5	Waste alkali	Photograph development waste liquid, waste soda liquid, metal alkaline waste liquid such as metal soap solution
6	Waste plastics	All synthetic polymer compounds such as synthetic resin scraps, synthetic fibre scraps, synthetic rubber scraps (including waste tyres), etc. and solid and liquid
7	Waste rubber	Natural rubber waste
8	Waste metals	Steel, non-ferrous metal polishing waste, cutting waste, etc.
9	Glass and cement and pottery waste	Glass (sheet glass, etc.), refractory brick scrap, gypsum board, concrete scrap other than demolition wastes, etc.
10	Slag	Casting waste sand, electric furnace, etc. Melting furnace residue, pot, poor coal, pulverised coal, etc.
11	Demolition wastes	Concrete fragments caused by new construction, remodelling or removal of workpiece, and other similar items
12	Soot and dust	Dust generated in the smoke-generating facility prescribed by the air pollution control law and captured in dust collection facilities
	Accompanying specific business activities	
13	Waste paper	Things related to the construction industry (those caused by new construction, rebuilding, extension, or removal of workpieces) Pulp manufacturing industry, paper industry, manufacturing industry of paper or paper processed goods, bookbinding industry, paper waste, etc.
14	Wood waste	Things related to the construction industry (as same as paper waste) Wood, wood products, furniture manufacturing industry, pulp manufacturing industry, wholesale business of imported timber, sawdust, barks, etc.
15	Waste textile	Natural fibre scraps such as cotton scraps and wool scraps generated from the textile industry other than the manufacturing industry (as same as paper waste) and clothing and other textile manufacturing industry
16	Animal and vegetable residue	Solid unnecessary matter on animals or plants used as raw materials in foodstuffs, medicines, and perfumery manufacturing industry

(continued)

Table 8.1 (continued)

Accompanying all business activities

17	Organic solid waste from glue factory	Unnecessary substances caused by dismantling of livestock at slaughterhouse and poultry processing place, solid residue such as bone
18	Animal excreta	Manure, cattle, horses, sheep, and chicken discharged from livestock farming
19	Animal corpse	Dead bodies of cattle, horses, sheep, and chickens discharged from livestock farming
20	Processed to dispose of the above industrial waste, which does not correspond to the above industrial waste	

Waste-generating businesses include large-scale manufacturers and construction companies that generate large quantities of homogeneous waste every day and small-scale offices that generate fixtures that become useless every several years. Situations are diverse among businesses, but regardless of profit or non-profit, all those who conduct business activities are held equally legally responsible as waste-generating businesses.

Industrial waste is the responsibility of waste-generating businesses, and any company can be contracted as long as they have a license to process waste. While waste-generating businesses can select their contractor freely, they are obligated to sign a contract with the contractor on the transportation route, processing method, annual throughput, processing fees, etc. and to confirm in written format that each waste item generated was appropriately processed to final disposal. Without such procedure, when a contractor performs improper processing such as illegal dumping, waste-generating businesses might be held responsible along with the contractor even if they did not actually commit illegal dumping.

Because the government is required to give permission when a request clears the minimum standard stipulated by the law, the processing ability of licensed companies varies greatly from superior contractors to those who barely pass the standard. Usually, simple facilities that crush and compress mixed waste and landfill cost less than superior facilities that fine-sort for recycling while considering the surrounding environment by installing devices to control odour and noise. When waste-generating businesses select their contractors through bidding (in order to lower the cost), the probability of using the latter type of contractors increases.

Some processing companies process waste improperly in order to minimise the cost following receipt of a consignment fee, and in the worst-case scenario, they may even resort to illegal dumping. This is a major social problem in many areas. Introduction of an industrial waste tax is often being discussed to prevent such improper processing and to secure financial resources to promote construction of superior processing facilities.

8.2 Developing a Legal System Towards a Recycling-Based Society

The Waste Management Law established a legal system that focuses on proper processing of waste, and via classification of "valuables" and "waste", hazardous substances and recycled resources are sometimes treated equally. For example, when a recycling company collects recycled resources for a fee, it must obtain a license to process industrial waste in the same manner as a company that handles hazardous substances. Waste-generating businesses that have recycled resources collected for a fee must confirm the processing until final disposal using a slip for industrial waste management.

Such legal system can no longer meet the requirements of modern recycling, and the Basic Act on Establishing a Sound Material-Cycle Society was enacted in 2000, establishing a legal system that incorporates recycling. This law stipulates in Article 2 that "recycling-based society" is "a society in which the number of products becoming waste is limited, generated waste is utilized as resource as much as possible, and burden on environment is minimized". The target of this law is all considered "waste" regardless of whether it is valuable, and the priority of the policy on waste was set in the following order: ① reduce, ② reuse, ③ recycle, ④ heat recovery, and ⑤ proper disposal.

Recycling laws enacted or revised based on the concept of the Basic Act on Establishing a Sound Material-Cycle Society include laws such as the Containers and Packaging Recycling Law (1997), the Home Appliance Recycling Law (2001), the Food Recycling Law (2001), the Construction Material Recycling Law (2002), and the End-of-Life Vehicles Recycling Law (2005).

The Waste Management Law is a general law on waste, and each recycling law is a special law. In other words, even when the waste is regulated by the Waste Management Law, if there is regulation by each recycling law—the special laws—these regulations would be given priority. For items that are not regulated, the Waste Management Law—a general law—is applied. In contrast, the Waste Management Law handles renewable resources that are not covered under the law and are classified as "valuable" as a "waste" renewable resource if it is stipulated by a recycling law. By establishing each recycling law, a uniform rule could be applied to waste that falls in the grey zone between "waste" and "valuables" and to that which may be non-industrial waste or industrial waste, depending on who generated the waste.

8.3 Current Situation of Industrial Waste in Japan

According to the FY2016 Annual Report on Environment in Japan (Ministry of the Environment 2016), the national total output of industrial waste decreased from 419 million t in FY2007 to 379 million t in FY2012, but in FY2013 (April 2013–March 2014), it was about 385 million t: a 1.5% increase from the previous year.

Processing in FY2013 was about 280 million t for recycling (54.0%), with a decrease of about 168 million t (43.5%), and the final disposal amount was about 12 million t (3.0%). The remaining years of the final disposal site is estimated to be about 14.7 years.

The number of illegal dumping cases is decreasing according to reports by municipalities (Ministry of the Environment 2016): 1150 cases in FY2001 to 165 cases in FY2014. The amount of illegal dumping decreased from 242,000 t in FY2001 to 29,000 in FY2014, excluding years where there were large-scale illegal dumping cases. However, it is possible that the government including regional municipalities is unaware of all illegal dumping cases and the individual amount of dumping cannot be accurately measured. Therefore, it is extremely difficult to accurately understand the actual situation and temporal changes. Those who committed illegal dumping described above are said to be waste-generating businesses (43%), unknown (27%), and unauthorised businesses (6%).

Contractors for handling of industrial waste are selected by each waste-generating business, and it is not uncommon for businesses to contract someone outside of their prefecture.

According to the Council Report on Industrial Waste Administration (Ministry of the Environment 2002), such wide-area processing is acceptable as long as the processing is proper. However, in large cities, the amount of waste generated by businesses usually surpasses the processing ability of local contractors, while the surrounding areas could accept more than what is generated. Under such circumstances, prefectures that have the capacity to process waste may stipulate that other prefectures must discuss and submit requests for transporting waste ahead of time. Although the council understands that citizens might not allow transport of waste from other regions due to illegal dumping cases in other prefectures, etc., they caution that such control of transport might become a limitation on a wide range of business development by superior businesses, and improper processing might occur as a result of the lack of proper businesses within the prefecture where the waste is generated. Therefore, influx control measures should be reviewed, and a method to tax industrial waste should be examined in order to establish superior industrial waste processing contractors as an industry to revitalise the area.

8.4 Discussions on Current Taxation on Industrial Waste and System Design

Let us now explain the classification and outline of the industrial waste tax introduced in Japan.

As of 1 April 2016, an industrial waste tax has been introduced in 27 prefectures, and other prefectures are considering introduction of such a tax. The industrial waste tax is applied to waste-generating businesses that ship waste to industrial waste processing facilities in each prefecture (including businesses from other prefectures) based on the amount of waste generated. Roughly divided, there are prefectures that require waste-generating businesses to declare and make the payment themselves and prefectures that have the final disposal contractor make special collections. Table 8.3 shows the present introduction status of the industrial waste tax as of 1 April 2016. To illustrate the difference between the self-declaration method and special collection method, we assume the following cases (Figs. 8.1 and 8.2).

In Prefecture A, industrial waste is taxed, while in Prefecture B, industrial waste is not taxed. In Prefecture A, there exists a large-scale waste-generating business (a1), a small-scale waste-generating business (a2), and a contractor (a3), while in Prefecture B, there are also large-scale and small-scale waste-generating businesses, along with a contractor (b1, b2, and b3). As we have already discussed, the contractor of industrial waste management is determined by the waste-generating businesses; thus, they are free to choose a contractor in or out of their prefecture. In the example, a contractor is selected as shown in the flow chart (block arrow), and a processing fee is paid.

Self-declaration tax by waste-generating businesses means, as in Fig. 8.1, waste-generating businesses declare the amount of tax they owe to the municipality and make the payment directly. Waste-generating businesses that use contractor a3, located in Prefecture A, must directly pay tax to the office of Prefecture A in addition to the fee they pay to the contractor a3. Waste-generating businesses that are the target of taxation are not limited to those in Prefecture A but include those that are located in other prefectures (Prefecture B). However, if all waste-generating businesses are targeted, it costs too much to determine taxpayers and tax collection; thus, it must be limited to businesses that generate a certain amount of waste or more (e.g.,

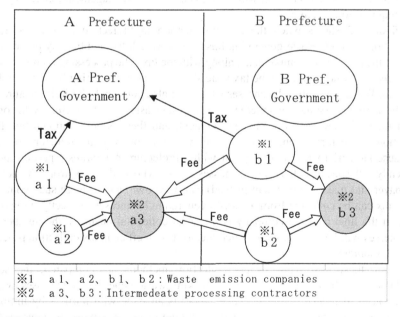

Fig. 8.1 Example of self-declaration method

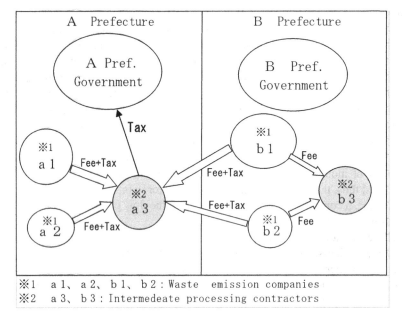

Fig. 8.2 Example of special collection method

annual waste generated of 1000 t or more). In this example, a1 and b1 would be classified as such businesses and must pay their tax to Prefecture A, while a2 and b2 are below such criterion; thus, while contracting waste management to a3, they are not required to pay any tax.

Figure 8.2 shows when the taxation method in Prefecture A is the special collection method. Waste-generating businesses, a1, a2, b1, and b2, pay processing fees to the processing company, a3, along with the tax. The processing company, a3, collects the money and pays the tax instead of the waste-generating business in this system. Waste-generating businesses b1 and b2 also contract to b3 in Prefecture B, but because it is assumed that there is no industrial waste tax in Prefecture B, the only cost for b3 is the cost of waste management, and there is no additional tax. For taxation, Prefecture A only needs to know contractors within Prefecture A, and because industrial waste management within Prefecture A requires a permit, theoretically, all special collection businesses (those who collect tax from the actual taxpayer and make the payment instead) can be known, and through such contractors, tax can be collected from all waste-generating businesses indirectly. In particular, if the final disposal company is a special collection business, the number of businesses will be quite limited, which means it is an efficient tax collection process for the municipality.

When these two types of tax collection methods are compared, the self-declaration method is more effective in making waste-generating businesses aware of the need to reduce waste. However, there is an issue with fairness by limiting taxation only to businesses with a certain amount of waste or more. In contrast, the special collection method can collect tax from all waste-generating businesses fairly

8 Overviews of Waste Management Policies in Japan 133

and efficiently, but it would be a major burden on contractors. Furthermore, contractors are in less powerful positions; thus, they may lower the taxation, meaning the actual waste-generating business might not be taxed. There are pros and cons.

As we saw in Table 8.3 earlier, the current industrial waste tax is mostly levied using the special collection method, and the self-declaration method is limited to two prefectures. In addition to regional bias in prefectures using one method or the other, the top three prefectures based on population and economy (Tokyo, Osaka, and Kanagawa Prefectures) have higher rates of contracting industrial waste management than other prefectures, yet an industrial waste tax has not been introduced in those prefectures.

As such, a different system was introduced in each area, and some areas have introduced no system. To examine the ideal system under such circumstances, the Ministry of the Environment established "A meeting to review industrial waste administration and taxation as a policy method" in January 2003 and presented the final report in June 2004. This meeting focused on the relationship between tax bearer and uses and avoidance of double taxation by multiple municipalities. Because data on the effects of taxation on prices are insufficient, the Ministry is limited to receiving reports from municipalities that have already introduced taxation on the changes in the final amount of waste processed and illegal dumping. At the meeting, discussion on whether introduction of an industrial waste tax was leading the treatment of industrial waste in a positive direction or whether it was an incentive to develop superior businesses remained insufficient. Thus, we summarise the points after analysis of effects from introducing an industrial waste tax.

Generally, introducing an industrial waste tax is said to increase the cost associated with waste generation, motivating suppression of waste generation. However, unlike domestic garbage changing from being free of charge to being charged, waste-generating businesses are paying a fee to processing companies for industrial waste before taxation; and thus, there should be a motivation to reduce industrial waste already. Increase in the cost (unit) to process industrial waste for waste-generating businesses due to introduction of tax is expected to be about 10–20%, and it is unlikely that this would suddenly reduce the amount of industrial waste. In Mie Prefecture where tax has been introduced, it has been reported that the amount of waste going through final disposal has decreased; however, Yamashita and Yokemoto (2004) indicated that a large company in the Prefecture has established treatment technology to effectively use sludge, and this has largely contributed to the reduction of waste.

It is more natural to think that the change in price due to taxation leads to a shift from actions that are taxable to those that are not, rather than to a reduction in the amount of waste. In other words, ① instead of using processing companies located in prefectures with industrial waste tax, those that are in a prefecture without tax will be used; ② if there is a criterion for taxation in a prefecture (e.g., 1000 t), a business may use multiple contractors in multiple prefectures, or branches may be created in order to lower the annual output of waste to below the criterion, and ③ in a prefecture with tax, if a certain situation (shipment to a superior facility with high recycling rate) is exempt, business might change from a contractor that is taxed to another without. In particular, the case of ③ is quite interesting in that the dilemma that the better the process is, the higher the processing cost is, might be mitigated or resolved by introduction of a tax.

8.5 Data Collection to Examine Effects of an Industrial Waste Tax

With Mie Prefecture—the first prefecture to introduce an industrial waste tax—as an example, we summarise the data necessary for analysis and the method to obtain such data.

Let us first outline the industrial waste tax system of Mie Prefecture. It uses the self-declaration method for waste-generating businesses, and those with annual output of less than 1000 t are exempt. Industrial waste processing facilities in the prefecture with 90% or higher recycling rate are designated as "recycling facilities" and are exempt from tax. Businesses that own recycling facilities have advantages compared to those without, in terms of tax-equivalent price competition.

To examine two types of effects we discussed in the previous section, each processing company is classified based on the presence or absence of a recycling facility, and the amount of waste processed for each site must be determined for each contractor.

We confirmed that data published in Mie Prefecture include "the list of industrial waste processing companies" and "the list of licensed recycling facilities", both as booklets and on the prefecture website. We cannot list all here, but we present excerpts of data items and content in Fig. 8.3. Actual names, addresses, telephone numbers, and licensed items for licensed companies are published, which are necessary for waste-generating businesses to select processing companies and to enter a contract.

Next, let us look at the amount of waste received by each processing company. This information is not generally published. However, we confirmed with Mie Prefecture that there is "a report on industrial waste processing performance" as an internal document for administrative guidance and regulation. "A report on industrial waste processing performance" refers to waste-generating businesses that generate large amount of industrial waste and to industrial waste processing companies (collections, transport, intermediate processing, and final processing) that report on their actual annual performance to the municipality that is responsible for waste management. Reports on the actual performance by intermediate processing and final disposal companies include the amount of waste processed annually for each type of waste from each waste-generating company, which is processed by each waste-processing company. Figure 8.4 shows an example of the form and entry of "a report on industrial waste processing performance" by an intermediate processing company. The form varies slightly between municipalities.

Because "a report on industrial waste processing performance" is not made public, one must follow a procedure for public document disclosure request to obtain

Permission Number	Name	Phone Number	Address	Type of Permission	Cinder	Sludge	Waste Paper	Wood Waste	Waste Textile	- - - - - - -
2422004237	Ada	0593-93-44	akita Komono-cho Mie-gun	processing			※	※	※	
2421073137	I·N·G	0567-68-33	i Kisomisaki-cho Mie-gun	processing			○	○	○	
2423049411	Asahi Doboku	0593-31-11	32-1 Kawahara-cho Yokkai	processing		※				
2422017848	Asahi Kinzoku	052-901-21	2768-1 Shouei-cho Yokkai	processing						
2401007009	Asahi Kougyou	0594-76-27	3-11-6 Sasaohigashi Toin –	processing	○	○	○	○	○	
2423049411	Asahi Shoukai	0593-31-11	32-1 Kawahara-cho Yokkai	processing		※				
2422004699	Aduma Kougyou	052-612-63	2-1584-3 Oinogawa Yokkai	processing		○				
2402066707	Awasawa	0593-63-38	245-1 Nishitomita-cho Yok	processing			○	○	○	
2408066480	Iga Ringyou	0595-21-11	661-1 Ouchi-cho Ueno-shi	processing			○	○	○	

Fig. 8.3 List of industrial waste disposal companies (Excerpt)

Postal Code *510–1234*

Adress of Contractor 20–2–3 Chuo Yokkaichi Mie

Name of Contractor Waste Management Co.Ltd

Number of Permission: 2 4 *2 0 × △ □ × □ △*

Waste Emission Companies: Name	Waste Emission Companies: adress emission	Code	Type of Waste	Name of Carrier / Prefecture of carrier / Number of Permission	Amount of Trust	Amount of Processing	Type of Processing	Code Processing	Code Prefecture
○× Construction	*5–7–9 Seihoku Suzuka* Code Prefecture *2 4*	(0) 1 2 3	*Demolition Wastes* Code Waste *1 5 1 0*	*△○ Transportation Mie 2410△○×△○×*	*1 5 0* t	*1 5 0* t	*Crush*	*1 4*	*2 4*
○× Construction	*8–1–3 Tonan Matsuzaka* Code Prefecture *2 4*	(0) 1 2 3	*Woods Waste* Code Waste *0 8 0 0*	*△○ Transportation Mie 2400△○×△○×*	*5 0* t	*5 0* t	*Incineration*	*3 1*	*2 4*
△□ Foods	*930–2 Yamagoe Higashiomi* Code Prefecture *2 5*	(0) 1 2 3	*Animal and Vegetable Residue* Code Waste *1 0 5 0*	*××Shipping Shiga 2410△○×△○×*	*7 0* t	*7 0* t	*Reuse as fertilizer*	*1 2*	*2 4*
......	Code Prefecture	0 1 2 3	Code Waste	......	t	t	......		

Fig. 8.4 Example of industrial waste performance report form (italic type, examples)

8 Overviews of Waste Management Policies in Japan

the data. Public document disclosure request means a member of the public requesting to view or obtain a copy of a document/public document processed by a government organisation. Documents for which a disclosure decision has been made are only given to the person who requested such document, but the content of such document can be handled in the same manner as a public document and, naturally, can be used for research publication, etc.

Definition of public document and determination of the procedure for disclosure or non-disclosure are determined by a law or ordinance for each government organisation. For example, if it is disclosure of a document owned by a national ministry, it is determined by information disclosure law, while documents owned by a city hall are determined by an ordinance on the information disclosure procedure of the city (the name of the ordinance used here is an example and it will vary). "The information disclosure law" and "ordinance on information disclosure" of each prefecture, city, town, and village are not subject to a hierarchy but are equal and parallel because they exist independently.

The ordinance on information disclosure of Mie Prefecture stipulates the following and more: whether "a report on industrial waste processing performance" submitted to Mie Prefecture would be a "public document". Also included are the criteria on disclosure and non-disclosure of private information that is redacted, the billing method, and the payment procedure.

Article 2 of the ordinance on information disclosure of Mie Prefecture defines a public document as "documents, drawings, photographs, films, and electronic records, prepared or obtained by staff of an executing agency as part of their work, and owned by the agency as it is systematically used by their staff". "A report on industrial waste processing performance" is a document acquired by the department that is in charge of waste management in Mie Prefecture and is, of course, considered public.

Article 5 of the same ordinance states that "there is no limit to number of people requesting disclosure of public documents owned by executing agency as per the ordinance" and accepts requests from many outside of the Prefecture.

Article 7 of the same ordinance clarifies the principle of disclosure and presents limited enumeration of non-disclosed items at the same time. Information owned by a government agency is not for staff to monopolise with privilege but is a common property with the public; and thus, it is disclosed on principle. However, disclosure could interfere with public interests or become disadvantageous to specific people. Thus, items that cannot be disclosed are enumerated by an ordinance, and all remaining items are disclosed. Information disclosure law and ordinances on information disclosure of many municipalities have similar stipulations, and items that cannot be disclosed are generally similar. Among the items that cannot be disclosed are personal information and corporate information (business activities), but this does not mean that if there is a slight reference to personal or corporate information, the whole document cannot be disclosed. Instead, personal and corporate information that meets certain criteria and conditions is not disclosed.

The criteria for non-disclosure vary greatly for personal and corporate information due to the difference in their nature. Specifically, the ordinance on information disclosure of Mie Prefecture defines "personal information" as "information on an individual with which the said individual can be identified"; thus, birthday, height, weight, etc. are not disclosed on principle. On the other hand, "corporate information" does not meet criteria for non-disclosure simply by "information that discloses the details of business activities", but it only becomes the subject of non-disclosure when it is clearly shown to be "harmful in terms of competition and legitimate interests". For example, all corporations are required to register information such as the date of establishment, capital, and business activities by the commercial code, and joint-stock companies are required to disclose their financial statement to protect investors. The underlying idea states that information on business activities should be disclosed; thus, the case of "being harmful in terms of competition and legitimate interests" is limited to situations such as information on development of new products.

If we examine whether the amount of waste industrial-waste processing companies accept each year could not be disclosed as "corporate information" through such viewpoint, it cannot be considered as information that harms legitimate benefits of the company through disclosure. If anything, it should be actively disclosed in order to check if waste exceeds the processing ability of a licensed facility. In Mie Prefecture, the prefectural advisory agency—the information disclosure review board—publishes the results of request on their homepage. According to this information, in cases of a disclosure request for "a report on industrial waste processing performance" by neighbouring residents of an industrial waste processing facility, in all cases, the prefecture is determined to disclose. When an affected company appealed the decision with "corporate information" as the reason, the information disclosure review board responded that the decision of the prefecture is valid as "generally, client information for a corporation is an important business information, and though it is not impossible to be disadvantaged depending on an effort by competitions, it cannot be considered as information that could immediately affect the company in terms of competition or legitimate benefits".

As such, data of "a report on industrial waste processing performance" can be obtained through requesting disclosure, but the amount of data would likely be massive. The original of "a report on industrial waste processing performance" is in print, but the definition of a public document includes "electronic records"; thus, data that were digitised from a printed record would be subject to a disclosure request. According to Mie Prefecture, not all items are digitised; for example, "name of waste-generating businesses" is not input, but instead, their prefecture is input as a code. As we considered this information sufficient for our study, we requested "electronic record".

When we requested computer input data of "a report on industrial waste processing performance" from 2001, prior to the industrial waste tax, and from 2003 following the industrial waste tax, as "electronic record", we were able to obtain a CD-R with data in Microsoft Excel format. Though reports submitted on paper have the name of waste-generating businesses and collection companies, only location code and permit number of collection companies were digitised, not the names. In this study, such permit number is not necessary; thus, we requested data without such number.

8 Overviews of Waste Management Policies in Japan

Obtained data were in the format shown in Fig. 8.5, but since the total number of reports (the number of rows in the Excel sheet) was massive (tens of thousands), we only present an excerpt.

Number Permission	Code Place of Disposal	Code Type of Waste	Amount of Trust (ton)	Amount of Disposal (ton)	Code Type of Processing	Code Place of Processing
2421007084	21	100	1,409	1,409	18	24
2421007084	23	100	5,525	5,525	18	24
2421007084	23	100	516	516	18	24
2421007084	24	100	1,180	1,180	18	24
2421007084	24	100	1,899	1,899	18	24
2421007084	24	100	683	683	18	24
2421007084	24	100	475	475	18	24
2421007084	25	100	570	570	18	24
2421007084	27	100	166	166	18	24
2421007084	27	100	312	312	18	24
2421007084	28	100	392	392	18	24
2421007084	16	220	242	242	18	24
2421007084	20	220	145	145	18	24
2421007084	23	220	614	614	18	24
2421007084	23	220	942	942	18	24
2421007084	23	220	270	270	18	24
2421007084	24	220	1,563	1,563	18	24
2421007084	24	220	62	62	18	24
2421007084	24	220	22	22	18	24
2421007084	24	220	60	60	18	24
2421007084	25	220	34	34	18	24
2421007084	25	220	20	20	18	24
2421007084	26	220	28	28	18	24
2421007084	26	220	5,886	5,886	18	24
2421007084	26	220	9,033	9,033	18	24
2421007084	27	220	167	167	18	24
2421007084	27	220	68	68	18	24
2421007084	28	220	104	104	18	24
2421007084	24	340	41,525	41,525	31	24
2421007084	13	610	46	46	31	24
2421007084	21	610	719	719	31	24
2421007084	21	610	15	15	31	24
2421007084	22	610	8	8	31	24
2421007084	23	610	1,070	1,070	31	24
2421007084	23	610	2,745	2,745	31	24
2421026889	24	210	4	4	11	214
2421026889	24	210	2	2	11	214
2421026889	24	1000	192	192	11	214
2421000220	24	1510	25,872	25,872	14	24
2421000220	24	1510	6,503	2,502	14	24
2421000220	24	1520	59,648	59,648	14	24
2421000220	24	1520	33,731	5,130	14	24

Fig. 8.5 Format of data obtained (partial excerpt)

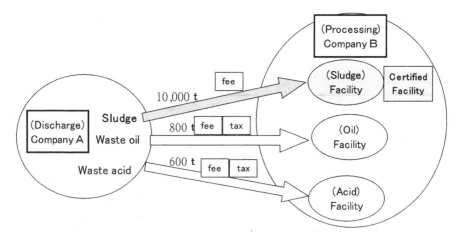

Fig. 8.6 Example of company which has certified facility and uncertified facilities

Table 8.4 summarises the general public data and data obtained through disclosure request. "Specially controlled industrial waste" may harm human health and living environment with their explosive, toxic, and infectious natures, and licensing and processing standards for such waste and other industrial waste are different. In this study, we excluded specially controlled industrial waste because such waste is not recycled, and for each type of waste, we summarised the amount of waste accepted at recycling facilities that are not taxed (hereinafter referred to as "certified facilities") and facilities that are not certified (hereinafter referred to as "uncertified facilities").

Certification of recycling facilities is reviewed by type of waste, and the same company might own both certified and uncertified facilities. As an example, let us assume that the waste-generating company A contracts intermediate processing company B to process "sludge", "waste oil", and "waste acid" (Fig. 8.6). The intermediate processing company B has a permit to process "sludge", "waste oil", and "waste acid", but only their "sludge" processing facility is certified as a recycling facility. In such a case, the company A would not be taxed for "sludge" despite generating a large amount while being taxed for "waste oil" and "waste acid" by the amount.

8.6 Examining the Effects of the Industrial Waste Tax

We classified the amount of waste accepted by certified facilities and by uncertified facilities for each type of waste. Table 8.3 shows changes from pre-tax (FY2001) to post-tax (FY2003) in these numbers.

The amount of waste accepted has mostly increased from FY2001 to FY2003. It is routine for industrial waste to be processed across prefectural lines, meaning waste

8 Overviews of Waste Management Policies in Japan 141

generated in Mie Prefecture may be processed in another prefecture while waste generated in another prefecture may be processed in Mie Prefecture; therefore, it does not necessarily mean that the amount of waste is increasing.

In terms of the type of waste, the rate of increase in the accepted amount of waste for the following seven, ① cinder, ② sludge, ④ waste acid, ⑥ waste plastic, ⑦ paper scrap, ⑩ animal and plant residue, and ⑫ metal scrap, was higher for the certified facilities than for uncertified facilities, while the opposite was true for the following six—③ waste oil, ⑤ waste alkali, ⑧ wood chips, ⑨ textile waste, ⑬ glass scrap, and ⑭ slag. For ⑪ rubber scrap, ⑮ animal faeces, urine, and carcasses, and ⑯ soot and dust, there were only either certified or uncertified facilities, making a comparison impossible. Because ⑰ rubble is tax exempt regardless of certification, we excluded it from our comparison.

The above summary shows that among the 13 types of industrial waste that could be compared, seven types saw an increase in the amount of waste processed at certified facilities, while six were opposite. Though the certified facilities had one more type of waste, it was nearly 50–50, making it difficult to conclude that there has been notable difference in the amount of waste accepted by certified or uncertified facilities before and after the introduction of the industrial waste tax.

However, the data obtained in this study include detailed information such as the name of each licensed company, the amount of waste accepted by type, and processing methods; thus, we could summarise again from a different perspective. A problem with the simple summary described above is that the rate of report submission is not 100% for both FY2001 and FY2003; thus, for example, facts such as "not submitting in FY2001 but submitting in FY2003" might be interpreted as an increase in the amount of waste accepted. To remove such misunderstanding, we must summarise the data again focusing only on companies that submitted reports in both FY2001 and FY2003. Handling of a company that owns both certified and uncertified facilities needs to be reviewed. In a case of intermediate processing company B as in Fig. 8.6, the amount of "sludge" commissioned was summarised as processed by a certified facility, while the amount of "waste oil" and "waste acid" commissioned was summarised as processed by an uncertified facility. However, if waste-generating company A selected their processing company mainly for "sludge", and selected processing company B to process "waste oil", "waste acid", and "sludge", increase in the amount of "waste oil" and "waste acid" commissioned accompanies the increased commission of the certified facility for sludge; meaning, it cannot be simply summed as increased commission by uncertified facility with companies without any certified facility. Thus, each waste must be classified into "a portion commissioned by a company with certified waste management facility", "a portion commissioned by a company with uncertified waste management facility but their other waste management facilities for other types of waste are certified", and "a portion commissioned by a company that has no certified facility for any type of waste".

Furthermore, depending on the type of waste, the number of companies that can process it may be quite small. In such a case, it is quite likely that the impact of a specific situation of one company on overall numbers could become large; thus, in order to include such situations in the discussion, we chose to present the number of companies that filed report both in FY2001 and FY2003 for each waste. We also examined the difference in the mean for changes from FY2001 to FY2003 for each type of waste/presence or certified facility with significance level of 5%.

Table 8.2 was prepared based on the above points. We summed the amount of commissions for each type of waste in Table 8.3 and compared this with the national data in Table 8.4.

According to Table 8.2, when changes in the amount of commission was compared for each type of waste, among the comparable 13 wastes, ① cinder, ② sludge, ④ waste acid, ⑥ waste plastic, ⑧ wood chips, ⑩ animal and plant residue, and ⑰ rubble saw the highest rate of increase in "a portion commissioned by a company with certified waste management facility", where the rate of increase in ① cinder and ⑥ waste plastic was statistically significant. In "a portion commissioned by a company with uncertified waste management facility but their other waste management facilities for other types of waste are certified", ⑤ waste alkali, ⑫ metal scrap, ⑬ glass scrap, and ⑭ slag had the highest rate of increase, where increase in ⑫ metal scrap was statistically significant. In "a portion commissioned by a company that has no certified facility for any type of waste", ③ waste oil, ⑦ scrap paper, and ⑨ textile waste saw the highest rate of increase, but none of the increase was significant. The last group ⑪ scrap rubber, ⑮ animal faeces, urine, and carcasses, and ⑯ soot and dust could not be compared because these entered either a certified or uncertified facility (not both), while ⑰ rubble is exempt.

Table 8.3 shows that, depending on the type of waste in Mie Prefecture, 12 types had increased amount of commission, while 5 had decreased amount of commission. There is a large difference in the amount of commission based on the type of waste, and the total sum shows that the reduction in "rubble" led to a slight increase at 2%. The national data are mostly the same, but ① cinder, ④ waste acid, ⑦ scrap paper, ⑨ textile waste, ⑪ scrap rubber, and ⑯ soot and dust show a large gap in points (50 or more) compared to Mie Prefecture data. Though there are regional characteristics, and we cannot generalise, those Mie Prefecture data with small number of businesses may reflect a special situation of one business in the overall result.

Among wastes for which the amount of commission by uncertified processing companies was shown to have increased in Table 8.4, scrap paper and ⑨ textile waste showed notable deviation from the national data. Especially for ⑨ textile waste, even when the commissioned amount of certified and uncertified facilities were combined, it did not reach the 1000 t criteria for taxation for one waste-generating company; thus, it can be considered to be off the comparison target. When these types of waste are excluded, the comparable waste types become 11, increasing the superiority of certified facilities even more.

As such, when pre-tax and post-tax are compared, only a few waste types showed statistically significant difference, but for almost all waste, companies with certified facilities tend to have greater increase in the amount of commissions compared to companies without any certified facilities. The cause for the increased amount of

Table 8.2 Contract amount by waste type

		Mie Prefecture (unit:ton)				2003	Nationwide unit:1000ton		2003
		※	2001FY	2003FY	2001→2003	2001	2001FY	2003FY	2001
①	Cinder	5	18,694	46,123	27,429	247%	1941	1949	100%
②	Sludge	26	390,208	513,513	123,305	132%	186,895	190,379	102%
③	Waste oil	15	44,913	57,661	12,748	128%	3089	3817	124%
④	Waste acid	7	3959	7064	3105	178%	2822	2662	94%
⑤	Waste alkali	7	25,200	42,062	16,863	167%	1528	1942	127%
⑥	Waste plastics	53	119,733	139,563	19,830	117%	5473	5462	100%
⑦	Waste paper	18	6345	9891	3546	156%	2159	1923	89%
⑧	Wood waste	35	86,638	74,698	▲ 11,939	86%	5357	5915	110%
⑨	Waste textile	13	281	459	179	164%	78	72	92%
⑩	Animal and vegetable residue	14	50,256	64,173	13,917	128%	4110	3393	83%
⑪	Waste rubber	5	21	8	▲ 13	36%	38	43	113%
⑫	Waste metals	34	20,345	24,488	4143	120%	8233	9044	110%
⑬	Glass and cement and pottery waste	38	28,905	31,260	2355	108%	4605	4273	93%
⑭	Slag	4	49,749	52,833	3084	106%	16,350	17,037	104%
⑮	Animal excreta	2	3150	3056	▲ 94	97%	90,094	88,977	99%
⑯	Soot and dust	3	251,796	239,729	▲ 12,067	95%	10,183	15,190	149%
⑰	Demolition wastes	54	1,339,873	1,188,011	▲ 151,862	89%	57,096	59,246	104%
Total		124	2,440,066	2,494,594	54,528	102%	400,051	411,623	103%

※Number of contractors. Generally, one contractor deals with multiple kinds of waste, so it is different from simple total value

Table 8.3 Amount of waste classified as "Recycling facilities" and "Ordinary facilities"

Unit: ton

			2001	2003	2003/2001
①	Cinder	Recycling facilities	11,828	35,291	298%
		Ordinary facilities	6968	10,832	155%
②	Sludge	Recycling facilities	349,512	468,795	134%
		Ordinary facilities	40,752	47,511	117%
③	Waste oil	Recycling facilities	34,458	42,989	125%
		Ordinary facilities	13,014	32,384	249%
④	Waste acid	Recycling facilities	1915	4340	227%
		Ordinary facilities	2044	2724	133%
⑤	Waste alkali	Recycling facilities	5538	6387	115%
		Ordinary facilities	19,662	35,895	183%
⑥	Waste plastics	Recycling facilities	37,147	46,555	125%
		Ordinary facilities	96,924	118,083	122%
⑦	Waste paper	Recycling facilities	143	372	260%
		Ordinary facilities	6984	14,238	204%
⑧	Wood waste	Recycling facilities	39,910	43,841	110%
		Ordinary facilities	53,956	64,648	120%
⑨	Waste textile	Recycling facilities	23	4	16%
		Ordinary facilities	277	1277	461%
⑩	Animal and vegetable residue	Recycling facilities	37,481	52,470	140%
		Ordinary facilities	12,775	11,669	91%
⑪	Waste rubber	Recycling facilities	0	0	–
		Ordinary facilities	21	8	36%

(continued)

8 Overviews of Waste Management Policies in Japan 145

Table 8.3 (continued)

					Unit: ton
⑫	Waste metals	Recycling facilities	11,507	15,829	138%
		Ordinary facilities	8291	9855	119%
⑬	Glass and cement and pottery waste	Recycling facilities	4601	3617	79%
		Ordinary facilities	23,374	39,324	168%
⑭	Slag	Recycling facilities	46,379	49,200	106%
		Ordinary facilities	3370	3642	108%
⑮	Animal excreta	Recycling facilities	0	0	–
		Ordinary facilities	13,096	3232	25%
⑯	Soot and dust	Recycling facilities	251,796	239,729	95%
		Ordinary facilities	0	0	–
⑰	Demolition wastes		1,490,022	1,428,607	96%
Total			2,623,768	2,833,349	108%
Subtotal(other than demolition waste)			1,133,746	1,404,743	124%

Table 8.4 Data obtained

		2001 Fiscal year	2003 Fiscal year
①	Number of intermediate processing companies which has permission	242	
②	Number of companies which submitted a report out of ①	145	163
③	Number of intermediate processing companies which has certified facilities	44	47
④	Number of companies which submitted a report out of ③	41	44
⑤	Total number of waste treated by processor	19,816	31,129

commissions includes multiple factors such as enactment of recycling related laws such as the 2002 Construction Material Recycling Law and the environment management system of ISO14000. Although we cannot simply state that recycling was promoted as an effect of the industrial waste tax, at the least, introduction of the tax promoted the use of recycling facilities.

8.7 Conclusions

The majority of prefectures with an industrial waste tax used the special collection method, but is it superior to self-declaration method? Generally, many areas with large cities have not introduced an industrial waste tax, but is this not a problem? Furthermore, the rate of taxation is uniformly 1000 yen/t, but is this a coincidence given that each area has a different situation? We would like to discuss these three points based on the above arguments.

First, we discuss the pros and cons of the special collection method and self-declaration method. In other words, it does not mean that one is better than the other, but depending on the situation of a given area, the more appropriate method should be selected. For example, a prefecture with a high rate of commissions from a large-scale waste-generating company could achieve the goal without collecting tax from waste-generating companies that are below a certain scale. To protect middle- to-small-scale companies, it is not necessarily appropriate to collect equally from all waste-generating companies. The self-declaration method can more surely shift the tax onto waste-generating companies, which should lead to more awareness of waste reduction. On the other hand, if there are more middle-to-small-scale waste-generating companies that may be able to reduce waste -generation, and they are not contracting superior processing companies, it would be better to exempt superior processing facilities and apply the special collection method as in Mie Prefecture. However, in reality, the special collection method is more common because it does not cost the government and is efficient. This may be advantageous if we only consider the cost to the government, but in terms of overall society, private businesses—final disposal companies—end up with massive administrative burden. Furthermore, there is no evidence that the tax is being shifted to waste-generating companies, which is the original objective. If these contractors decide to provide a discount on the tax, it would become a double burden. If the special collection method is to be employed, it must be via a system that guarantees appropriate shift of tax (e.g., processing cost is regulated by the government), so that processing cost and tax can be clearly separated. In addition, tax collection cost needs to be compared and examined not only for government but also for the cost to processing companies.

Next, let us discuss the regional bias. Areas with large cities, in particular, often do not have enough processing facilities to accept the large amounts of industrial waste they generate; thus, it would be significant to introduce a tax. Some argue that when waste processing is dependent on other prefectures, it is inappropriate to be taxed. However, if we consider the original objective of the industrial waste tax, this is an incorrect way of thinking. Industrial waste management is a private trade, and the government simply plays the roles of monitoring and guidance. If the number of industrial waste processing companies is low under free competition, government taxing waste-generating companies in order to build superior industrial waste processing facilities is desirable because it leads towards municipalities processing their own waste in their own area. Given this, an industrial waste tax should be introduced in large cities and surrounding areas.

As for introduction of an industrial waste tax, prefectures that led such introduction had higher policy building ability because they began their examination from nothing. However, those prefectures that followed might have simply followed. In terms of the method of taxation, the fact that there were prefectures that adopted a special collection method different from that of Mie Prefecture, the leading prefecture, should be acknowledged. However, the processing fee being uniform 1000 yen/t in 26 of 27 prefectures cannot be a coincidence and is difficult to assume that this price was determined upon much consideration. Because the industrial waste tax is to be reviewed after 5 years in all prefectures, we hope the taxation method will be re-examined to fit the actual situation of each area.

Further Reading

Kaneko R, Togawa K (2004) Environmental taxes. Toyo Keizai Inc, Tokyo

Kurasaka H (2003) Trends and issues on Industrial Waste Tax. J Japan Soc Waste Manag 14 (4):171–181

Morotomi T (2003) Theoretical grounds and institutional design of industrial waste tax. J Japan Soc Waste Manag 14(4):182–193

Nagasaki T (2003) Introduction of industrial waste tax ahead of the nationwide Monthly The Waste 2003-1 Nippo Business Co. Ltd.

Uga K (2001) Information disclosure law and information disclosure ordinances. Yuhikaku, Tokyo

Washida T (2004) Environmental policy and general equilibrium. Keiso Shobo, Tokyo

Chapter 9
Methods of Environmental Risk Management for Land Contamination Problems: Suggestions for Japan

Miwa Ebisu and Kiyoko Hagihara

Abstract In Japan, the Soil Contamination Countermeasures Act was enacted in 2002. Since then, implementation of the required countermeasures to tackle land contamination in urban areas has improved considerably. However, the pollution of soil on private land may spread undetected. Moreover, contaminated land may be left untreated because ridding soil of contamination is very expensive. Therefore, further countermeasures to reduce the environmental risk of land contamination in urban areas are necessary. This study's purpose is to suggest methods of environmental risk management for urban land contamination in Japan.

First, we consider sources of contamination, differentiating point sources and nonpoint sources, to evaluate how best to manage the environmental risk of land contamination. The characteristics of these two source types are explained through the concept of transaction costs.

Second, we discuss how Japan has approached land contamination problems and adopted regulations since the period of high economic growth. We also briefly discuss foreign countries' regulations. We then examine what kinds of typical environmental policy measures are effective in environmental risk management for land contamination.

Finally, we suggest practical methods of environmental risk management for land contamination in urban areas. This requires efficient methods to reduce contamination with low transaction costs. In particular, the costs of monitoring and enforcing to reduce contamination caused by nonpoint sources are high. Therefore, it is important to manage these sources appropriately.

Keywords Land contamination · Nonpoint sources · Transaction costs · Environmental risk management · Soil Contamination Countermeasures Act

---

M. Ebisu (✉)
Doctoral Program, Department of Urban Science and Policy, Graduate School of Urban Environmental Sciences, Tokyo Metropolitan University, Hachioji-shi, Tokyo, Japan

K. Hagihara
Tokyo Metropolitan University, Tokyo, Japan
e-mail: khagi@tb3.so-net.ne.jp

© Springer Nature Singapore Pte Ltd. 2019
C. Asahi (ed.), *Building Resilient Regions*, New Frontiers in Regional Science: Asian Perspectives 35, https://doi.org/10.1007/978-981-13-7619-1_9

9.1 Introduction

In Japan, the Soil Contamination Countermeasures Act (SCCA) was enacted in 2002, after the problem of contaminated land in urban areas became a cause of public concern. Before this law was enacted, the 'polluter pays principle', i.e. that the person or the party causing pollution should bear costs for the resultant damage, was the common way of thinking in the environmental policy field. The SCCA, however, provided that the person responsible for investigating a situation of soil contamination and conducting removal, etc. of contamination is the owner, manager, or occupier of the affected land (hereinafter referred to as the 'owner, etc.'). Furthermore, in 2009, the SCCA was revised, focusing particularly on the following three points: (1) expanding opportunities to investigate a soil contamination situation; (2) clarification of the measures that the owner, etc. should take, corresponding to the classification of a given area targeted for regulation; and (3) securing appropriate management of removed contaminated soil.

Thus, countermeasures for land contamination problems have been systematically improved in Japan. However, it is fundamentally difficult to implement countermeasures for this problem for two reasons.

First, soil contamination often occurs on private land. While investigating the environmental conditions in public domains, such as the air, rivers, and seas, is relatively easy, such investigation on private land is difficult. Therefore, pollution of the soil on private land may spread undetected. Second, contaminated land may be left untreated because the polluter or owner of the land cannot bear the high cost of ridding the soil of contamination.

In light of these challenges, further countermeasures to reduce the environmental risk of urban land contamination are necessary. In this study, methods of environmental risk management for urban land contamination in Japan are suggested.

9.2 Environmental Risk of Land Contamination in Urban Areas

9.2.1 Causal Substances of Soil Contamination and Their Environmental Risk

Substances which can cause soil pollution include heavy metals, volatile organic compounds, agricultural chemicals, dioxins, nitrate-nitrogen, radioactive materials, pathogenic organisms, etc. If these substances are treated appropriately, they are less likely to have detrimental effects on humans; however, if they are treated inappropriately, they can threaten human health and the environment.

9 Methods of Environmental Risk Management for Land Contamination... 151

The risk of land contamination is mainly classified into four types: (1) the risk of ingesting hazardous substances by eating foods, for example, crops or livestock produced on contaminated farmland and seafood sourced from public water contaminated by soil or groundwater containing hazardous substances; (2) the risk of ingesting hazardous substances by drinking water contaminated by soil containing hazardous substances; (3) the risk of inhaling hazardous substances scattered as dust or volatilised into the air from contaminated land; and (4) the risk of ingesting hazardous substances via the skin by touching contaminated soil.

In urban areas, there are various types of sites, such as those of stores, factories, and residences; moreover, agricultural lands also still remain. Put simply, all of the aforementioned risks can exist in these areas. In addition, there are many sources of contamination in urban areas. Some sources may continue to pollute lands undetected, and polluted lands may be left untreated. Furthermore, some sources may be unconsciously polluting land through emissions containing substances whose risks are still unknown. Accordingly, the risk that people face comprises exposure to (1) various kinds of hazardous substances, (2) hazardous substances over a long time period, and (3) potential hazardous substances whose risks are unknown.

9.2.2 Two Types of Contamination Sources: Point Sources and Nonpoint Sources

9.2.2.1 Social Attributes of Contamination Sources and the Relationship Between Polluters and Victims

Many urban contamination sources can be roughly classified into two types as regards social attributes. One comprises large corporations, possessing a strong economic base and high social status. The other comprises individuals and, in some cases, small companies with relatively low socioeconomic status. As members of the first group are relatively few in number, each of them is relatively easy to monitor as potential contamination sources. However, the second group is formed of many individuals and small companies; therefore, it is difficult to monitor them all. Thus, from the perspective of monitoring, contamination sources can be classified into point sources and nonpoint sources. A point source is an identifiable source of contamination, such as emissions from a factory or a house. By contrast, a nonpoint source is an unidentifiable source, such as air pollution by exhaust emissions from automobiles and water pollution by runoff from agricultural lands or urban areas.

As soil contamination occurs on land, the source of contamination is relatively easy to identify. An identified source can be controlled as a point source. However, there are many sites with the potential to become contaminated, and only a small proportion of them is discovered. Contamination occurring on the site of a small company is hard to discover, and such sites are not few in number. For problems of groundwater contamination, even if the contamination is discovered, its source

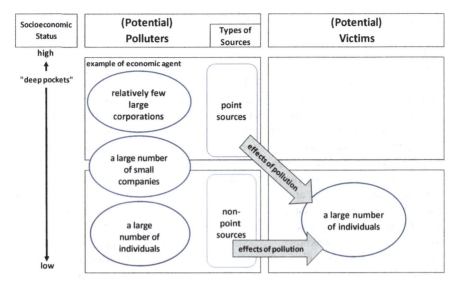

Fig. 9.1 Ordinary relationship between polluters (involving sources of pollution) and victims

cannot be identified in some cases, thus possessing the characteristics of nonpoint sources. Figure 9.1 shows the relationship between contamination's sources and the people it affects, i.e. polluters and victims. As indicated in Fig. 9.1, individuals can be not only victims but also polluters: the latter category is not limited to large corporations and can include households. Although small companies are enterprises, their socioeconomic position is lower than that of large corporations; therefore, small companies are placed between large corporations and individuals in the model.

9.2.2.2 Characteristics of the Two Contamination Source Types in Terms of Transaction Costs

Introduction of the Concept of Transaction Costs

As discussed in the previous section, in terms of monitoring, contamination sources can be classified into point sources and nonpoint sources. Furthermore, the characteristics of these two source types can be explained by the concept of transaction costs.

When 'negative goods' are not exchanged appropriately in a market, negative externalities, such as environmental pollution, occur. If people try to exchange 'negative goods' appropriately, transaction costs arise in the exchange.

Coase (1960) proposed that transaction costs are necessary to exchange something in a market. Thereafter, Dahlman (1979) proposed that transaction costs are classified into three types, namely, the cost of (1) searching for an exchange partner, (2) striking the bargain, and (3) monitoring the other party's actions and (where necessary) enforcing fulfilment of their obligations pursuant to the contract. Cooter

9 Methods of Environmental Risk Management for Land Contamination... 153

Table 9.1 Factors affecting transaction costs

Lower transaction costs	Higher transaction costs
1. Standardised good or service	1. Unique good or service
2. Clear, simple rights	2. Uncertain, complex rights
3. Few parties	3. Many parties
4. Friendly parties	4. Hostile parties
5. Familiar parties	5. Unfamiliar parties
6. Reasonable behaviour	6. Unreasonable behaviour
7. Instantaneous exchange	7. Delayed exchange
8. No contingencies	8. Numerous contingencies
9. Low costs of monitoring	9. High costs of monitoring
10. Cheap punishments	10. Costly punishments

Source: Cooter and Ulen (2016)

and Ulen (2016) termed these three transaction cost types 'search costs', 'bargaining costs', and 'enforcement costs' (used hereinafter in this paper) and indicated the factors affecting each transaction cost, as summarised in Table 9.1.

As discussed above, transaction costs are various costs necessary to conduct an exchange in a market. How, then, is the concept of transaction costs related to solving problems of externalities? It is considered that one way to solve an externality problem is to exchange through voluntary negotiations, the interventions of public institutions, etc. (negative or positive) goods that are not exchanged in a market. If a victim affected by pollution sues the polluter, both must directly bear the bargaining costs, such as court costs or legal fees. If a municipality tries to regulate pollution, it must find the polluters, observe the emissions for which they are responsible, and compel them to comply with regulations. Therefore, the municipalities must pay the administrative costs of implementing their regulations. In such a case, the costs of regulation are borne by society as a whole, as the financial resources of municipalities comprise taxes from citizens and enterprises, subsidies from the national government, etc.

In other words, although the costs for solving such negative externalities as environmental pollution are termed judicial or administrative costs, depending on the situation, they are essentially transaction costs.

The Characteristics of Transaction Costs in Bargaining Between Polluters and Victims

In this section, we assume that each of two different pollution source types affects each of two different victim types. As Fig. 9.2 shows, the bargaining between polluters and victims can be classified into four types. In these cases, we consider how transaction costs in bargaining are.

A: A few identifiable polluters (point sources) affect a few identifiable victims.

In this case, there are a few polluters and a few victims, identifiable to each other.

In the simplest case, one victim confronts one polluter. For example, a manufacturing factory may emit water that includes toxic substances used in a

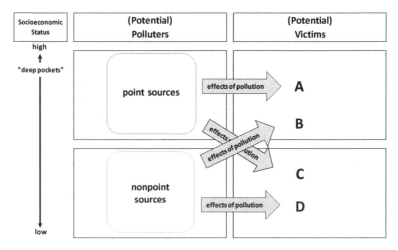

Fig. 9.2 Relationship between polluters (involving sources of pollution) and victims—four cases

manufacturing process, causing the neighbouring factory to be adversely affected by the polluted water. (Of course, the relationship of polluters vs. victims can be that of factories vs. factories, factories vs. individuals, or individuals vs. individuals.) In such cases, when polluters and victims try to solve their problem through voluntary bargaining, the transaction costs have the following characteristics:

1. Search costs: These can be relatively low, as it is comparatively easy for both polluters and victims to identify each other.
2. Bargaining costs: These can be relatively low, as a bargain between a few parties is easier to achieve than one between many parties.
3. Enforcement costs: These can be relatively low, as it is easier to monitor a few polluters and to enforce their compliance with agreed obligations, compared with a case of many polluters.

B: Many unidentifiable polluters (nonpoint sources) affect a few identifiable victims. For example, we assume that a manufacturing factory needs clean air (or water) for its manufacturing process. If the air (or river) near the factory is polluted by neighbourhood residents (exhaust gas of automobiles, domestic waste water, etc.), the factory may have to instal purification facilities. The costs of purifying air (or water) are then reflected in the price of the product, of which the residents may be buyers. In this case, voluntary bargaining between the factory and the residents is not necessary, because the pollution, which is a 'negative service', is exchanged in the market through the price of the product. In practice, it is difficult for the factory to solve this problem by voluntary bargaining with many residents.

C: A few identifiable polluters (point sources) affect many unidentifiable victims.
   A typical example of this case is the pollution that damages residents' health through their consumption of polluted crops or seafood. In such a case, when the polluters and their victims try to solve their problem through voluntary bargaining, the transaction costs have the following characteristics:

1. Search costs: These can be high for polluters, as it is necessary to gather information to identify each of many victims. By contrast, these costs can be relatively low for victims, as it is easy to identify a few polluters.
2. Bargaining costs: These can be high for both polluters and victims, as bargains between many parties are difficult to achieve.
3. Enforcement costs: These can be relatively low, as it is not difficult to monitor a few identified polluters and to enforce their compliance with agreed obligations.

D: Many unidentifiable polluters (nonpoint sources) affect many unidentifiable victims.
   In this case, there are many polluters and many victims, neither of which is easily identifiable to the other. For example, there may be a case in which the exhaust gases of many automobiles affect many residents' health. In urban areas, we often observe such relationships. In such cases, when polluters and victims try to solve their problem through voluntary bargaining, the transaction costs have the following characteristics:

1. Search costs: These can be high for both polluters and victims, as it is difficult to search for and identify one another among many parties.
2. Bargaining costs: These can be high for both polluters and victims, as bargains between many parties are difficult to achieve.
3. Enforcement costs: These can be very high, as it is difficult to monitor many polluters who are difficult to identify and to force them to take action to reduce pollution.

When polluters, victims, or both are many and unidentifiable, both search costs and bargaining costs tend to be high. In particular, when polluters are many and unidentifiable, enforcement costs also tend to be high. This section has discussed the trends of transaction costs in voluntary bargaining, and it is considered that these trends are the same in cases of municipalities seeking to control pollution. When municipalities try to regulate pollution from nonpoint sources, the monitoring and enforcing costs will be high because it is not easy to monitor many sources and compel them to reduce pollution appropriately. Therefore, the transaction costs for managing nonpoint sources can be considered relatively high, and those for managing point sources relatively low.

Environmental risk management for land contamination in urban areas needs to appropriately address both point sources and nonpoint sources. In particular, the costs of monitoring and enforcing to reduce contamination caused by nonpoint sources are high. Accordingly, it is important to manage them appropriately.

9.3 Outline of Countermeasures for Land Contamination

9.3.1 Countermeasures for Land Contamination in Japan

In Japan, countermeasures for land contamination began in earnest after the outbreak of Itai-itai disease ('itai-itai' means 'ouch-ouch'). Itai-itai disease is a pollution-related disease contracted by eating rice polluted by cadmium, which originated in the Jinzu River Basin in Toyama Prefecture. Itai-itai disease was first detected around 1910 but only became widely known around 1955. Finally, in 1968, the Ministry of Health and Welfare announced that the cause of itai-itai disease was the contaminated water discharged by a mining industry facility. (Itai-itai disease and its countermeasures are detailed in Yoshida et al. 1999.) Against this social background, 14 laws regarding environmental pollution were established or revised at the extraordinary session of the Diet (the so-called Pollution Session of the Diet) in 1970. One of the major legal reforms at that time was the addition of 'soil contamination' as a typical pollution under the 'Basic Law for Environmental Pollution Control' (enacted in 1967 and replaced by the 'Basic Environment Law' in 1993). Furthermore, at the Pollution Session of the Diet, the 'Act to Prevent Soil Contamination on Agricultural Land' (APSCAL) and the 'Act on Entrepreneurs' Bearing of the Cost of Public Pollution Control Works' (AEBCPPCW) were enacted. The APSCAL provides that a prefectural governor must establish a plan for countermeasures against soil contamination on contaminated or potentially contaminated agricultural land. The AEBCPPCW provides that even if a prefectural authority carries out remediation of contaminated agricultural land, the party responsible for the contamination can be compelled to bear the costs. Following the establishment of this law, the 'polluter pays principle' became a common rule in the field of environmental pollution control measures.

Thus, legislative countermeasures for agricultural land contamination were introduced; no legislation was enacted to provide countermeasures for urban land contamination. The policy of soil environment conservation in urban areas focused mainly on preventing pollution. For example, waste water, soot, or smoke discharged from factories or workshops were regulated by the 'Water Pollution Control Act' or 'Air Pollution Control Act'. In addition, the disposal of waste materials was regulated by the 'Waste Management and Public Cleansing Act'. These laws were all passed at a time when environmental pollution was a significant social problem in Japan (between 1968 and 1970). This policy perspective on soil environment conservation persists today (Ministry of the Environment 2009).

In the 1990s, at sites of closed factories or laboratories in urban areas, soil contaminated with hazardous substances was often found, and such cases became social problems. To address these problems by setting targets for environmental management, environmental quality standards (EQSs) for soil pollution were issued in 1991, and EQSs for groundwater pollution were issued in 1997. Two years later, the 'Act on Special Measures against Dioxins' was enacted to tackle pollution by dioxins.

9 Methods of Environmental Risk Management for Land Contamination... 157

Subsequently, the 'Soil Contamination Countermeasures Act' (SCCA) was enacted in 2002, and countermeasures for land contamination in urban areas began in earnest.

The end of this section outlines the APSCAL and SCCA (see Table 9.2).

The common features of these two laws are as follows. First, the purpose of both is to prevent harm to human health from soil contaminated with designated substances (though the designated hazardous substances differ in each law). Second, a regulator needs to designate any area that may harm human health through contaminated soil. When the regulator recognises that the reason for the designation has

Table 9.2 Outline of the two laws for tackling land contamination

Name of law	Act to Prevent Soil Contamination on Agricultural Land (APSCAL)	Soil Contamination Countermeasures Act (SCCA)
Year of enactment	1970	2002
Object of protection	Citizens' health	Citizens' health
	Living environment	
Purpose	Preventing the soil of agricultural land from being contaminated by designated hazardous substances	Facilitating the implementation of countermeasures against soil contamination by formulating:
	Ridding the soil of agricultural land of such contamination	
	Rationalising the use of contaminated agricultural land	measures to understand a situation of soil contamination by designated hazardous substances
		measures to prevent harm to humans resulting from such contamination
Facility or land to regulate	Agricultural land, such as land used for cultivation, livestock pasturage, or harvesting grasses to use in the livestock pasturage	Land formerly used as a site for the plant or workplace of a now-defunct specified facility which used hazardous substances[a]
		Land exceeding 3000 m^2 intended for excavation and other changes to the form or nature
		Land suspected of posing a health hazard due to soil contamination
Designated hazardous substances[b]	Cadmium and its compounds	26 kinds of substances, such as volatile organic compounds, heavy metals, and pesticides
	Copper and its compounds	
	Arsenic and its compounds	
Person obliged to investigate soil contamination	Prefectural governor	Owner of the site
		Manager of the site
		Occupier of the site
		('Owner, etc.')

(continued)

Table 9.2 (continued)

Main role of regulatory authority	Designating an area with the potential to harm human health, etc. as an area for countermeasures against soil contamination on agricultural land (or cancelling that area's designation)	Designating an area that does not meet the designated standard, etc. as one of the two types of designated areas, depending on the situation of soil contamination (or cancelling that area's designation)
	Establishing a plan for countermeasures against soil contamination	
	Implementing undertakings to rid the soil of the agricultural land of contamination, etc.	
	Continually monitoring the soil condition of agricultural land	Instructing owner, etc. to remove soil contamination, etc.
		Management of the processes for transporting contaminated soil from the designated area, etc. to other places
Person who must implement remediation, etc. of contaminated land	Prefectures, municipalities, etc.	Owner, etc.
		The person responsible for the contamination
Person who must bear the costs for remediation, etc. of contaminated land	Government (grant of subsidies)	Owner, etc.
	Prefectures	The person responsible for the contamination
	Municipalities	
	The person responsible for the contamination (based on AEBCPPCW)	The SCCF (grant of subsidies)

Notes: The above-mentioned contents include provisions of related laws, ordinances, government notifications, etc.
[a]A specified facility is defined in Article 2, Paragraph (2) of the Water Pollution Control Act
[b]These laws exclude radioactive substances from regulation

ceased to exist, due to removal, etc. of contaminated soil, the regulator must then cancel the designation of that area.

By contrast, the person who must investigate a situation of soil contamination and take action to remove, etc. contaminated soil differs in the two laws. Under the APSCAL, a prefecture, etc. is the responsible party; however, under the SCCA, the owner, etc. of the site is responsible. Accordingly, the legal scheme in terms of the burden of costs of removal, etc. also differs. On agricultural land, governed by the AEBCPPCW, the costs for removing contamination or improving soil are borne by the nation, the prefecture, or the polluter. The costs that the polluter must bear are decided according to their contribution to the pollution. By contrast, the SCCA provides that a prefectural governor can order the owner, etc. to remove contaminated soil, etc.; however, when the owner, etc. is not responsible for the contamination, the prefectural governor can order the polluter to do so. When an owner, etc.

without responsibility for the contamination has taken action to remove contaminated soil, etc., the owner, etc. can claim the cost of these actions from the party responsible for the contamination. If an owner, etc. without responsibility for the contamination cannot afford to take action for removal of contamination, etc., they may apply for a subsidy from the so-called Soil Contamination Countermeasures Fund (SCCF) established under the SCCA.

9.3.2 Introduction, Background, and Outline of Laws on Land Contamination in Western Countries

In the United States, to protect human health and the environment from harm by hazardous substance pollution, the 'Comprehensive Environmental Response, Compensation, and Liability Act' (CERCLA; the so-called Superfund Act) was enacted in 1980. The introduction of this law was prompted by one incident. In the 1970s, at Love Canal, New York, buried toxic waste materials were pushed up to ground level by heavy rain, etc., and these materials damaged local residents' health. This event shocked US society, leading to the establishment of this law (United States Environmental Protection Agency 2000, Kato et al. 1996). In the Netherlands, in a residential area in the suburbs of Rotterdam, the drinking water system was polluted by toxic materials in 1981. The following year, the 'Interim Act of Soil Remediation' ('*Interim Wet Bodemsanering*') was enacted and later revised to the 'Act of Soil Protection' ('*Wet Bodembescherming*') in 1994 (Kato et al. 1996).

These laws of both countries prescribe who is obliged to remove, etc. soil contamination. Such regulations have also been adopted in other countries, including by Japan in the SCCA.

Under the US Superfund Act, a fund was established to enable the federal government to conduct removal, etc. of soil contamination in cases in which the polluter is unknown, insolvent, etc. That is one of the law's most significant features.

Other than the laws considered above, in areas or countries which often use groundwater to supply the drinking water system, countermeasures for groundwater pollution have long been implemented. One of the methods to protect groundwater quality is to classify an area to be protected into several zones, depending on the distance from a groundwater source. Designated actions which can cause pollution are restricted in each zone. Known as 'zoning', this method is widely used in Western countries (Europian zoning is detailed in Fujinawa 1994 and Yanagi 2001).

9.4 The Effectiveness of Typical Environmental Policy Measures for Land Contamination

This chapter examines what kinds of typical environmental policy measures, such as command-and-control regulation, economic incentive-based approaches, and decentralised approaches, are effective in environmental risk management for land contamination, from the perspective of point sources and nonpoint sources.

9.4.1 Command-and-Control Regulation

This is a measure to control pollution by requiring certain actions of polluters, such as discharging pollutants at levels lower than designated standards or producing products without using designated materials that cause pollution. Such measures mainly comprise setting emission standards, specifying production methods, and zoning.

9.4.1.1 Setting Emission Standards

In this approach, a regulatory authority sets an emission standard for each emission source and monitors the situation of compliance with each source's standard. A regulatory authority may be able to achieve the aim of reducing pollution in society through this measure. When the marginal private cost of a firm that discharges a pollutant does not equal the marginal social cost, including the marginal cost of pollution damage imposed on a victim, a negative externality occurs. In such a case, a socially optimal amount of pollution is the amount at which the marginal social benefit equals the marginal social cost. Therefore, the regulatory authority can achieve the socially optimal amount of pollution by requiring firms to discharge pollutants below that level.

To make such regulation effective, a regulator needs to collect information regarding the marginal social cost curve, marginal social benefit curve, and marginal private cost curve of each firm. However, it is difficult to obtain such information. Accordingly, this measure is often implemented by requiring each emitter to uniformly comply with a target emission limit, which is decided by the regulator. However, it is generally considered that regulation using uniform standards, while feasible, is not efficient.

Furthermore, to monitor the situation of firms' emissions, a regulator needs to periodically measure the concentration of contamination within a certain area to be protected. However, unlike the air, rivers, or lakes, etc., land usually belongs to private individuals or organisations. It is, therefore, difficult for a regulator to periodically measure the concentration of contamination within a certain area of private land. Consequently, the effectiveness of using emission standards is low as a measure for tackling land contamination.

9.4.1.2 Specifying Production Methods

In this approach, a regulatory authority requires producers who are also potential polluters to use a particular pollution control technology or to instal a particular equipment. This measure is also known as specifying technology standards. For example, a regulator may require farms to use particular methods for controlling insect pests to reduce pollution by agricultural chemicals. In another case, a regulator may require factories to instal particular equipment for controlling pollutant emissions to reduce pollution. Such regulations, however, may prevent producers from efficient production, denying them the freedom to choose and adopt technologies. Consequently, producers may be disincentivised from developing more efficient technologies for controlling emissions. For regulators, it may be easier to monitor the use of particular equipment or technologies, rather than the emissions, of each factory or farm. However, regulators need to frequently monitor whether factories, etc. use the particular equipment or technologies. Moreover, regulators also need to continually monitor the development of more efficient new technologies for controlling emissions. Therefore, regulators' administrative costs can be high.

As regards feasibility, this measure has an advantage over using emission standards, as regulators can manage hazardous substances at the production stage. In particular, it is effective for managing nonpoint sources, whose emissions are difficult to monitor. Furthermore, in many cases, small firms have no ability to develop technologies for reducing pollution. Accordingly, to specify particular technologies for small firms is effective for managing nonpoint sources.

9.4.1.3 Zoning

Also known as land use controls, zoning is an approach in which a regulatory authority restricts particular actions, such as the use of hazardous substances which cause pollution, within designated areas. It is also referred to as limits on input, because a regulator sets restrictions on the kinds of materials permissible as inputs in production processes. Prohibiting the use of designated substances within designated areas is very effective in reducing pollution in those areas. Accordingly, this measure is often used in areas sensitive to pollution, such as water source areas, river basins, or lakes.

Western countries often use this measure to protect groundwater recharge areas. It is effective for preserving the quality of groundwater used as a drinking water source. Therefore, zoning is a practical and effective measure to prevent land pollution, particularly to prevent groundwater pollution through contaminated land. Zoning is considered effective to manage both point sources and nonpoint sources.

9.4.2 Economic Incentive-Based Approaches

9.4.2.1 Taxes and Charges

Emission Charges

To achieve the optimal pollution level in cases of a negative externality, a regulator may impose a tax on a firm's emissions corresponding to the difference between the marginal social cost and the firm's marginal private cost. The so-called Pigovian tax is the price of the emissions that cause pollution. To implement a Pigovian tax, regulators must know such information as the marginal social benefit curve, marginal social cost curve, and each firm's marginal private cost curve. However, it is difficult for regulators to obtain such information. A Pigovian tax, therefore, is difficult to use as an environmental policy measure.

As a second-best alternative to a Pigovian tax, regulators can implement an emission charge, for which purpose they do not need to obtain information on either polluters or victims. This is a measure to reduce pollution by setting a targeted (desirable) ambient standard and the amount of the charge per unit of emission. The amount of the charge is adjusted many times until the ambient standard is achieved. This measure is cost-effective to achieve desirable ambient standards. Moreover, it is possible to incentivise polluters to develop new technologies to reduce pollution. However, to implement an emission charge effectively, regulators must monitor the emissions of all sources, the (frequently changing) numbers of sources, and changes in the available technologies for reducing pollution. Furthermore, regulators need to adjust the amount of a charge periodically, in accordance with the results of their ongoing monitoring.

Even if an emission charge can be implemented as an environmental policy, it has some drawbacks. First, the effectiveness of emission charges as a measure to reduce extremely hazardous substances is low, as the use of such substances is not banned, unlike under command-and-control regulation. Second, several problems in terms of setting or changing the amount of charges are highly likely to occur. For example, it is not possible to achieve targeted ambient standards if emission charges amounts are set too low. Furthermore, if the emission charge amounts are frequently changed, firms must contend with operational uncertainties. Consequently, regulators are likely to be resisted by the targeted firms (or the targeted industry) and will, therefore, face greater difficulties in seeking to implement the measure.

As a measure to tackle land pollution, the effectiveness of emission charges is low, as monitoring emissions on private land is difficult, even if the sources are identified.

Taxes and Charges at the Production Stage

An alternative to emission charges is imposing taxes or charges at the production stage. For example, imposing taxes on particular substances that are inputs in production processes will increase firms' marginal production costs and decrease their production processes using those substances. Thus, this measure is effective to reduce the use of particular substances.

However, this measure also has some drawbacks. First, it does not prompt the users of targeted substances to strive to reduce pollution. Second, regulators must continually research technological progress in pollution reduction, as this may change the marginal costs or marginal benefits. Moreover, regulators must amend the amount of taxes or charges in accordance with any change in the marginal costs or the marginal benefits. Third, it is difficult to determine the appropriate amount of taxes or charges depending on the conditions in each area, even if the urgency of pollution reduction differs between areas. Fourth, after successfully reducing the use of a targeted hazardous substance, alternative hazardous substances may often come to be used by firms, potentially causing new pollution problems. Fifth, this measure's effectiveness in reducing pollution by extremely hazardous substances is low, as the use of such substances is not banned.

While imposing taxes or charges at the production stage evidently has some drawbacks, this measure can be implemented without monitoring the emissions from all sources. Therefore, as a measure for tackling land pollution, it is relatively easy to implement and effective for managing both point sources and nonpoint sources.

The Use of Taxes Revenue
As noted in each of the above sections, the characteristics of the taxes and charges system differ between the approaches; however, they share the fundamental purpose of making each economic agent take appropriate actions to achieve socially efficient levels of pollution. Therefore, compensating victims from tax revenue is not particularly necessary. Taxes or charges, however, can be used by administrative authorities to reduce pollution or develop pollution-reducing technologies.

Under the US Superfund Act, a trust fund is operated to cover the costs of removal, etc. of contaminated soil when the party responsible for pollution is unknown or unable to bear the costs, etc. This fund was mainly supplied by taxes on crude oil, petroleum products, specific chemical substances, etc., in the 15 years following this law's enactment. (Since these taxes were scrapped in 1995, funding has been sourced through contributions from the government's general account, etc. (Japan Environmental Management Association for Industry 2014).) In other words, taxes on inputs or products were used as the financial resources for removal, etc. of contaminated soil. Such taxation, therefore, has the advantage of providing financial resources for pollution control and contamination reduction. However, these financial resources are not stable, as tax revenue depends on the amount of production of petroleum or chemical products or the amount of usage of their feedstock.

Thus, it is considered that taxes on inputs or products may be used to generate financial resources to fund countermeasures for contaminated land.

9.4.2.2 Subsidies

The measure of providing subsidies for polluters to reduce pollution is difficult to implement, as regulators need to obtain information about polluters, such as the amount of emissions from all sources. This challenge is the same as that posed by emission charges. Emission subsidies, moreover, have several further disadvantages distinct from those of emission charges.

As subsidies increase profits for firms that emit pollutants, this measure may decrease firms' inclination to withdraw from industries generating pollution. On the contrary, it may increase new entrants and, thereby, increase pollution. Where subsidies are sourced from tax revenue, this may cause distortion in the redistribution of income. Furthermore, subsidies to polluters are contrary to the 'polluter pays principle' and may, therefore, struggle to obtain social consensus.

However, as with taxation, subsidies are useful and practical measures if regulators subsidise efforts to reduce the use of hazardous substances in production processes. Under one measure in the United States, the Federal or state governments subsidise farmers that voluntarily adopt a best management practice ('BMP') for the reduction of pollution due to agriculture. A BMP is a measure to mitigate particular types of pollution, and it is considered effective as a countermeasure against nonpoint source pollution. However, Prato (1998) demonstrated that subsidies for adopting BMPs were not efficient in reducing pollution when their implementation did not correspond to differences in the pollution in each area. He claimed that, to address this systemic weakness, such subsidies should be implemented in serious pollution areas where BMPs were found to be effective.

As noted above, subsidies have some problems. Subsidy systems, however, are often implemented because they easily gain acceptance by production firms and it is reasonable that society, as the recipient of pollution reduction benefits, bears the cost of funding subsidies.

Large corporations with sufficient funds can voluntarily accommodate requirements to reduce pollution; accordingly, entrusting pollution reduction to the discretion of each large corporation is efficient. However, voluntary pollution reduction is more difficult for small companies with limited funds. Such companies can be nonpoint sources of soil pollution. Subsidies for small companies can be considered an effective measure for managing these nonpoint sources.

9.4.2.3 Emission Permits Trading

Issuing transferable emission permits is an alternative measure to efficiently reduce pollution. First, a regulator sets an allowable concentration of contaminants or an upper limit of total emissions in a particular area. Second, the regulator issues emission permits within these limits and assigns a certain number of permits to each emitter. Emitters can then trade these permits freely. If the price of the permits is cheaper than their marginal abatement costs, emitters will purchase additional permits and increase emissions. Conversely, if the permit price is higher than their marginal abatement costs, emitters will reduce emissions and sell their surplus permits. Therefore, a socially optimal reduction of pollution can be efficiently achieved through market mechanisms, even if the regulator does not obtain information about each polluter's marginal cost and marginal benefit. Given this point,

9 Methods of Environmental Risk Management for Land Contamination... 165

emission permits trading is considered more effective than command-and-control regulation, taxes, or subsidies.

To make an emission permits trading system effective, regulators need to investigate whether emitters holding emission permits comply with the permits. Moreover, regulators also need to investigate the amount of emissions from all emitters and keep up-to-date records of the holders of all transferred emission permits. Therefore, the regulators' administrative costs can be expensive. Furthermore, when emitters trade their emission permits, they must bear the transaction costs. Depending on the state of emission permit markets, transaction costs may be high. As a measure for tackling land pollution, emission permits trading is not effective, as regulators need to always monitor the emissions of the land of all emission permits holders.

9.4.3 Decentralised Approaches

These are measures to achieve a socially optimal pollution reduction without enforcement by regulators. One example is voluntary bargaining between polluters and victims, as discussed in Sect. 9.2.2.2. In addition to being the most motivated to solve the problem that they confront, these parties are closest to the information about their respective marginal costs and benefits. Such an approach, therefore, is efficient to solve certain pollution problems.

This chapter discusses liability and the pollutant release and transfer register (PRTR) system.

9.4.3.1 Liability

A scheme using liability laws is an approach to control pollution through compensation from polluters to victims. It is based on the idea that an injured party must be compensated by the wrongdoer. This scheme motivates potential polluters to prevent pollution and has the effect of internalising the costs of pollution damage.

Generally, liability laws are considered effective not only to relieve pollution victims financially but also to prevent pollution. A scheme using liability laws does not require each emitter to perform uniform actions, unlike under command-and-control regulation. In other words, each emitter is allowed to take the necessary actions corresponding to each situation. Consequently, the administrative costs are low, as regulators do not need to monitor each emitter. However, if it is unlikely that the victims will sue the polluters, this scheme is ineffective as an approach to control pollution. Lawsuits against polluters may not necessarily be raised, as victims need to bear (at least until a successful judgement) the cost of filing and sustaining a lawsuit. Furthermore, this scheme does not work when damage caused by pollution is undetected, despite that pollution's evident occurrence, or when the victims cannot identify the party who caused the pollution, because the victims cannot sue the polluters. Even if the polluters are identified, when they are bankrupt or likely to be so rendered by a huge compensation award, the victims may not be compensated in any event. Because this scheme is premised on litigation, judicial costs may be high, even if the administrative costs are low.

A scheme using liability laws is intended to incentivise each emitter to take appropriate actions voluntarily; accordingly, it can efficiently reduce pollution. Consequently, it is effective for managing point sources. However, companies whose socioeconomic status is low, such as small firms, may be unable to voluntarily accommodate the demands of efficiently preventing pollution; accordingly, this scheme may not be effective in incentivising them to prevent pollution. Therefore, it is considered that such schemes are not effective for managing nonpoint sources.

Prescribing the party that is obliged to remove soil contamination by law, such as under the Superfund Act in the United States, is also effective to make potential polluters prevent pollution. However, this causes new problems. Across the world, including in Japan, contaminated land or land that may be contaminated is often left untreated for many years. Referred to as 'brownfield sites', this land poses significant problems. Usually, the cost for remediation of contaminated land is very high. Consequently, litigation between the parties over the burden of the cost may be prolonged; alternatively, it may be difficult to find a willing buyer of such land. This leads to the long-term neglect of contaminated land. From this perspective, a scheme using liability laws alone is insufficient, and countermeasures against brownfield sites are required.

9.4.3.2 PRTR System

The PRTR system is a measure to incentivise specific companies to control chemical substances voluntarily. This system, first, requires companies to report to the administration the amount of specific chemical substances that they release or transfer. Second, the data thereby collected from the companies are disclosed by the administration. In Japan, this system was established in 1999, under the 'Act on Confirmation, etc. of Release Amounts of Specific Chemical Substances in the Environment and Promotion of Improvements to the Management Thereof'.

Disclosing each company's emission data is intended to urge voluntary pollution control. However, even if their data is disclosed, this may be not effective for controlling pollution by small companies that could be nonpoint sources, as their limited resources may preclude voluntarily reducing pollution.

This system is also expected to enhance risk communication: a measure to manage environmental risk in a region through companies and residents sharing risk information and communicating about risks. Land contamination problems are often regional in nature; accordingly, risk communication between the parties in a region is relevant to tackling land contamination problems.

9.4.4 The Effectiveness of Each Approach for Land Contamination Problems

As discussed in each of above sections, effective approaches to land contamination problems are measures to prevent pollution, particularly at the production stage. These are effective to manage both point sources and nonpoint sources. Furthermore, decentralised approaches are particularly effective to manage point sources, incentivising each emitter to prevent pollution while allowing them freedom to adopt the most efficient means.

9.5 Risk Management Methods Required for Land Contamination Problems in Japan's Urban Areas

This chapter suggests a risk management framework and concrete management methods required for Japan's urban land contamination problems.

9.5.1 The Range of Required Risk Management

First, the range of required risk management for land contamination must be clarified. Currently, the scope of Japan's land contamination policy is to prevent land pollution by substances with known harmfulness or remediate land contaminated by such substances. There are many potential sources of pollution in urban areas; however, the sites on which contamination is discovered are only a small proportion of very many potentially contaminated sites. There is also contaminated land yet to be discovered and land contaminated with substances whose harmfulness remains unknown. Such potential contaminated land also poses environmental risks. Therefore, risk management, including that of potential land contamination risk, is required going forward.

In addition, radioactive substances were historically outside the regulation of Japan's environmental contamination policies. In 2011, however, radioactive substances were discharged because of the accident at the Fukushima Daiichi nuclear power plant operated by Tokyo Electric Power (TEPCO), caused by the Great East Japan Earthquake. Since then, measures to prevent environmental contamination by radioactive substances have been subject to the Basic Environment Law. However, neither the SCCA nor the APSCAL has so far classified radioactive substances as designated hazardous substances. It is desirable for these laws to be extended to cover radioactive substances.

9.5.2 Relationship Between Environmental Management Measures and Transaction Costs

This section discusses the relationship between environmental management measures, as discussed in Sect. 9.4, and transaction costs.

Command-and-control regulation or economic incentive-based approaches are classified into measures at the production stage and measures at the emission stage. The latter measures require monitoring by regulators of the emissions from each emitter; consequently, the enforcement costs can be high. However, the enforcement costs for measures at the production stage are relatively low, as regulatory authorities do not need to monitor the emission of each source. Of course, although regulators need to investigate the contamination in a certain environment, the production levels of target industries, etc., these tasks are not less costly than monitoring each source's emissions.

By contrast, the transaction costs incurred in decentralised approaches have different characteristics from those under command-and-control regulation or economic incentive-based approaches.

A scheme using liability laws is often relevant to litigation; accordingly, search costs, bargaining costs, and enforcement costs are borne by the parties concerned. The PRTR system's aim is for each emitter to voluntarily control the emission of chemical substances. Therefore, as the required extent of regulatory monitoring is low, enforcement costs are also low. Furthermore, if a firm emitting chemical substances and the neighbouring residents engage in risk communication, the bargaining costs are borne by both parties.

Decentralised approaches require emitters (the parties closest to their own information) and (potential) victims to bargain among themselves (including through litigation) or to manage environmental risk voluntarily. These approaches, therefore, can reduce the transaction costs of society as a whole, compared with the measures in which regulatory monitoring is necessary. However, the transaction cost burden of the parties may be heavy.

9.5.3 Required Framework of Risk Management

Based on the above sections, this section discusses the required framework of risk management for land contamination.

As regards feasibility, desirable measures to manage the risk of land contamination in urban areas are those in which the transaction costs for society as a whole are low. In particular, as the costs of monitoring and enforcing to manage nonpoint sources are high, only measures in which the transaction costs are inexpensive can actually be implemented. Therefore, this paper proposes the following required framework of risk management.

9 Methods of Environmental Risk Management for Land Contamination... 169

(a) Utilisation of decentralised approaches

Urging each polluter to control pollutants voluntarily through decentralised approaches is important, as regulators cannot monitor all the emissions at every site. However, these approaches may not work in isolation, as the heavy burden of transaction costs tends to fall on parties, whether the polluters or victims, with insufficient financial strength. Therefore, such measures as 2 and 3 (below) are also required.

(b) Prompt and reliable implementation of required measures for contaminated land

Establishing a system that prescribes parties and procedures for conducting remediation of contaminated land is important to ensure that dangerous situations caused thereby are not left unattended for a long time.

(c) Thorough prevention measures at the production stage

Preventing pollution with measures at the production stage is important, as the enforcement costs for these measures are low.

(d) Comprehensive risk management without limiting targeted substances

Establishing a flexible and comprehensive risk management system without limiting the range of targeted substances is important, as substances which are not subject to regulations and those whose risks are unknown can also cause land pollution.

9.5.4 Concrete Risk Management Methods

Based on the previous section, this section suggests concrete risk management methods for land contamination by point sources and nonpoint sources. Of course, a method effective as a measure for nonpoint sources is also effective for point sources.

(a) Risk management method for point sources pollution

1. Prescribing the range of persons responsible for remediating contaminated land

This facilitates the prevention of pollution and promptly addressing contaminated land.

In Japan, the SCCA has already prescribed such a rule, the effects of which are expected to be as described above.

(b) Risk management method for nonpoint sources pollution

1. Implementation of zoning corresponding to the nature of the soil or groundwater system

2. For small companies, specifying production technologies (pollution reduction technologies) and supporting with subsidies
3. Establishment of a fund for contaminated land remediation, etc.
4. Utilisation of risk communication

1. Implementation of zoning corresponding to the nature of the soil or groundwater system

The most problematic aspect of land contamination is that, when neglected, it affects other environmental media, such as groundwater and rivers. Even if each firm strictly controls hazardous substances, accidental emission or leakage can occur. In this respect, it is desirable to implement zoning. Watanabe (1997, 2000) demonstrated that the frequency of detection of organochlorine compounds and nitrate-nitrogen ions was higher in groundwater at Musashino Plateau (located mainly in western Tokyo) than in groundwater at the alluvial lowland (located mainly in eastern Tokyo). Watanabe also concluded that geological differences may have affected the ease of movement of pollutants.

The Examination Committee on Countermeasures for Brownfield Surrounding Soil Contamination (ECCBSSC) (2007) reported that, in Tokyo, according to the divisions of 'use districts' under the 'City Planning Act', the probability of soil contamination in industrial districts was 35% higher than in residential districts.

In Japan, urban areas have small sites of various types of use, and people are exposed to the risk of soil or groundwater contamination. Even if pollution occurs accidentally, it is necessary to avoid spreading the resulting damage. To do so, regulators need to set zoning corresponding to the different nature of soil or groundwater systems and to regulate actions that can cause pollution. This measure can comprehensively manage the risk of land contamination without limiting the range of targeted substances.

2. For small companies, specifying production technologies (pollution reduction technologies) and supporting with subsidies

According to the questionnaire survey on companies conducted by KBETI (2012), as a desirable measure to promote soil pollution control during the operation of factories, etc., nearly 70% of respondents expressed that subsidy systems for soil contamination investigation and countermeasures were necessary. Regarding the implementation of soil pollution investigations and countermeasures during the operation of factories, etc., the survey also reported that a high proportion of large companies conducted these, but the implementation ratio was lower among smaller enterprises. This indicates that, for small companies, it is difficult to voluntarily reduce pollution.

According to the Environmental Management Bureau, Ministry of the Environment (2016), in Japan, about 30 municipalities have subsidies and loan systems for soil contamination countermeasures; however, these systems are rarely used. Therefore, it is considered necessary, particularly for small companies, to expand the specifying of technologies and supporting with subsidies.

9 Methods of Environmental Risk Management for Land Contamination... 171

3. Establishment of a fund for contaminated land remediation, etc.

To prevent pollution, such regulations as above 1 and 2 are effective. However, already contaminated land requires other measures. To properly address contaminated land, it is important to prescribe, in advance, the person(s) who must implement soil remediation. Establishing a fund is also required for cases in which the polluter, etc. cannot bear the costs.

In recent years, the balance of Japan's SCCF has been approximately 1.5 to 1.7 billion yen (Ministry of the Environment 2015, 2016). However, from the establishment of the SCCF to today, there have been only two cases in which the grant of a subsidy was permitted, totalling 95 million yen (Japan Environment Association n. d.) This may be seen to suggest the SCCF is unnecessary; however, according to the ECCBSSC (2007), Japan's brownfield sites are estimated to cover 28,000 ha, and the total countermeasure cost is estimated to be 4.2 trillion yen. Investigating the probability of land becoming a brownfield site in Japan, Yasutaka et al. (2008) demonstrated this to be high for the sites of medium- and small-sized manufacturing factories, gas stations, and dry cleaning shops in rural areas with low land prices; there are estimated to be 260,000 such sites. They also suggested that countermeasures for brownfield sites pose major economic problems for small- and medium-sized companies with limited funds.

Considering this situation, a larger scale fund is necessary. The key issue to resolve in this approach is how to finance the fund. Japan's SCCF is financed by subsidies from the national government, donations from companies involved in the repair or investigation of soil contamination, etc. To secure greater financial resources, using a taxation system can be considered.

Using taxation on particular hazardous substances, as under the US Superfund, is effective; however, financial resources generated using it may be unstable, as revenues depend on the amount of these substances' use.

Using another form of taxation can be considered, namely, taxing on landowners depending on the usage of their lands. Soil pollution is generated by people's or companies' activities on land. Every economic agent, whether individual or company, uses the emission absorption capability of the environment. Therefore, users should arguably bear the costs of exploiting the capability of the environment, such as through land use. Taxation based on the use form of land, such as residential, commercial, industrial, etc., can internalise part of the costs of pollution by nonpoint sources. Furthermore, the revenue from this taxation can be a stable source of financial resources.

4. Utilisation of risk communication

There are two stages when risk communication is required in land contamination problems. One is the stage that companies notify neighbourhood residents of the information about discharging or transferring hazardous substances. In Japan, under the PRTR system, the information about discharging or transferring of designated substances by certain companies is disclosed. Another is the stage that companies notify neighbourhood residents of information about the contaminated land which may be discovered. If companies discover pollution in their sites, they need to inform the residents of the situation of the contaminated land, its risk to human health or environment, the plan for soil remediation, etc.

In Japan, the association specified by SCCA sets up a guideline to progress common understanding environmental risk of land contamination and supports risk communication among polluters, residents, and municipalities. Although risk communication is basically between polluters and residents, in fact, municipalities which stand between both have a significant role. In particular, when small companies are responsible for contaminated land, the municipalities in charge of the area can support a smooth risk communication.

The urban areas in Japan have sites of a variety of uses, which exist closely to each other. In particular, the polluters who can be nonpoint sources often exist near the daily life of residents. Accordingly, it is inevitable that residents are exposed to the environmental risk of land contamination to some extent. Residents need to obtain information about the risk of land contamination by neighbourhood companies which discharge pollutants and to understand the risk. Risk communication between both is essential.

9.5.5 Recent Japanese Land Contamination Experiences

Recently, there have been two major events concerning land contamination in Japan.

One is the soil and groundwater contamination at the new site of the Tokyo central wholesale market. In around 2001, the Tokyo Metropolitan Government (TMG) began planning the relocation of the wholesale market at Tsukiji in Tokyo's Chuo Ward; the market was scheduled to relocate to 40 ha of land in Toyosu, Koto Ward, in November 2016. However, due to doubts about safety, huge costs, and the lack of appropriate information disclosure of the relocation project, Governor of Tokyo Yuriko Koike announced the postponement of the relocation at the end of August 2016 (Koike 2016). Shortly afterwards, it was revealed that part of the embankment construction work, which had been planned as one of the soil contamination countermeasures, had not been conducted. Furthermore, at the end of September, benzene and arsenic exceeding environmental standards were detected in groundwater at the new site in Toyosu, which inevitably became a significant issue. The new site for the wholesale market had previously accommodated a gas manufacturing plant of Tokyo Gas, and it was known to be contaminated by a high concentration of benzene and heavy metals. Having purchased this site from Tokyo Gas as the new site for the wholesale market, TMG announced that new buildings would be constructed, after implementing a series of soil contamination countermeasures, such as removal of contaminated soil, replacing it with decontaminated soil, and piling up new soil. However, in some of the new buildings, the basement floors were established; consequently, in the ground underneath these buildings, the space left by removing contaminated soil was not filled with uncontaminated new soil. This contradicted what TMG had publicly announced to citizens and was, therefore, an especially controversial event. This is a typical case of land contamination by a point source. The polluter and the current landowner both have high socioeconomic status and, naturally, the ability to address the land contamination problem. However, the risk communication between the TMG and Tokyo's citizens was inadequate, resulting in a significant, complicated problem. In addition, if strict zoning had been adopted and the sites in the industrial district had been restricted to use for industrial factories, etc., this problem would not have occurred. (Although the new site in Toyosu is located in the industrial district according to the City Planning Act, under the current legal system, a wholesale market can be built regardless of the use district through a decision by municipalities' city planning authorities, etc. or with the permission of a specified administrative agency.)

The second major event is the spread of radioactive substances by the 2011 accident at Fukushima Daiichi nuclear power station, in Fukushima Prefecture, Tohoku region (north-east of Honshu). Radioactive substances released into the air were diffused from Tohoku region to Kanto region (seven prefectures centring on Tokyo), leading to land contamination of residential areas, agricultural lands, forests, etc. This accident profoundly impacted the daily lives of many residents living in these areas, particularly in Fukushima Prefecture. Although many areas have now completed decontamination work, such work in some areas, mainly in Fukushima Prefecture, still continues (as of the end of March 2017). In this case, the polluter was a large electric power corporation, TEPCO, which accepted responsibility for carrying out the decontamination work, compensating residents, etc. Furthermore, the national government was actively involved due to the seriousness of this accident. Therefore, the required measures have mostly been progressed. However, an extremely serious problem remains to be settled: how to ultimately dispose of the huge amount of soil and waste contaminated with radioactivity that has been generated by the decontamination work. National consensus is necessary on how to proceed. An unprecedented level of risk communication between the national government and the people is required.

From the above two examples, it can be seen that conventional environmental measures, centred on countermeasures for point sources, are not enough. Furthermore, the adoption of zoning, risk communication, etc., which are effective as nonpoint source countermeasures, will enhance coping with unexpected pollution problems in the future.

9.6 Concluding Remarks

In this paper, we focused on point sources and nonpoint sources and suggested methods of risk management for land contamination problems. This classification of pollution sources is an important perspective when addressing all environmental pollution problems.

People cannot equally monitor all sources of contamination due to limitations in their observational capability. Accordingly, the management of nonpoint sources with monitoring incurs high enforcement costs. In Japan, countermeasures for land contamination have been focused on the management of point sources, through preventing emissions of hazardous substances and formulating clean-up processes for contaminated land. However, there are many nonpoint sources in current urban areas, and these pollution sources cannot be ignored in society as a whole. To manage nonpoint sources, it is necessary to understand their characteristics and to implement effective measures with relatively low transaction costs.

In Japan, some of the methods we propose have already been implemented; however, it is apparent that some are insufficiently effective at present. The next issue to investigate is how to make these more effective. Furthermore, as discussed in the previous section, in the recent significant cases of land contamination in Japan, soil remediation works, etc. require huge expenditures due to the size of land contamination. In the future, as Japan's decreasing birth-rate and the ageing of society progress, the financial resource shortage of society as a whole is expected to become serious. How to use the limited financial resources for tackling land contamination is a further issue to consider.

Acknowledgements We would like to thank Editage (www.editage.jp) for English language editing.

Note This paper is a revision to Ebisu and Hagihara (2002).

References

Coase RH (1960) The problem of social cost. J Law Econ 3:1–44
Cooter R, Ulen T (2016) Law and economics. 6th ed. Berkeley Law Books. Book 2. http://scholarship.law.berkeley.edu/books/2. Accessed 16 Feb 2017
Dahlman CJ (1979) The problem of externality. J Law Econ 22(1):141–162
Ebisu M, Hagihara K (2002) Methods of environmental risk management for contaminated land problems: management of sources of contamination in urban areas. Compr Urban Stud (77):39–53. (in Japanese)
Environmental Management Bureau, Ministry of the Environment (2016) Results of the survey on the enforcement status of the soil contamination countermeasures act and soil contamination investigations and countermeasures in FY 2014 (in Japanese). http://www.env.go.jp/water/report/h28-01/full.pdf. Accessed 25 May 2017

9 Methods of Environmental Risk Management for Land Contamination... 175

Examination Committee on Countermeasures for Brownfield Surrounding Soil Contamination (ECCBSSC) (2007) Actual situation of brownfield problems surrounding soil contamination (Interim report) (Dojo Osen wo Meguru Brownfield Mondai no Jittai tou ni tsuite (Chukan torimatome)) (in Japanese). http://www.env.go.jp/press/files/jp/9506.html. Accessed 5 June 2017

Fujinawa K (1994) Protection of groundwater source in Europe (Europe ni okeru Chikasui no Suigen Hogo ni tsuite). Water Sci (Suiri Kagaku) 38(1):31–50. (in Japanese)

Japan Environment Association (n.d.) The accomplishments of granting subsidies (Josei-Kin Kofu Jisseki) (in Japanese). http://www.jeas.or.jp/dojo/business/grant/record.html. Accessed 14 May 2017

Japan Environmental Management Association for Industry (2014) Report of global warming issue countermeasures research project in FY 2013: survey on trends concerning conservation of soil environment (Heisei 25 Nen-do Chikyu-ondanka Mondai tou Taisaku Chosa Jigyo (Dojo Kankyo no Hozen ni Kansuru Doko Chosa) Hokokusyo) (in Japanese). http://www.meti.go.jp/meti_lib/report/2014fy/E003731.pdf. Accessed 5 June 2017

Kanto Bureau of Economy, Trade and Industry (KBETI) (2012) Survey on industrial pollution prevention measures for small and medium enterprises in FY 2011: report of survey on soil pollution control in the Kanto Bureau of Economy, Trade and Industry (Heisei 23 Nen-do Chusho-kigyo tou Sangyo Kogai Boshi Taisaku Chosa: Kanto-Keizai-Sangyo-kyoku kannai ni okeru Dojo Osen Taisaku ni kakaru Chosa Hokokusyo) (in Japanese). http://www.kanto.meti.go.jp/seisaku/kankyo/recycle/data/20120409dojoosen_chousa.pdf. Accessed 5 June 2017

Kato I, Morishima A, Otsuka T, Yanagi K (eds) (1996) Soil contamination and corporation responsibility (Dojo Osen to Kigyo no Sekinin). Yuhikaku, Tokyo. (in Japanese)

Koike G (2016 August, 31) 'Governor's Room'/Press conference. (Koike Chiji 'Chiji no Heya'/Kisha Kaiken) (in Japanese). http://www.metro.tokyo.jp/tosei/governor/governor/kishakaiken/2016/08/31.html. Accessed 20 May 2017

Ministry of the Environment (2009) 2009 edition's white paper on the environment, the sound material-cycle society and biodiversity (PDF version) (Heisei 21 Nen-ban Kankyo, Junkangata-shakai, Seibutsu-tayousei Hakusyo PDF-ban), pp 332–333 (in Japanese). http://www.env.go.jp/policy/hakusyo/h21/pdf.html. Accessed 21 Mar 2017

Ministry of the Environment (2015) The Fund Sheet in FY 2014: The Fund Sheet No. 26-009 (Heisei 26 Nen Kikin Sheet: Kikin Sheet Bangou 26-009) (in Japanese). https://www.env.go.jp/guide/budget/spv_eff/review_h26/funds_sheets_h26.html. Accessed 14 May 2017

Ministry of the Environment (2016) The Fund Sheet in FY 2016: The Fund Sheet No. 28-007 (Heisei 28 Nen Kikin Sheet: Kikin Sheet Bangou 28-007) (in Japanese). https://www.env.go.jp/guide/budget/spv_eff/review_h28/funds_sheets_h28/28-007.pdf. Accessed 14 May 2017

Prato T (1998) Natural resource and environmental economics. Iowa State University Press, Ames

United States Environmental Protection Agency (2000) Superfund: 20 years of protecting human health and the environment

Watanabe M (1997) Chemical substances in undergroundwater (part 1). Annual report of the Tokyo Metropolitan Institute for Environmental Protection 1997, pp 121–127 (in Japanese)

Watanabe M (2000) Chemical substances in undergroundwater (part 4) (Chikasui-chu no Kagaku Busshitsu (sono 4)). Annual report of the Tokyo Metropolitan Institute for Environmental Protection 2000, pp 25–31 (in Japanese)

Yanagi K (2001) Environmental law policy: environmentally conscious laws and policies in Japan, the EU, and the UK (Kankyo Hou Seisaku: Nippon, EU, Eikoku ni miru Kankyo-Hairyo no Hou to Seisaku). Seibunsya, Tokyo. (in Japanese)

Yasutaka T, Makino M, Matsuda H (2008) Estimation of the probability of a potentially contaminated site becoming a brownfield site in Japan. Environ Sci 21(4):291–306. (in Japanese)

Yoshida F, Hata A, Tonegawa H (1999) Itai-itai disease and the countermeasures against cadmium pollution by the Kamioka mine. Environ Econ Policy Stud 2:215–229

Chapter 10
The Role of Parks in the Inheritance of Regional Memories of Disasters

Noriko Horie

Abstract The inheritance of disaster memory is considered an important issue. Disaster prevention is one of the main functions of urban parks, and every time a catastrophe occurs, disaster prevention functions have been improved. For disaster prevention, in addition to 'public assistance' such as maintenance of facilities and systems (hardware) by the administration, 'self-help' and 'co-aid' by each citizen are indispensable. Besides the infrastructure or hardware aspect, urban parks become places to convey memories of disasters and potential contributors to 'software' such as raising the consciousness level of disaster prevention and improving the ability to prevent local disasters. In this research, I focus on the inheritance of local memories in order to enhance the disaster prevention function of urban parks. After reviewing past researches, I examined the evidence of memories of disasters in parks in Naka Ward, Yokohama City. As a result of my study, I discovered that there are some monuments mentioning earthquake disasters in the inscriptions, although communicating memories of disasters is not the main purpose of the monuments. There are some monuments that are memorials to war damage and accidents. I consider parks' function of inheriting memories of disasters as still insufficient. It is necessary to clarify the purpose of inheritance, the subject of inheritance, and the measures taken to nurture inheritance of disaster memories in order to make better use of parks to improve the ability of the area to prevent disasters.

Keywords Inheritance of memory · Disaster · Urban park · Monument · Disaster prevention education

---

N. Horie (✉)
Department of Public Policy, Faculty of Sociology, Bukkyo University, Kyoto, Japan
e-mail: horie@bukkyo-u.ac.jp

© Springer Nature Singapore Pte Ltd. 2019
C. Asahi (ed.), *Building Resilient Regions*, New Frontiers in Regional Science: Asian Perspectives 35, https://doi.org/10.1007/978-981-13-7619-1_10

10.1 Introduction

Urban parks have precious resources and hold the history and memories of their regions. Among their inheritance is the memory of regional disasters. Conventionally, urban parks play an important role in disaster prevention by becoming evacuation areas and disaster prevention hubs in the event of disasters. As a result of the Great Hanshin-Awaji Earthquake, parks were promoted nationwide. The disaster prevention park system was launched in 1978, with the main purpose of establishing urban parks as wide-area evacuation spaces and evacuation routes during emergencies. When the Great Hanshin-Awaji Earthquake struck in January 1985, many parks were effectively utilised in various ways. Following this, the primary evacuation site was added to the disaster prevention park in 1986, and the wide-area disaster prevention base was added in 1988. Furthermore, when the Chūetsu Earthquake occurred in the Niigata Prefecture in October 2004, the park demonstrated its function as a base for restoration and reconstruction. Self-defence forces and other relief units used the park as a site to distribute supplies to municipalities affected by the disaster. Thus, in 1995, a regional disaster prevention base was added to the disaster prevention park. As described above, the disaster prevention park system was established in concurrence with major earthquake disasters.

In addition to 'public assistance' such as the maintenance of facilities and systems by the administration, 'self-help' is essential for every citizen in order to protect life and property from disasters. It is essential to conduct disaster prevention awareness programmes and carry out disaster management measures (White Paper on Disaster Management, 2010). After the Great East Japan Earthquake that occurred on 11 March 2011, the necessity of 'self-help' and 'mutual aid' as well as 'public assistance' is increasingly emphasised. When a disaster occurs, individuals must survive by themselves or by helping each other.

Additionally, local residents should be able to recognise possible disasters beforehand, by studying records of past disasters. This will improve the disaster prevention capability of the area and enable people to act consciously about disaster prevention or disaster reduction. Even in urban parks, which are local public goods and infrastructure, there is a possibility of contributing not only to the hardware aspect but also to the software aspects. By becoming places that inherit memories of regional disasters, parks can potentially improve the disaster prevention consciousness of citizens and improve their ability to prevent local disasters.

Therefore, in this research, I focus on the handing down of local memories that enhance the disaster prevention function of urban parks. After reviewing past researches, I examined the evidence of the memories of disasters in urban parks in Naka Ward, Yokohama City. I organise and examine the purpose, subject, and measures of the inheritance of memories of areas from the point of view of the role that urban parks play in disaster prevention.

10.2 Review

Many researches have explored the history, existence, or transformation of regional resources such as ruins and cultural properties, and their inclusion in the park system (e.g. Tabata et al. 1990, Neki and Kishimoto 1997, Hayashi et al. 2003, Nishisaka et al. 2008).

Among them, Nishisaka and colleagues examined the location and actual utilisation of stone monuments and ruins at 103 urban parks in the Hyōgo Prefecture (in the cities of Ashiya and Kobe). He demonstrated that parks play a role in conveying history through the conservation of diverse regional resources.

On the other hand, a vast amount of research has accumulated on the disaster prevention function of urban parks. This includes research on the refractory function of trees (e.g. Nakamura 1956); reconstruction of a park after the Great Kantō Earthquake, air defence green space, and park maintenance by war damaged reconstruction project (Imamura 2009); utilisation of urban parks in the Great Hanshin-Awaji Earthquake (e.g. Wako et al. 1998); and disposition and satisfaction of urban parks from the viewpoint of disaster prevention (Masuda 2003).

As has been pointed out, it is important to study not only the development of physical infrastructure, or the 'hardware', such as spaces and facilities, but also 'software' aspects such as the formation of local communities that function effectively in the event of disasters and the necessity of imparting disaster education.

An investigation of the situation at the disaster prevention park in Saito in 2009 revealed issues like 'ground water pump for emergency stopped working, but the repair cost is enormous due to custom equipment and it cannot be repaired', 'the grating which is put on the cooking oven for emergency is lost', and 'Person in charge changed and the operation manual was missing'. In addition, not knowing when an earthquake disaster will happen increases the tendency to fall into a negative chain of 'management costs of things that are not immediately needed are reduced → insufficient management → failure → not useful at times of disaster'. Minimising necessary hardware facilities, and using the park for educating people and creating awareness about disaster prevention in peacetime, points to the necessity for improving the ability to prevent regional disasters, including the resourcefulness to tackle community-based disaster prevention storytelling.

In view of the importance of park management in disaster prevention, Hiramatsu and Aoki (2017) also point out evidence from the Kumamoto Earthquake Survey Report (2016).

This research deals with the inheritance of memories of disasters of regions, from the viewpoint of disaster prevention. The following studies were examined: research that explores the present condition of the Hiromura embankment (Hirokawa Town, Wakayama Prefecture), which was made a historical site park for regional heritage and resident consciousness (Katayanagi et al. 2009), and international comparison study on the succession of earthquake memory (Sakamoto et al. 2009). Katayanagi et al. showed that the Hiromura embankment is not only a disaster prevention facility but also plays a great role in creating awareness of regional disaster prevention.

Sakamoto et al. suggest that museums and parks related to natural disasters in Turkey, Taiwan, and Indonesia inherit the memories of the disasters. Yamori (2002) focuses on the memory of earthquake disaster experiences and its communication via storytelling activities when he studies the Hokudan Earthquake Memorial Park and Nojima Fault Preservation Museum that preserves the epicentre of the Great Hanshin-Awaji Earthquake.

The Great East Japan Earthquake (2011) has made us aware of the importance of the succession of memory of tsunami disasters that have occurred in the past. Tachibana and Hirata (2013) explores suggestions for the park plan in the disaster-affected areas of Tohoku from the present situation and problems faced when the park intends to convey the memory of the Great Hanshin-Awaji Earthquake.

As described above, parks are expected to play a vital role for disaster prevention in the area, in various aspects of hardware and software. However, there is insufficient research on the role of urban parks in the succession of memory of regional disasters.

10.3   Parks Built with Local Disasters

The Oxford Dictionary of English defines 'disaster' as 'a sudden accident or a natural catastrophe that causes great damage or loss of life'. Natural disasters include damage caused by meteorological disasters such as winds, floods, earthquakes, and volcanic activities. Artificial disasters include damage caused by wars, fires, industrial accidents, accidents, etc.

Table 10.1 lists examples of parks that can be considered as built with local disasters. In addition to being listed in Table 10.1, there are several parks that convey the memory of the Great Hanshin-Awaji Earthquake (Tachibana and Hirata 2013). After the Great East Japan Earthquake, some plans of memorial parks, such as Millennium Hope Hills (Iwanuma City, Miyagi Prefecture) and Great East Japan Earthquake Memorial Park (temporary name), are in progress. Also, in Oshima-Machi, Tokyo, the area of the sediment-related disaster that occurred in 2013 will be converted into the Oshima Town Memorial Park.

10.4   Traces of Disasters in Urban Parks in Naka Ward, Yokohama

In this section, I examine the ruins of disasters memorialised in urban parks in Naka Ward, Yokohama. The documents referred to in this survey are Naka Ward and Yokohama City (2001), Yokohama City (1976) and the Homepage of Naka Ward. Naka Ward, a charming tourist destination of Yokohama, encapsulates a historic atmosphere of modernisation, as it was a site of the Great Kanto Earthquake. The area was also damaged during the war. Currently, as the centre of Yokohama, a

10 The Role of Parks in the Inheritance of Regional Memories of Disasters   181

Table 10.1 Major parks with memories of local disasters

Disasters		Name of park and location	Overview
Natural disasters	Earthquakes	Yokoamicho Park, Taitō, Tokyo	Memorial to the many victims burned to death in the Great Kantō earthquake
		Yamashita Park, Yokohama	Built with the reclaimed rubble of the Great Kantō Earthquake
		Motomachi Park, Yokohama	Displays the remains of a memorial dedicated to the earthquake reconstruction work of the time
		Hokudan Earthquake Memorial Park, Awaji	The Nojima Fault Preservation Museum preserves a section of the Nojima Fault that was exposed when the Great Hanshin-Awaji Earthquake struck
		Minato no Mori Park, Kobe	Built as a symbol of the city's recovery after the Great Hanshin-Awaji Earthquake
		Port of Kobe Earthquake Memorial Park, Kobe	Preserves a part of the quay as it was during the Great Hanshin Earthquake
	Tsunamis	Hiromura Levee, Horokawa Town	Built with the damage of the tsunami caused by the Great Ansei Earthquake
	Landslides	Jidukiyama Park, Nagano City	Memorial park built on the site of the 1985 landslide
		Momijidani Park, Hatsukaichi City	Built utilising rocks of debris from the 1945 Makurazaki typhoon
	Floods	Kasekiko Park, Kakamigahara	Memorial park built on the Teppougawa river flood site
Human disasters	Wars	Hiroshima Peace Memorial Park, Hiroshima	Memorial with a prayer for the peaceful repose of victims of the atomic bombs and a pledge of peace
	Fires	Oomori Park, Hakodate City	Built in memory of the many citizens who died in the river at the Hakodate Great Fire in 1934

major city, it has a population of nearly 4 million people including residents, workers, and tourists. Therefore, disaster prevention is a big consideration.

Yamashita Park, a park representative of Yokohama City, is a disaster recovery park built by reclaiming the rubble of the Great Kanto Earthquake. Before the earthquake, Yokohama had only two parks: Yokohama Park (Naka Ward) and Kamonyama Park (Nishi Ward). The reconstruction project by the country after the earthquake resulted in the addition of three new parks: Nogeyama Park (Nishi Ward), Kanagawa Park (Kanagawa Ward), and Yamashita Park. At the same time as the restoration, a baseball stadium was set up, and the Kamonyama Park site was expanded. Landscaping was carried out at other parks, including Hodogaya Children's Park (Hodogaya Ward), Motomachi Park (Naka Ward), Yamate Park (Naka Ward), and Okinacyo Park (Naka Ward). Thus, although many parks in Yokohama

City are closely related to the earthquake disaster, it is not always easy to find traces of the disaster at their sites.

In 2001, Naka-ku produced a booklet presenting 239 monuments within the Naka Ward. This information was updated with 78 more monuments on their website as of April 2009.

Table 10.2 summarises the names of the parks, the names of the monuments, the year of installation of the monuments, and the purpose of the monuments for the 50 monuments found in parks, out of the total of 239 monuments in the Naka Ward published in the 2001 booklet. Looking at the purposes of these monuments, the most references are to the origins of the existing facilities or the places of origin of something (32 monuments). The second highest number of references is to honourable achievements (12 monuments), followed by commemoration of friendships (8 monuments), and memorialisation of earthquake disasters (6 monuments). The monument of 'the oldest park in Japan' in Yokohama Park makes a reference to the time of the Great Kantō Earthquake, but does not mention it as the main purpose of the creation of the park. Other examples of monuments preserving the memory of disasters include the 'Indian Water Tower' in Yamashita Park and 'Gerard's tile' in Motomachi Park.

For example, the inscription on the monument to 'The oldest park in Japan' in Yokohama Park (Fig. 10.1), in addition to stating the origin of the park installation, also mentions that the park protected people from the flames of the big fire during the Great Kantō Earthquake.

Similarly, the Indian Water Tower monument in Yamashita Park (Fig. 10.2) has an inscription from the Indian commerce association in Japan, thanking the citizens of Yokohama City for their relief efforts during the Great Kantō Earthquake and commemorating the friendship.

In Motomachi Park, and the ruins of Yamate no. 80, there are inscriptions with details of the damage created by the earthquake and information on Mr. Gerard who operated the water supply industry and the tile manufacturing industry. These descriptions contain some memories of the earthquake disaster.

The Odori Park contains a peace monument of the Second World War as a record of the damage wrought by the war.

A monument in French Hill has immortalised the record of the American military plane crash in Midori-ward in 1977 with a statue of a mother and a child who were sacrificed in the accident.

In addition to monuments, the explanation boards in some parks that describe the origins of the parks with letters, photographs, pictures, drawings, etc. refer to earthquakes.

For example, the explanation board in Yamashita Park (Fig. 10.3) has some pictures and text in Japanese and English that describe its historical background. This includes a picture of the Yokohama port in the early Meiji period that shows the rubble of the Great Kantō Earthquake strewn on the coastline. It makes it easy for viewers to understand the extent of the devastation.

Setting up such explanation boards is an effective means of communicating regional memories – if people can read it. However, when the information is too far from the current reality, it may be difficult for viewers to conceive the situation

Table 10.2 Monuments in parks in Naka Ward, Yokohama City

Park	Monument	Established year	Purpose and contents of the monument						
			Origin	Friendship	Honour	War	Earthquake	Accident	Others
Yokohama Park	Oldest park monument in Japan	1929	O				△		
	Stone lantern of Gankirou	1982	O						O
	Bust of Richard Henry Brunton	–			O				
Yamashita Park	Statue of a large head commemorating the introduction of the Western haircut to Japan	1989	O						
	Indian Water Tower	1939		O			△		
	Girl Scout Statue dedicated to Japan-US friendship	1962		O					
	Statue of the Girl with Red Shoes	1979	O						
	Monument of the Children's Song 'Seagull Sailor Man'	1979	O						
	The Guardian of Water sculpture	1960		O					
	25 Perimeter Monument of Yokohama-San Diego Sister City Partnership	1982		O					
	El Camino Real mission bells	1982		O					
	Monument of General Artemio Ricarte	1971		O	O				
Odori Park	Memorial with a plaque on the origin of peace	1992				O			
	Memorial of Kiyoshi Hasegawa	1981			O				
	Memorial of Kanzan Shimomura	1998			O				
Honmoku Sancho Park	Yokohama Hizakura (cherry tree) boasting scarlet cherry blossoms	1997	O						

(continued)

Table 10.2 (continued)

Park	Monument	Established year	Purpose and contents of the monument						
			Origin	Friendship	Honour	War	Earthquake	Accident	Others
Kominatosyo Park	A monument of the Northern Fisheries Cooperative Association	–	O						
Honmoku Citizen Park	Honmoku citizen pool	1969	O						
	Monument of the Honmoku Fisheries Cooperative Association	1980	O						
Sankeien Garden	Shanghai Yokohama friendship garden	1989	O	O					
	Traditional Japanese style garden	–	O						
	Memorial of Sankei Hara	1959			O				
	Haiku monument of Kyoshi Takahama	–			O				
Negishi Forest Park	Morgan Plaza	–	O		O				
	Negishi Racecourse Site	1994	O						
	Haiku monument of Taiho Furusawa	1986			O				
	Hayagriva (Kannon with horse head shaped decoration)	1954							O
Motomachi Park	Historical remains of Alfred Gerard's tile and brick factory and water reservoir	1993	O		O		△		
	Gerard's Western-style tiles	1985	O		O		△		
	Monument of the ruins of Yamate Number 80 house	1985	O				△		
	Memorial of the birthplace of painting in Japan	–							
	Ruins of Taisyokatuei film studio	1984	O						
	Motomachi Park	1930	O				△		
	Bluff groove monument	1986	O						
	Water wall spring of old children's pool	2000	O						

Park	Feature	Year				
Minato-no-Mieru Oka Koen (Harbor View Park)	Monument of Minato-no-Mieru Oka Koen	—	O			
	A monument of a popular song	1999	O			
	Rose Garden	—	O	△		
	Osaragi Jiro Memorial Museum	—			O	
Furansu Yama (French Hill Park)	Yokohama Bowling birthplace monument	—	O		O	
	Pavilion Baltal	—	O			
	Haiku monument of Rinka Ohno	1983			O	
	Statue of a mother and child	2005				O
	Birthplace of cleaning industry	1973	O			
Yamate Park	A monument to the birthplace of tennis in Japan	1978	O			
	Yamate Park 20th Anniversary	1990	O			
	Japan's first Western-style park	—	O			
	Yamate Park and Himalayan cedar	—	O			
Kirin Park	Memorial of the origins of Kirin Brewery	1937	O			
	Cultural remains	1963	O			

O Built on the site of the disaster; △ Disaster is mentioned in the inscription

Fig. 10.1 Monument to the Oldest Park in Japan in Yokohama Park

Fig. 10.2 Indian Water Tower monument in Yamashita Park

Fig. 10.3 An explanation board in Yamashita Park

during the disaster, even if they have all the facts. I want a device that allows viewers to get a deeper experience of the memory of disasters.

The Zou-no-hana Park was built to celebrate the 150th anniversary of the port of Yokohama. The masonry of the breakwater that collapsed at the time of the Great Kantō Earthquake was preserved locally, and an explanatory board was set up to convey the memory of the disaster. It may be necessary to show evidence of disasters on the actual site in this way, both for historical cultural integration and for becoming fully aware of disasters.

However, such polite explanation boards are installed only in famous sightseeing spots such as Yamashita Park. In addition, inscriptions such as that on the 'The oldest park in Japan' monument in Yokohama Park are too old and difficult for modern citizens to understand.

10.5 How to Preserve the Inheritance of Memories of Disasters in Parks

Even in areas where many citizens have died due to great earthquake disasters, people's memories will diminish, and the awareness of disaster prevention will dull as the years go by. In other areas, it will become more difficult to convey the memory of disasters to people.

In Naka Ward, Yokohama, there are many historical resources of modernisation since the opening of the port, and the earthquake disaster has greatly influenced the creation of some parks. Not only tourists but many citizens use parks that are superb both historically and aesthetically. However, only a few parks communicate the memory of disasters in a positive manner. Parks are also not places to encourage judgement on the methods of evacuation and the actions to be taken in order to survive in the event of a disaster.

Many precious lives were lost in the Great East Japan Earthquake, despite the fact that measures were taken to address both infrastructure and awareness to protect against potential tsunamis.

The disaster was certainly of an unexpected scale, but from survivors' testimonies, it seems that in many scenarios, judgement and timely action meant the difference between life and death. In order to contribute to the improvement of a region's ability to prevent disaster, parks should be used as places to impart the memory and wisdom of disasters and to develop self-help capabilities that each person can use to evaluate and act during a disaster.

Below, we will examine the inheritance of regional memories in parks. That is, (a) for what (the purpose), (b) what (the subject), and (c) how (the measures taken).

(a) **Purpose of Inheritance**

The purpose of inheritance is to improve the capability to prevent disasters. In order to improve the disaster prevention capability of an area, it is important to improve facilities and systems. In addition, it is equally important for each individual to acquire the ability to prevent disasters. It is an individual's disaster prevention capability that will enable them to recognise the possibility of local disasters from the records of past disasters, act with an awareness of disaster prevention techniques, gain knowledge of disasters, and help others.

There are museums playing institutional roles in the inheritance of memory. However, when museums try to inherit the memories of people, a value judgement has to be made on whether incidents are particularly worthwhile in the context of historical culture. Particularly in the case of history, there are disagreements to interpretations. Moreover, the handling of certain incidents may be delicate, for example, discrimination problems. Parks, on the other hand, can avoid ideological conflicts by expressing the improvement of regional disaster prevention ability straightforwardly, as a realistic purpose.

(b) **Subject of Inheritance**

What people inherit from disasters are its memories and its wisdom, in other words, the kinds of disasters that occurred in the past, the kinds of situations that occurred in the past, how people responded, and the wisdom and lessons. The wisdom includes providing judgement materials on the possibilities of future disasters and how each person should behave when it occurs.

Although parks are evacuation sites to avoid fires, there is a possibility that parks itself and the roads to parks may be destroyed depending on the ground, topography, and surrounding environment. Of course, there are risks of tsunamis in coastal parks.

Moreover, parks may be very dangerous places during weather situations in upstream areas, as proved in the serious accident of July 2008, caused by flash floods that occurred in a river friendly park on Togagawa River that runs through Nada Ward in Kobe. Depending on the location of the park, it may be useful as an emergency shelter or disaster prevention base, but it may also be dangerous. Information on the negative as well as the positive aspects of parks must be inherited.

In addition, memories of social unrest caused by disasters are also inherited. For example, in the case of the Great Kantō Earthquake, while there was friendship that went beyond nationality, as can be seen in the 'Indian Water Tower' monument at Yamashita Park, many Koreans were massacred in the confusion that resulted from social unrest and wrong information. Such negative memories should never be forgotten. It is important to provide a place to think about how to act as human beings during emergencies.

(c) **Measures Taken to Support Inheritance**

Inheritance methods require actualising. In particular, in order to raise the disaster prevention capability, it is necessary not only to transfer knowledge but also to urge people to understand situations and to improvise.

In terms of a deeper emotional understanding of disasters, it is effective to show evidence of disasters as they are, as seen in Port of Kobe Earthquake Memorial Park (Fig. 10.4). However, opinion is divided among victims over leaving afflicted buildings on the site, even though they survived the earthquake disaster of the Great East Japan Earthquake.

Fig. 10.4 Port of Kobe Earthquake Memorial Park

Therefore, while it is necessary to gain consensus and take consideration of the area, it is also true that the number of people of future generations who have no direct experience of disasters is increasing year by year. In order to communicate disaster situations and improve disaster prevention abilities, it will be required to leave disaster-affected remains in parks so that everyone can encounter it on a daily basis.

In some parks, there are buildings that effectively improve disaster prevention capabilities instead of showcasing disaster-affected remains. There are parks that relocate and preserve old private houses from the area and use them for educating the public on disasters. For example, when the lifeline is destroyed, the wisdom of predecessors' lives is effectively preserved. Old folk-style tools in old houses do not need a modern lifeline to be explained (Fig. 10.5).

The wisdom contained in old private houses that did not depend on electricity, gas, and water provides an insight into lives that were devised with materials available in the era without electric energy.

The wisdom and patience of those who have survived the tough times may give us hints to survive disasters and may evoke the essential life force we should have.

It is not enough to only explain information at museums but also to deliver knowledge while utilising the actual experience through the experience program. Parks can be used as a place of experience for this.

Fig. 10.5 Old traditional houses and folk-style tools

It is believed that the awareness of residents is progressing through the implementation of disaster drills and the dissemination of information on hazards at the time of disasters, such as the distribution and disclosure of hazard maps, but in the event of emergencies, each person must judge and act.

An examination of the Great Hanshin-Awaji Earthquake has pointed out that people use parks that they are familiar with on a daily basis even during emergencies (Saito 2009). It would be desirable for parks that are used on a daily basis to provide guidance on emergency actions to be taken during disasters.

10.6 Conclusion

Even after the Great East Japan Earthquake, a massive earthquake such as the Kumamoto Earthquake occurred. Volcanic disasters, floods due to heavy rains, and sediment-related disasters are occurring repeatedly. There is concern that the occurrence of large-scale tsunamis and the frequency of super typhoons will increase. Before the recovery and reconstruction of disaster areas are completed, it may be hit by the next disaster. We must acquire the ability to survive and prepare for the next disaster.

The Tokyo Rinkai Disaster Prevention Park opened in the Tokyo bay area in July 2010. When a large-scale disaster occurs in the Tokyo metropolitan area, this park will be a local countermeasure headquarters, not an evacuation site, and the entire park will be responsible for the wide-ranging command function. In peacetime, citizens can enjoy it as a recreational place. A vast park, it becomes a place that provides disaster prevention drills and conducts events. It also has a disaster prevention experience-learning facility, which is responsible for educating people on disaster prevention. The maintenance of such facilities and systems by the administration, and each person's capability to live, will be the two wheels that drive the improvement of disaster prevention. Because it is a life-threatening problem, it is required that each individual be able to judge and act based on inherited memory and wisdom and that opportunities and places to nurture such strengths are provided.

From the present situation in Naka-ku, Yokohama, it turns out that the park is not sufficient despite the possibility that it could play a role in the succession of memory for improving disaster management capacity. The park needs to function on a daily basis as a place where citizens can come in contact with the memory of the area's disaster, not only for those who have a specific interest in history and disaster prevention but also for ordinary people who are not interested in such matters. Due to the different types of disasters that can occur depending on the area, the way parks administer the inheritance of disaster prevention memories may differ in different communities. Studies by region and disaster types are left as future tasks.

Acknowledgements This work was supported by JSPS KAKENHI Grant Number 16 K01203.

References

Hayashi Y, Kobayashi A, Fukuoka T (2003) A study on the Boat Basin in Yamashita Park. Yokohama. J Jpn Inst Landsc Archit 66(5):447–452

Hiramatsu R, Aoki A (2017) Roles and current issues of urban parks for the evacuation site at the 2016 Kumamoto earthquake. Park Adm Manag Res 10:24–30

Imamura Y (2009) A study on the conversion policy of the former military grounds in the post-war plan and the conversion to the open spaces'. City Planning Review Special Issue, Papers on City Planning 44(3):817–822

Katayanagi T, Tajima H, Hurukawa M et al (2009) The condition of the Hiromura Levee as regional heritage and the consciousness of the community. Bull Geo Environ Sci 11:131–138

Masuda N (2003) Urban Park planning from the point of view of the safe and secure urban environment. J Jpn Inst Landsc Archit 66(3):180–184

Naka Ward, Yokohama City (2001) Naka-ku no Rekishi wo Hi-mo Talk (to unravel the history of Naka-ku)

Naka Ward, Yokohama City. http://www.city.yokohama.lg.jp/naka/sighthist/etizu

Nakamura S (1956) Fundamental studies on fire protection plantings. Bull Kyoto Univ For 26:10–58

Neki A, Kishimoto M (1997) Preservation of archaeological sites, new movement of "Ecomuseum" and its significance in urban design and in creating new community. Bull Nagaoka Univ Technol 19:105–113

Nishisaka R, Tahara N, Kamihogi A (2008) A study on existence situation and use realities of regional resources in City Park. J Jpn Inst Landsc Archit 71(5):615–618

Saito Y (2009) What is required of the park manager at the time of the earthquake – its task and correspondence. Public Parks (186):2–5

Sakamoto M, Kimura S, et al (2009) The comparative study of earthquake memory and transference: case studies of Turkey, Taiwan and Indonesia. Disaster Prevention Research Institute Annuals B 52:181–194

Tabata S, Miyagi S, Uchida K (1990) Several issues on the development of historic parks in the old castle sites. J Jpn Inst Landsc Archit 53(5):169–174

Tachibana T, Hirata F (2013) Present situation and issues of parks and park facilities which transmit memories of great Hanshin-Awaji earthquake disaster. J Jpn Inst Landsc Archit 76(5):517–520

Wako K, Shimizu M, Tanaka T et al (1998) A study on park users, their selection and uses of evacuation site after the great Hanshin-Awaji earthquake. J Jpn Inst Landsc Archit 61 (5):773–776

Yamori K (2002) How to prevent records of disaster experiences from weathering in terms of museum display?: the case of Nojima fault preservation museum. Annual Reports of the Graduate School of Nara University 7:331–358

Yokohama City (1976) Yokohama City history, the second half of Vol. 5

Chapter 11
Measuring the Public Supply of Private Hedges for Disaster Prevention

Noriko Horie

Abstract Although typically considered private goods, some private hedges are supported by the public sector through subsidies or regulations because they serve a public function such as contributing to the environment, landscape, and disaster prevention. When a big earthquake occurs, death or injury often is a result of collapsing structures such as concrete brick fences. A pressing problem is converting unsafe structures into safe structures as soon as possible. This chapter examines the current state of public supply to privately owned hedges as private goods. Various measures of direct supply are considered such as regulation, induction and attraction, and enlightenment concerning hedges in Japan. The main means of promoting the public supply of hedges is induction, particularly the subsidy system. Enlightenment measures are performed in specific ways. However, direct supply and direct regulation are not typical. Considering public support of hedges, the systems should be enriched to aggressively advance hedge-ization.

Keywords Private hedge · Disaster prevention · Public supply · Subsidy · Regulation

11.1 Introduction

The supply systems of various public goods are changing as socioeconomic circumstances also change. Green space in urban areas such as parks and roadside greenery serves various functions such as environmental and landscape preservation, recreational areas, and disaster prevention. Today, many cities are attempting to increase both publicly and privately owned green space. However, it is necessary to clarify the relationships between the characteristics of non-excludability

---

N. Horie (✉)
Department of Public Policy, Faculty of Sociology, Bukkyo University, Kyoto, Japan
e-mail: horie@bukkyo-u.ac.jp

© Springer Nature Singapore Pte Ltd. 2019
C. Asahi (ed.), *Building Resilient Regions*, New Frontiers in Regional Science: Asian Perspectives 35, https://doi.org/10.1007/978-981-13-7619-1_11

and non-competitiveness of green space as public goods and their supply to determine their sector – public or private (Horie et al. 2015).

We concentrate on the relationships between the existence effects and the supply of privately owned green space by the public sector (Horie et al. 2016). That is, by examining public documents on privately owned greenery from the viewpoint of existence effects such as environmental preservation, landscape, recreation, and disaster prevention in Saitama City, we consider the relationships between the existence effect and the supply of privately owned green space by the public sector. Various existence effects are described to explain the necessity of public supply for private green space. Particularly, the amount of description concerning the excludability and competitiveness of greenery was higher than other descriptions of existence effects. There are more descriptions of 'landscape' in supply to management than installation, and the number of descriptions for regulation is higher than the number of descriptions for other effects. However, there are few descriptions that include references to 'disaster prevention'.

The Kumamoto Earthquake occurred in April 2016, and measures to manage seismic hazards are urgent business once again. Many local governments set up subsidy systems when removing dangerous block fencing and replacing it with hedge after the Miyagi Earthquake that occurred in 1978, and many people were killed or injured by collapsing concrete block walls.

These subsidy systems are considered public supply for private goods based on the existence effects of hedges. For hedge installation, there are other measures like regulation, leading means, and others.

There are studies on the environment protection effect of hedges (e.g. Nitta 1949, Suzuki and Nagata 2014), the psychological effect (e.g. Nakamura and Fujii 1992), hedge history (e.g. Hida 1999), hedge installation promotion (e.g. Mitsuyoshi et al. 1986), and the management of hedges (e.g. Tsuruwa and Nohara 2013). However, studies on the state of the public supply of hedges are insufficient. Particularly, it is necessary to examine supply means from the perspective of disaster prevention.

In this chapter, the current state of the public supply of privately owned hedges as private goods will be discussed from the perspective of disaster prevention.

11.2 The Function of Hedges

A hedge is a fence formed by closely growing bushes, shrubs, or trees.

Manyoshu shows that a hedge of deutzia was made during the Nara era (710–784). In the Heian era (794–1192) and the Kamakura era (1185–1333), hedges that were made from the smaller branches of trees were the mainstream. In the Kamakura era, a hedge using thorny trees emerged for crime prevention. Hedges came into fashion in the Muromachi era (1336–1573) to the first term of the Edo period (Edo era; 1603–1867). Hedge pruning became possible with pruning scissors that could be used by both hands and that appeared during the mid-Edo period (Hida 1999).

11 Measuring the Public Supply of Private Hedges for Disaster Prevention 195

Hedges have various functions such as boundary fencing, prevention against physical and observational invasion, control of wind and fire prevention, a barrier to weather, contribution to biodiversity, landscape, a sense of the seasons, and disaster prevention.

Table 11.1 shows the effects of green space and hedges. Items enclosed by a thick frame in the table provide a disaster prevention function, which is directly related to

Table 11.1 Functions of green space and hedges

Functions of green space			Explanation	Hedge
Existence effects	Environmental preservation	Weather modification	Relief of temperature, humidity, and wind in urban areas	○
		Air purification	Purifying air pollutants and reducing noise	○
		Noise reduction		
		Biodiversity	Habitat for wildlife	○
		Water circulation	Collecting rainfall, ploughing ground-water, and adjusting water by transpiration	○
		City development regulation	Urban regulation and the formation of green belts	–
		Preservation of cultural assets	Preserves historical and cultural resources	○
	Landscape	Beautiful landscape	Creates a rich landscape	○
		Regional landscape	Creates a distinctive local landscape	○
		Seasonal landscape	Reflects the season	○
		Disaster prevention	Prevents fires from spreading and prevents mudslides	○
Use effects	Disaster prevention	Refuge	Offers refuge and escape routes for evacuees	○
		Relief and restoration	Provides a basis for relief and restoration	–
	Recreation	Dynamic recreation	Sports, exercise, play	–
		Static recreation	Relaxation, walking, observation, artistic activity	–
	Production	Food production	Produces food and food ingredients	–
		Materials production	Produces materials for buildings and industries	–
		Plants production	Produces plants and flowers for gardens	–

human life, such as the prevention of the spreading of fire and the securing of an escape route for evacuees.

Brick fences that are constructed in congested housing districts with high-density use are particularly hazardous during earthquakes. These structures collapse on roadsides causing danger to individuals and obstructing emergency vehicles and rescue operations.

11.3   Hedges and Disaster Prevention

In Omiya Bonsai Village, hedge making began after the Great Kanto Earthquake. Bonsai traders in Tokyo hit by the Great Kanto Earthquake in 1923 moved to the current Bonsai-cho, Kita-ku, Saitama City, in 1925, and the village was opened. In 1928, village residents agreed to the following: ① to maintain more than ten Bonsai pots, ② to keep gates open, ③ to only construct single-story buildings, and ④ to only use hedges as fences.

The Takagi-cho residents' association in Kokubunji City is a case where hedge making began for safety and began after the Miyagi Earthquake. To minimize the damage from the disaster, the Takagi-cho residents' association attempted to change the fence weight (brick fence, tuff fence, and concrete fence) to hedge and safety fence weights. After conducting condition surveys and questionnaire surveys on wall improvements, the fence became the focus of activity because, although hedges are individual possessions, they play a variety of roles in the region.

In 1986, a 'Declaration for fence making in Takagi-cho' was announced that included the following: (1) protect our rich green town by hedges, (2) build a fence where you can enjoy conversation with a neighbour, (3) build fences that save pedestrians, (4) make fences that protect children's lives, and (5) make the streets beautiful with fences. In 1995, after the Hanshin-Awaji Great Earthquake, the 'Declaration for town planning in Takagi-cho' was introduced, which promoted the concept of fences among the community and building contractors.

The Hanshin-Awaji Great Earthquake Memorial Research Institute reported that the damage in parks and open spaces was relatively slight, and these areas had played a significant role in rescue operations. Particularly, trees and hedges had prevented many houses from falling and allowed many roads to remain passable.

During the Geiyo Earthquake in 2001, the Fukuoka-ken Western Offing Earthquake in 2005, and the Kumamoto Earthquake in 2016, people were killed or injured by a collapsing concrete block wall. In 1981, an enforcement ordinance of the Building Standards Law set the earthquake standards for concrete block walls. The aim of the standard was the following: almost no damage by a moderately strong earthquake (seismic intensity of five according to a Japanese scale of zero to seven) and no damage to human life from a strong or severe earthquake (seismic intensity of six and seven). However, when the damage caused by a large-scale earthquake occurs, such as that caused by the Kumamoto Earthquake, concrete block walls should be converted to safer hedges.

11.4 The Current State of the Public Supply of Hedges

The means of public supply for public goods are direct supply, direct regulation, induction, and enlightenment. Since a private hedge in private land constitutes a private good, the owner should supply the hedge directly by paying all expenses. But many local governments are formulating support systems and regulation because hedges function as public goods.

Table 11.2 shows public supply measures for hedges. That is, public supply means are categorized. We outline examples of each official supply type and discuss some cases from the perspective of disaster prevention. We examine public documents that are publicized on municipal homepages and in booklets.

Table 11.2 The outline of a public hedge supply plan

Type	System	Outline	Main examples
Direct supply	Public sector planting	Local governments plant hedges	–
	Provision of saplings	Provision of hedge saplings	Akita City
	Provision of seedlings	Provision of ivy seedlings for hedges	Atami City, Himeji City
	Provision of skills and labour	Provision of the required skills and labour for planting	Kikuyo Town (Kumamoto Prefecture)
Regulation	Hedge obligation	Hedge obligations are imposed in a specific area	Omiya Bonsai Village
	Tree planting proposal	Local governments require developers or land owners to report their tree planting proposals and guide them to install hedges	Shinagawa Ward, Nakano Ward
	Residents' agreement	Residents conclude an agreement for the installation and maintenance of hedges	–
	Hedge protection	Local governments designate existing hedges as protected hedges	Kawasaki City
Induction and attraction	Subsidy	Subsidies for the removal of concrete brick walls and hedge plantings	Ichikawa City, Niigata City
		Subsidies for hedge planting	Toyonaka City
		Subsidies for hedge maintenance	Hakodate City
	Tax reduction, tax exemption	When installing and maintaining a hedge, a tax is reduced or exempted	Kawaguchi City

(continued)

Table 11.2 (continued)

Type	System	Outline	Main examples
	Deregulation	When installing a hedge, the building coverage ratio or the floor area ratio is eased	Oosaka Prefecture
	Interest rate discount	When installing a hedge, the interest rate of a housing loan is discounted	Nagareyama City
	Sapling purchase subsidy	When installing a hedge, good quality purchases are inexpensive	Kawaguchi City
	Exemption of pruning processing costs	Branch and leaf disposal costs from pruning are exempted	Nagareyama City
	Eco-point	Eco-points are given for hedge installation	–
Enlightenment	Providing information	Information is provided on the function, installation, and maintenance of hedges	Hedge exhibitions, green consulting office
	Charter statement	Charters or statements persuade people to plant and upkeep hedges	Takagi-cho in Kokubunji City
	Campaigns	Some companies plan hedge promotions	Disinfection spray-free campaign
	Commendation contest	Excellent hedges are commended	Kai City
	Study activities	Provision of study activities such as independent study groups, special hedge courses	–
Others		Hedges are used for sightseeing and regional development	Hirakawa City

11.4.1 Direct Supply

The measures considered as direct supply are direct establishment by the public sector, the material provision of saplings for hedges and ivy plants, and the supply of skills and labour necessary for planting.

Regarding material provision, Akita City had a hedge provision system that provided saplings where hedges formed part of a strong community effort to build structures to protect against disaster from 1984. However, in 2007 this system was abolished, and, instead, a local government corporation in Akita City began to subsidize hedges. There is no clear documentation of disaster prevention by the new system, and the purpose of measures seems to be centred on aesthetic appearances.

Regarding ivy plants, Atami City and Himeji City have a provision system. However, there is no clear documentation of disaster prevention in the provision system.

There seem to be almost no system that offers technology and labour. However, operational support is provided by a volunteer group. A students' group from Tokai University has been supporting hedge management in Kikuyo town in Kumamoto prefecture. The total length of hedge development increased from 1 to 3 km in approximately 30 years, and this development was also supported by Kikuyo town. Residents were informed that a hedge is also effective for community empowerment as well as aesthetics, disaster prevention, and environmental preservation.

11.4.2 Regulation

The measures considered as direct regulation are to place hedges in designated areas, to require the submission of a tree planting proposal, to require a guide to hedge installation, to designate existing hedges as protected hedges, and to obtain a residents' agreement as a self-imposed control or gentleman's agreement on the installation and maintenance of hedges.

Omiya Bonsai Village was designated as a special scenic district in addition to the resident agreement. Some residents decided to create an agreement whereby hedges and fences were recommended, but high concrete brick walls over 1 m were prohibited. Although the hedge creation in Omiya Bonsai Village was stimulated by the Great Kanto Earthquake disaster, the main purpose of the hedges is to maintain the scenic beauty of the residential area rather than to prevent the effects of a disaster.

Regarding tree planting proposals, in Shinagawa Ward, the plan covers over 300 square meters, and the area is obligated to produce a hedge planting proposal. There is no reference to disaster prevention, but the managing jurisdiction is 'Park section, disaster prevention town development department'.

11.4.3 Induction and Attraction

The measures for induction and attraction are the subsidy, tax reduction, tax exemption, easing deregulation of the building coverage ratio or the floor area ratio, a housing loan discount of interest rates, the introduction of nursery trees, and the exemption of processing costs of pruned branches and eco-points.

According to an investigation in July 2012 by the Economic Research Association (https://www.zai-keicho.or.jp/about/english.html), 355 local governments in Japan have public subsidy systems for hedges, and 203 cases of 355 clearly state 'hedge' in the system name. Some cases mention improvements in disaster prevention by a hedge, and some cases have almost no reference to disaster prevention.

Hakodate City is promoting 57 yen per meter each year to maintain hedges designated as hedge preservation in the subsidy system. However, this subsidy is not for disaster prevention but for aesthetics maintenance.

Cases of reduction and the exemption of taxes for hedge installation cannot be found although there is a system that reduces the municipal tax on real estate, which is through the authorization system of the Law for the Preservation of Urban Greenery.

Regarding deregulation of the building coverage ratio or the floor area ratio, a deregulation system called the 'Green wind project area' exists in Osaka prefecture. Although not explicit, there is a reference to disaster prevention in the relaxation terms.

In Nagareyama City, 'Green chain approval' certification obtained by planting trees and setting hedges discounts housing loan interest rates and processes the costs of pruned branches, which is free. This is an environmental protection system to improve the effects of urban weather, but the system's application to disaster prevention is explained in the hedge subsidy.

Kawaguchi City subsidizes the cost of nursery trees by 50% with a view to disaster prevention.

11.4.4 Enlightenment

The measures considered as enlightenment are providing information, charters, statements, campaigns, commendations, and learning activities.

Regarding the provision of information, there are 103 urban arboretum and green consultation offices (Aoki and Morimoto 2012). These offices offer technical information on hedges and showcase hedge exhibition gardens. There are many hedge exhibitions in parks, botanical gardens, and nongovernment parks. In the hedge exhibition garden in a park in Nakano Ward, there is a clear explanation of disaster prevention on an instruction card, and there is also a hedge exhibition garden with no reference to disaster prevention.

Regarding charters and statements, the 'Declaration for fence making in Takagi-cho' and 'Declaration for town planning in Takagi-cho' in Kokubunji City refer to disaster prevention as 'safety'.

Some local governments commend excellent hedge making or plan hedge contests. Some companies plan hedge promotions. These instances are typically from the perspective of aesthetics, and the disaster prevention perspective is not indicated.

There are cases where gardening companies promote discounts on pruning and sterilization costs for damages caused by diseases or pests.

Additionally, Hirakawa City uses 'hedge load' for sightseeing and area activation but has no disaster prevention perspective.

11.5 Conclusion

This chapter examined the current state of public supply to privately owned hedges as private goods. The means of public supply of public goods are direct supply, direct regulation, induction, and enlightenment. The main means of promoting the public supply of hedges is induction, particularly the subsidy system. Enlightenment measures are performed in specific ways. However, direct supply and direct regulation are not typical.

The institutional purpose varies depending on the public document, which contains the explanation of each system. There are some cases for which the main purpose is disaster prevention, such as Takagi-cho and Kokubunji City. The declaration of Takagi-cho residents' association clearly describes preparation for earthquake disaster, and Kokubunji City promotes hedge installation by subsidizing the removal of brick fences and planting hedges with an appealing homepage headline 'Let's plant hedges to prepare for earthquake disasters'. On the other hand, many cases have no reference to disaster prevention. Hedge functions (see Table 11.1) include high exteriority existence effects, and each local government emphasizes the priority functions depending on the perspective, such as environmental effects and the landscape in addition to disaster prevention and regional needs.

However, the view of disaster prevention by hedge-ization should be explained more clearly to the public in the form of an appeal. This should be the case even when other functions are emphasized because of regional needs bearing in mind that the hedge is effective against unforecastable seismic hazards. Considering that hedges have a significant public role, we should enrich more systems and aggressively advance hedge-ization. In congested housing districts and along school routes, particularly where safety improvements are critical, it is necessary to strengthen regulation. At the same time, it is necessary to reduce the burden on residents by combining economic guidance and informational support. Considering the aging of residences and vacant house-ization, abandoned dangerous brick fences and unmanaged hedges may increase. In such cases, we should consider mechanisms to enrich direct supply such as direct establishment and labour.

Acknowledgements This work was supported by KAKENHI (15K00666).

References

Aoki A, Morimoto C (2012) A survey on management of urban greenery arboretum. Park Adm Manag Res 6:37–42

Hida N (1999) Historical transition of Japanese Hedge. J Jpn Inst Landsc Archit 62(5):413–416

Horie N, Hagihara K, Kimura F, Asahi C (2015) A study on the use and the supply of greenery in Saitama City-from the view point of the character as public goods of greenery. Stud Reg Sci 45 (3):333–349

Horie N, Hagihara K, Kimura F, Asahi C (2016) Existence effect and supply of private greenery – from descriptions in public documents of private greenery in Saitama City. Stud Reg Sci 46 (3):295–307

Kenji Mitsuyoshi, Noboru Iwao, Tetsu Hagishima 'A study on promoting hedge creation part 1 summaries of technical papers of the annual meetings, Architectural Institute of Japan, Hokkaido, pp.15–16, 1986

Nakamura R, Fujii E (1992) A comparative study on the characteristics of electroencephalogram inspecting a Hedge and a concrete block fence. J Jpn Inst Landsc Archit 55(5):139–144

Nitta S (1949) On the effect of hedge on dust abatement. J Jpn Inst Landsc Archit 12(2):7–8
Suzuki M, Nagata A (2014) 'Effects on heat and wind environment caused by hedge' Summaries of technical papers of the annual meetings. Archit Inst Jpn(Environmental Engineering) 1:1135–1136
Tsuruwa S, Nohara T (2013) A study on methods of community management of hedge landscape in former Samurai district. J City Plann Inst Jpn 48(3):369–374

Part IV
Evaluation of Regional Vulnerability and Resilience

Chapter 12
Environmental Valuation Considering Dual Aspects of an Urban Waterside Area

Kiyoko Hagihara and Susumu Shimizu

Abstract In this study the authors aim to clarify the role of environmental valuation in public policymaking through a case study of valuing the waterside along a river in an urban area. First, it is indicated that the role of urban waterside has dual aspects: one role is to mitigate damages from various disasters such as earthquakes and fires, and the other role is to provide a comfortable environment for residents along the river. Then, in order to identify residents' demands concerning the waterside in particular from the viewpoint of their daily life, a discrete choice model is set up. The model is then applied to a case study. Not only revealed preference data but also stated preference data are used in the case study. Finally, the limited role of the value of the waterside environment that is obtained from the model is shown.

Keywords Dual role of waterside · Disasters · Amenity space · Environmental valuation · Policymaking

12.1 Introduction

Environmental valuation in various fields has become a necessary process in public policymaking in Japan. Already established is that all public policies must be justified in terms of not only cost but also benefit. In the determination of the benefit of public policy, environmental valuation, among others, is still a difficult task. Therefore, all levels of government, from central to local, are anxious for an easy valuation method for environments. Under this situation, the former Ministry of Construction, for example, has formulated a manual

---

K. Hagihara (✉)
Tokyo Metropolitan University, Tokyo, Japan
e-mail: khagi@tb3.so-net.ne.jp

S. Shimizu
Sewage Works Division, Nihon Suido Consultants Co., Ltd., Tokyo, Japan
e-mail: simizu_su@nissuicon.co.jp

© Springer Nature Singapore Pte Ltd. 2019
C. Asahi (ed.), *Building Resilient Regions*, New Frontiers in Regional Science: Asian Perspectives 35, https://doi.org/10.1007/978-981-13-7619-1_12

outlining the valuation of environments. This manual is similar to the chapter on 'Appraisal and evaluation in central government' in the Treasury 'Green Book' of the United Kingdom (Hanley 2001).

A theory and method for environmental valuation have been developed, and there has already been a tremendous amount of research on environmental valuation (e.g. Hagihara and Hagihara 1990; Freeman 1993; Hanley and Barbier 2009). Recently, several studies on a number of environmental resources, such as rivers and bogs, and environmental problems, including air and water pollution, have been conducted in Japan. However, we are concerned with situations in which only values obtained under different conditions can be easily used in the manual.

In this study, the role of environmental valuation in public policymaking will be shown through a case study that values the waterside along a river in an urban area in Japan. In the process of improving urban waterside during the 1990s, the Great Hanshin-Awaji Earthquake that occurred in 1995 around the Kobe areas emphasised that waterside is amenity space used on a daily basis and also provides secure place during disasters such as earthquakes and fires. The waterside prevents the spread of fire and provides water for washing clothes and dishes. The role of urban waterside has the characteristic of duality (Hagihara et al. 1998a, b; Hagihara and Hagihara 2010). Section 12.2 shows that waterside has dual roles. One role is preventing and mitigating damages from disasters, and the other role is providing a comfortable environment for residents along a river. Therefore, the waterside is typically a place for playing and walking but provides a secure place and water utilization in the event of a disaster. We will consider the environmental valuation of waterside taking into account the dual role of waterside; residents usually enjoy the waterside area, but they will be able to use some roles of the river.

Then, in Sect. 12.3, the philosophy under which the Japanese government has established policies is shown through a brief history of previous river policies in Japan. One objective of planning a public policy for watersides is, first of all, to develop a waterside that will be appreciated by the residents in the area. Thus, in Sect. 12.4, the desired components of the waterside are shown with the aid of a discrete choice model based on a random utility theory. Then, in Sect. 12.5, the model is applied to a case study on an urban waterside area. In the process, in order to determine the components of the waterside actually desired by residents, not only revealed preference data but also the stated preference data are used in the case study. Moreover, how the residents value this waterside area is examined. Finally, the limited role of environmental valuation is shown through the example of the case study.

12.2 Dual Aspects of Urban Waterside

Japan has experienced earthquake disasters in the past 20 years. These disastrous experiences emphasized that the security of urban area relies on their resilience to disasters. Although a river brings disasters in the form of flooding and tsunamis, a river also provides transportation, prevents fires, and provides water in the event of a disaster. The river is a source of enjoyment by users every day and has a role in fighting disasters. Consequently, the state of resilience of an urban area depends on how the waterside is improved for use in daily life and in the event of a disaster. The urban waterside provides open space in an urban area and is a component of the water and greenspace network. Moreover, the waterside's role is as an amenity for space and the prevention and mitigation of disasters. Thus, the waterside offers a dual relationship of comfort and safety.

We describe the role and functions of the waterside as follows (Hagihara et al. 1998a, b):

1. Disaster prevention and mitigation functions:
   Providing evacuation space and water utilization
2. Recreation functions:
   Providing a place for recreation, sports, and event staging
3. Aesthetic functions:
   Colour, smell, sounds, and motion
4. Ecology functions
   Cultivation of flora and fauna
5. Cultural functions:
   Providing materials for education, research, and creativity

Consequently, desirable design of urban waterside should include the above diverse roles of the waterside. One example of urban waterside improvement is the following. Since 1963, just in a period of high economic growth in Japan, a shape of one small river named Horikawa which flows almost through the centre of Kyoto city, near Kyoto Imperial Palace, is so-called a river covered bank with concrete, and few water flows usually. However, the river fills up in a short period when it rains. Residents enjoy walking near the river but consider it dangerous when it rains much. Therefore, Kyoto city government planned to improve the river in 2002 considering the dual role of the waterside. People in Kyoto city could participate in the planning process. Now people have greater enjoyment when walking along the river, and even some events along the river are planned every summer. Not only residents but also some other people who do not live near are now able to enjoy walking along the river. Tremendous amounts of water when it rains are flowing in sewerage under the river. This type of improvement will become more necessary considering global climate change.

As mentioned above, the design of waterside includes both aspects of providing amenities and preventing and mitigating damages from disasters. However, it is desirable that people usually enjoy the waterside and the area be useful only when disasters occur. Consequently, we consider a desirable design of waterside to allow daily enjoyment in the remainder of this study.

12.3 Brief History of the Policies Concerning Rivers in Japan

The first River Law was established in 1896 during the Meiji era. The purpose of the Law was mainly flood control and the establishment of water rights. Until the end of the Second World War and the time of the high economic growth, this purpose was maintained. However, the disaster that occurred from the Ise Bay typhoon has cause the government to establish the new River Law in 1964. The purpose of the new River Law was not only strengthening flood control but also increasing the use of water, because many industries required additional industrial water to increase their production and also water use had increased in highly populated urban areas.

In order to control flooding and provide sufficient water to both industry and urban areas, the Nagara River Estuary Weir Development (NREWC) Project was initiated. This project attracted substantial national media attention and led to further opposition movements supported by various actors, including stakeholders and negotiators. Among others, the conservation group of the Nagara River's environment has been much attention from the media. Locals become involved in one of the opposition movements. Nevertheless, the NREWC Project began in 1988 and was completed in 1995, when Japan had a relatively strong economy.

The Nagara project became a turning point. The Japanese government made a full revision to the River Law in 1997, the purpose of which was the 'improvement and preservation of the river environment in addition to the traditional purposes such as flood control and an increase in the use of water. Further improvements to the river should reflect locals' opinions'. Opposition movements changed because of more detailed criteria required for planning and designing projects.

On the other hand, Japanese people desired more comfortable surroundings since economic growth has brought a level of affluence and the problems associated with recreational waterside use for recreation attracted significant attention in the 1990s. Behind this lies the consideration that too much emphasis had been placed on the economic efficiency of water resource usage, a metalogic of the period of high economic growth. The aim of spatial planning during that period was to maximize the distance between water and people. In that period, the waterside was viewed as a dangerous place for residents or as not useful and/or wasteful if not used for economic activities. Numerous small rivers and ponds were converted into roads or parking lots during that time. However, in these eras many people have been reconsidering these strategies and advocating a new metalogic in the spatial planning of watersides, in which the distance between water and people is minimized, not maximized. Corresponding to this new metalogic in the waterside, it could be stated the current River Law was established.

Here we will take a brief look at the history of the rivers that have been opened to the public (Hagihara et al. 1995). In 1964 when Japan hosted the Olympic Games for the first time, the public was permitted to use flood plains or high water channels for sports activities. Since then, only a few flood plains or high water channels have remained in use for sports and recreational purposes. From 1975 to 1980, a spatial planning program was laid out for the Tama River, and the report of the River Council of the Ministry of Construction in 1981, entitled 'River environmental management policy', emphasized the need for the preservation of the water quality of rivers and for open-space planning. As a lot of rivers had been contaminated through industrialization and urbanization and as the construction of infrastructure for river conservation had been delayed, especially in urban areas, during the 1960s and 1970s, the government finally recognized the importance of the environmental aspects of rivers.

In 1985, the Ministry of the Environment selected the '100 best bodies of water' (Environment Agency 1985). This was an attempt to rediscover the high value of good-quality water resources, especially spring and surface water, and to stimulate public pride in, enthusiasm for, and interest in the conservation of the water environment in their respective areas. We can regard the mid-1980s as a period in which development proponents and environmentalists began to accommodate each other. The past sharp rivalry between these two groups was gradually replaced by attempts to strike a balance between them. In other words, the age of government-led water environment conservation ended and that of local and municipal government-led water environment creation began.

The River Council's report in 1991, 'Policy for Future River Improvements', took up the subject of 'attractive and beautiful water environments'. The keywords in the report included 'charm' and 'peace of mind', 'diversity of fauna', 'ecologically friendly', 'plentiful water', 'good water quality', and 'beauty'. The report also recommends the following measures to realize what these keywords mean: the creation or protection of good-quality watersides, the preservation or improvement of the environment of major watersides, the improvement of the biodiversity of rivers, the improvement of the water environment, and river beautification. It then proposed the development of watersides to make the most of regional characteristics and river culture, to achieve an orderly use of rivers in response to a diversity of values, to realize proper water circulation systems, and to take action to conserve the global environment.

According to the 'White paper on water resources', published annually by the former National Land Agency (NLA), the Japanese government—mainly the former Ministry of Construction—carries out many projects involving the environment and water resources. These projects were mostly started around 1985. They may be roughly classified into the following seven categories: (1) construction of brooks and tree planting, (2) consideration of water quality and quantity, (3) ecosystem conservation, (4) recreation, (5) waterside improvement projects undertaken as part of urban planning, (6) public participation, and (7) modification of river configurations.

However, there is no clear relationship between these projects nor any concept that governs them all. If the administration is to pursue only the needs of the public, this situation is probably unavoidable. However, if we view things from the taxpayers' viewpoint, it is only natural that we would want to find a clear and consistent philosophy or idea as a basis for these projects. It seems that we must describe these projects as consecutive but as being unrelated to each other, with no consistent underlying ideology.

This lack of any consistent philosophy may be the result of the efficiency-only strategy adopted in the planning process. The projects related to watersides had no established technical standards for hardware in most cases, though there was a clear recognition of the need for such standards. Because of this, these projects were undertaken only in an experimental and partial manner. For example, tree planting projects for riverbanks were carried out as follows. Following the River Council's recommendations in 1981, a draft tree planting standard was adopted in 1983 (Ministry of Land, Infrastructure and Transport 1983). After 6 years of experimental implementation, the draft was reviewed in 1990 (Ministry of Land, Infrastructure and Transport 1990). The government was customarily not very supportive of tree planting on riverbanks because it feared that this would hinder flood control measures. However, it gradually began to provide technical support and to plant trees in limited areas of the country. Here again, we can see the intention, on the part of the government, to encourage the public to use rivers for recreational activities, which represents a shift from the traditional policy of keeping them away from rivers—an environment originally close to citizens' lives—to pursue the aim of flood control.

In short, the government policies on waterside projects have changed from the traditional efficiency first principle that focused on maximizing the distance between people and water to a new philosophy of minimizing that distance.

12.4 Model Setup

As we have already mentioned above, the waterside has dual roles, that is, one role for amenity space and another role for preventing and mitigating damages from disasters. However, it is desirable that people enjoy watersides without fear of disasters in their daily lives. Therefore, we focus on the amenity aspects of the waterside.

In order to improve watersides in urban areas for recreational purposes under the new philosophy of minimizing the distance between water and people, we must take into account some of the following issues. In particular, many people live around and near the waterside in urban areas in situations different from those of watersides in natural areas. Therefore, the waterside must be planned based on the desires of the residents who live there. These desires must be taken into account in the form of participation, of which there are two types: participation through a survey process and participation in the decision-making process. The survey type of participation will be considered in this paper.

Although several methods, such as a hedonic approach and a contingent valuation method, can be used for the valuation of a waterside area, a discrete choice model based on the random utility theory is applied to the case study in this paper. The hedonic approach and the contingent valuation method are regarded as inappropriate for valuing the waterside environment, for the following reasons. In the hedonic approach, the valuation by nonresidents cannot be represented; in addition, the value of land or of a house depends mostly on the distance from the central business district (CBD). With regard to the contingent valuation method, the environmental value as obtained by this method is not yet seen as reliable by many researchers in Japan, though some studies based on the contingent valuation method have been attempted for the valuation of several environmental qualities (see papers in the journal of the *Japan Society of Civil Engineers, Environmental Systems Research,* and *Environmental Science*).

Moreover, discrete choice theory based on random utility theory is applicable to determine how changes in attributes and in the quality of a recreational site affect consumers' choice behaviour. Furthermore, as discrete choice theory is based on actual behaviour, or revealed preference, the result is considered to be valid and reliable. We will go into more detail later in this paper, but, in short, the revealed preference data used in our study concern whether or not the respondents visit the river at present and on the stated preference data concern whether or not the respondents would visit the river were certain attributes of the river to be improved to a level satisfactory to the respondents. Consequently, even in the case of using stated preference data in discrete choice theory, the data will reflect the activities of residents, not their willingness to pay, as it is considered that people will more readily reveal their activities than any monetary values, especially in Japan, where people are not accustomed to stating monetary values, even of market goods.

The utility function is separated into an observable part and into a non-observable part that is described as a random variable:

$$U_{ij} = V_{ij} + \varepsilon_{ij}. \tag{12.1}$$

Here, U_{ij} is the utility for an individual i when that individual chooses behaviour j; V_{ij} is a definite term; and ε_{ij} is a stochastic term. When $U_{ij} \geq U_{ik}$, behaviour j, rather than behaviour k, is chosen by individual i.

The probability that individual i will choose behaviour j, π_{ij} is given by

$$\pi_{ij} = \Pr\left[\left(V_{ij} + \varepsilon_{ij}\right) \geq (V_{ik} + \varepsilon_{ik}); j \neq k, j, k \in A_i\right], \tag{12.2}$$

where A_i is the choice set of individual i.

V_{ij} is assumed to be an indirect utility function as follows:

$$V_{ij} = V_{ij}\left(q, p_{ij}, y_i, m_i\right), \tag{12.3}$$

where q represents attributes of the waterside, p_{ij} is the cost when individual i chooses behaviour j, y_i is the income of individual i, and m_i represents other characteristics of individual i (see Hagihara et al. 1998a, b). In this paper, q is a vector of objective measures of attributes and of the respondent's subjective perceptions of attributes. A respondent's subjective perceptions of attributes include consideration of the quality and quantity of water as well as abundance of plants and the possibility of walking comfortably along the waterside and so on. Objective measures of attributes include distance to the waterside from place of residence and time required to reach the waterside. The m_i attributes include components such as whether the individual has children, keeps pets such as a dog, has plenty of leisure time, and so on.

In the above indirect utility function, attributes of the waterside are described by perception data. Choices are usually made on the basis of perceptions, and not on the observed quality of the attributes, regarding the waterside. In other words, people's decisions are based not on the observed water quality described in units of pollution in parts per million (ppm), but on whether the water quality is good for swimming, for example. Recently a paper was published that introduced perceptions data (Adamowicz et al. 1997). If these perception data can be used and the relationship between perception data and observed data can be clarified, a more desirable design for planning for people can be realized.

Assuming that the stochastic term ε_{ij} has a Gumbel distribution, our model is described through the following logit model:

$$\pi_{ij} = \frac{\exp V_{ij}}{\exp V_{i1} + \exp V_{i2}} \qquad (12.4)$$

where behaviour $(j)1$ indicates the individual goes to the waterside and behaviour 2 indicates the individual does not go to the waterside.

12.5 Application of the Model

A survey questionnaire was conducted with residents living near a small river located in Kawasaki city, near Tokyo. During the period of high economic growth, in the 1960s, the population surrounding the river increased rapidly, and the river became polluted. Recently, some projects, mentioned in Sect. 12.3, to improve the water quality of the river were carried out, supported by grants from the former Ministry of Construction.

We conducted a mailed survey, sending questionnaires to 900 residents living near the river. The questionnaire covered observed data (such as distance from the river), perception data, and individual attributes. For perception data, respondents were asked to rank 26 attributes (including water quality, quantity of grass, number of trees, quantity of waste in or around the river, feeling of familiarity with the waterside, and so on) as 1 (very bad), 2 (bad), 3 (neutral), and 4 (good) or 5 (very good) (see Table 12.1). The response rate was 44%, and 90% of respondents lived within 500 m of the river. The survey instrument, in Japanese, is available from us.

12 Environmental Valuation Considering Dual Aspects of an Urban Waterside Area

Table 12.1 Waterside environment: observed and index variables covered in the survey questionnaire

Observed variable		Index variable	
No.	Attribute	No.	Attribute
1	Water quality	19	Quality of landscape
2	Presence of odour	20	Ease of walking along the waterside
3	Quantity of waste	21	Quietness
4	Quantity of water	22	Ease of approach to the water
5	Number of trees	23	Existence of danger
6	Quantity of flowers	24	Ease of access to the waterside
7	Quantity of grass	25	Ease of finding the way to the waterside
8	Quantity of fish	26	Feeling of familiarity of the waterside
9	Quantity of insects		
10	Quantity of birds		
11	Number of people		
12	Existence of pavement		
13	Slope of bank		
14	Existence of play area		
15	Existence of park		
16	Existence of bench or something on which to rest		
17	Existence of toilets		
18	Existence of parking area		

Note: each item in the questionnaire was graded according to five rank; for example, for water quality, 1 corresponds to 'very bad', 2 corresponds to 'bad', 3 corresponds to 'neutral', 4 corresponds to 'good', and 5 corresponds to 'very good

12.5.1 Use of Grouped Data

A model was estimated by using the maximum likelihood method. The model is not significant when all data from all samples are included. The reason why is considered to be as follows. Our method depends on people's revealed preference. The term 'revealed preference' in economic theory is based on people's rational behaviour. In other words, there is no contradiction between people's preference and their behaviour. But, the results of our survey questionnaire show that there are people who like the waterside but who do not go there; in addition, there are people who do not like the waterside but who do go there. The relationship between the preferences and behaviour of these people does not coincide with economic theory. Therefore, all samples were divided into four groups: group 1 for people who like the waterside and who go there; group 2 consists of people who like the waterside but who do not go there; group 3 consists of people who dislike the waterside but who do not go

Table 12.2 Waterside environment: peoples' preference as described by revealed preference and perception data

Attribute	Parameter	t-value
Water quality	1.101	3.87
Quantity of trees	0.653	2.71
Existence of bench or something on which to rest	0.508	2.09
Distance to the waterside from one's residence	−0.002	−1.36
Plenty of leisure time	1.361	2.77
An interest in the river	1.868	5.07
Goodness of fit ρ^2	0.60	

Source: Authors' survey

Note: these results were obtained from respondents in groups 1 and 3 (those liking the waterside and going there and those not liking the waterside and not going there, respectively)

there; and group 4 consists of people who dislike the waterside but who go there. When samples of groups 1 and 3 are used to estimate the model, the result is highly significant. This result is shown in Table 12.2.

12.5.2 Incorporation of Latent Variables

When it comes to making a decision on whether to enjoy the waterside, people perceive an impression, such as of atmosphere, safety, and comfort, of the waterside rather than of individual components of the waterside, such as water quality and number of trees. Therefore, we assume that some latent variables exist behind some subjective perception data. We will thus attempt to express latent variables by using subjective perception data. If the relationship between perception data and latent variables can be elucidated, we can obtain more of the components of the attributes of the waterside that are used by people in deciding whether or not they will go to the waterside. As a result, we can gain a clearer image of how to improve watersides.

The multiple indicator multiple cause (MIMIC) model can be applied to express causal relationships between observed subjective perception data and latent variables. The structure of the model is constructed by using observed subjective perception data as a cause and latent variables (i.e., ambiguous impression) as a result of valuing the waterside as a whole (for the structural equations, see Bollen 1989; Duncan 1975).

The structural equation and measurement equations for the MIMIC model may be described as follows (Morikawa and Sasaki 1993):

structural equation

$$\eta = \beta x + \zeta \tag{12.5}$$

12 Environmental Valuation Considering Dual Aspects of an Urban Waterside Area

measurement equation

$$y = \lambda \eta + e \tag{12.6}$$

Here, η represents the latent variable, x represents the observed subjective perception data, y is the observed index vector, β and λ are unknown parameter vectors, and ζ and e are error terms.

The structural equation expresses the causal relationship between latent variables and the observed subjective perception data. It also shows the structure of perception of the waterside environment. The measurement equation shows the relationship between the latent variables and the observed index variables. Observed index variables reflect people's feelings about the waterside.

Unknown parameters are estimated in order to correlate theoretical covariance matrices obtained from Eqs. (12.5) and (12.6) to sample covariance matrices obtained from the questionnaire.

From the questionnaire, 18 observed variables and 8 index variables (see Table 12.1) are used as the components that describe the waterside; from these the latent variables are derived. Grouped data are also used to derive these variables. We used a software package, AMOS (SPSS Japan Inc., Tokyo), for our analysis.

The results of estimating the structural equations and measurement equations are shown in Table 12.3. In Table 12.3, only the results that satisfy certain indices are given (i.e. that meet the requirements for the fitness of the model as a whole; i.e., where the goodness of fit is greater than 0.9, the root mean square error of approximation is less than 0.05, and the t-values of each parameter is greater than 1.96). In addition to the above test, the model must satisfy the condition that the p value must be greater than 0.5. If this condition is met, the given model of structural and measurement equations is valid. Finally, two latent variables are obtained. One expresses a 'good atmosphere at the waterside', η_1, and the other expresses a 'feeling of affinity with the waterside', η_2.

From Table 12.3, we can see that η_1 is obtained from indices such as 'good landscape' and 'quiet' and that η_2 is obtained from indices such as 'easy access to the waterside' and 'feeling of familiarity of the waterside'.

The latent variable, η_1, expressing a 'good atmosphere at the waterside', includes 'good quality of water', 'little waste', 'plenty of flowers', and 'existence of pavement', and the latent variable, η_2, expressing a 'feeling of affinity with the waterside', includes 'plenty of trees', 'plenty of birds', and 'gentle slope at bank'.

Thus, Eq. (12.1) is estimated by using these latent variables. The result of the estimation is shown in Table 12.4. In Table 12.4, t-values for each latent variable are greater than 1.96, with 95% reliability, making them statistically significant.

Consequently, we can obtain other components that express the waterside environment through the latent variables and thus can obtain more information that can be used for the improvement of the waterside.

216 K. Hagihara and S. Shimizu

Table 12.3 Waterside environment: relationship between observed subjective perception data and index data and latent variables η_1 (good atmosphere at the waterside) and η_2 (feeling of affinity with the waterside)

	η_1		η_2	
Observed variable	Parameter	t-values	Parameter	t-values
Structural equation				
X_1: good quality of water	0.192	2.32	0	–
X_2: little waste	0.076	1.08	0	–
X_3: plenty of trees	0	–	0.179	2.83
X_4: plenty of flowers	0.288	3.84	0	–
X_5: plenty of birds	0	–	0.114	1.94
X_6: existence of pavement	0.345	4.42	0	–
X_7: gentle slope at bank	0	–	0.228	3.47
X_8: existence of play area	0	–	0	–
X_9: existence of parking area	0	–	0	–
Measurement equation				
Y_1: Good landscape	1.000	–	0	–
Y_2: Easy to walk along the waterside	0	–	0	–
Y_3: Quiet	0.402	4.26	0	–
Y_4: Do not feel danger	0	–	0	–
Y_5: Easy access to the waterside	0	–	1.000	–
Y_6: Easy to find the way to the waterside	0	–	0	–
Y_7: Feeling of familiarity of the waterside	0	–	1.294	5.90
Goodness of fit of the model				
χ^2-statistic	1.75		1.22	
p value	0.63		0.54	
Goodness of fit, ρ^2	1.00		1.00	
Root mean square error of approximation	0.00		0.00	
Not applicable				

Source: Authors' survey

Table 12.4 Waterside environment: peoples' preference, as described by latent variables

Attribute	Parameter	t-value
η_1: good atmosphere at the waterside	1.84	3.67
η_2: feeling of affinity with the waterside	1.61	2.25
Distance to the waterside from place of residence	−0.0003	−0.26
Respondent has plenty of leisure time	0.86	1.86
Respondent has an interest in the river	2.35	5.26
Goodness of fit ρ^2	0.57	

Source: Authors' survey

12.5.3 Combining Revealed and Stated Preference Data

Revealed preference data are useful for obtaining information on what attributes are inducing residents to use the waterside at present. However, the use of only the revealed preference data will not be sufficient for obtaining other information that will be useful for the construction or improvement of waterside areas in the near future. The stated preference data are obtained by asking respondents whether or not they would go to the river in a hypothetical situation where, for example, their requirements were realized to a satisfactory level. The stated preference data would be able to supply more useful data for planning a waterside area.

In the questionnaire, we asked the residents which attributes they want to be added to the waterside environment. Each respondent was allowed to list five attributes. Then we asked the respondents whether or not they would go to the waterside if each attribute were improved to a satisfactory level. Based on the survey results, the most desirable attribute is 'improved water quality of the river', with almost 60% of the people who now do not go to the waterside saying they would do so if the water quality were improved.

In the model based on revealed preference data, three components—water quality, number of trees, and presence of benches or something on which to rest—are included. Besides improved water quality, the survey results indicated that reduced waste, easily accessible toilets, and benches or something on which to rest are components considered by people to improve the waterside. Nevertheless, not all components that people desire always appeared in the revealed preference model. In the case of planning to improve the waterside, it is necessary to include components other than those appearing in the revealed preference model, particularly in the case of evaluating the effects of newly added components at the waterside.

Consequently, it is useful to use stated preference data where respondents are asked to describe their own predicted (not real) behaviour in a situation which some improvement is hypothetically carried out. Such data, however, have a low reliability. A useful method that treats both revealed and stated preference data simultaneously and has the advantages of each type of data has been proposed (Adamowicz et al. 1997; Mizokami and Kakimoto 1999; Morikawa and Moshe 1992; Morikawa and Sasaki 1993).

The results of our estimation with use of the combined revealed and stated preference model are shown in Table 12.5. By using the combined model, we can introduce other attributes such as the provision of toilets as information to be led to improvements in the waterside area.

218 K. Hagihara and S. Shimizu

Table 12.5 Waterside environment: peoples' preference as described by combined revealed and stated preference data

Attribute	Description	Parameter	t-value
Good quality of water	Five ranks	0.2172	4.48
Existence of a bench or something on which to rest	Five ranks	0.3083	3.48
Existence of a toilet	Five ranks	0.0927	1.51
Distance to the waterside from place of residence	Meters	−0.0010	−3.97
Respondent has an interest in the river	Yes = 1; No = 0	0.7365	7.26
Respondent desires an improved water quality	Yes = 2; No = 1	0.9384	7.74
Respondent desires a bench or something on which to rest	Yes = 2; No = 1	0.8253	5.58
Respondent desires to have toilets available	Yes = 2; No = 1	0.1770	2.48
Number of samples	1235		
Goodness of fit, ρ^2	0.20		

Source: Authors s of fi

12.5.4 Benefit Measure of the Model

In this section, the benefit of a change in the quality of attributes of the waterside is considered. An individual's indirect utility function satisfies the following equation:

$$V_j\left(q_j^1, p_j, y - CV, m\right) + \varepsilon_j = V_j\left(q_j^0, p_j, y, m\right) + \varepsilon_j, \qquad (12.7)$$

where CV is a compensating variation, q_j^0 is the initial quality of the waterside, and q_j^1 is the subsequent quality of the waterside, index i, which indicates 'individual' is omitted.

The indirect utility function is specified by

$$V_j = \alpha_j + \beta(y - p_j) + \gamma q_j + \zeta m. \qquad (12.8)$$

If the indirect utility function is linear, the marginal utility of income is constant.

Consequently, the value of the waterside environment is measured as the difference in utility before and after the planning of the waterside, as follows:

$$CV = -\frac{1}{\beta}\left\{\ln\left(\sum_{j=1}^{2}\exp\left[V_j(q^1, p_j, y, m)\right]\right) - \ln\left(\sum_{j=1}^{2}\exp\left[V_j(q^0, p_j, y, m)\right]\right)\right\}.$$

$$(12.9)$$

12 Environmental Valuation Considering Dual Aspects of an Urban Waterside Area 219

It is generally said that one of the problems of the travel cost approach is the conversion of travel time value into monetary terms. Much research has been presented on the solution to this problem. For example, one of the approaches involves use of a wage rate, and another involves use of a distribution of time values with wage rate.

However, in our case study, the wage rate itself cannot be used to convert time value into monetary terms. As the waterside in our study is used by residents ranging from children to the elderly, most of whom do not work at all, the wage rate itself is unsuitable for use in the calculation. Instead, time value must be converted according to the respondents' sense of value. However, these values are not yet clear. The problem of determining a monetary value for time for all generations is the theme of our next study.

As we have already mentioned, in Sect. 12.1, the aim of public policies is, in the case studied here, to provide an improvement to waterside that residents indeed desire. Environmental values of waterside areas should be used only to compare one plan with another. One idea for the effective use of environmental values is to compare values with each other only where they are calculated for each alternative plan with use of the same time value. That is, environmental values should be estimated for several alternative plans and be used only to evaluate which plan is 'the best'. For example, in our case study, with the combined revealed and stated preference data, we identified three alternative plans—improving water quality, providing a bench or something on which to rest, and providing a toilet. The benefits of each of these plans can be evaluated as follows. The benefit of improving the water quality is \3461 (approximately €28.42 at €1.00 = \121.78); that of providing a bench or something on which to rest is \5276 (approximately €43.32); and that of providing a toilet is \1830 (approximately €15.03). Consequently, it is judged that provision of a bench or something on which to rest at the waterside will yield the greatest benefit among these three plans.

12.6 Concluding Remarks

The role of environmental valuation in public policymaking has been considered in this study. Recently, all levels of government have been required to consider the effectiveness of their expenditure given the constraint that the revenue of the Japanese government is not expected to increase. Therefore, central government in particular is undertaking to measure environmental values for all kinds of public investment. To evaluate the environment, several easy procedures are currently available.

First, the dual aspect of the waterside in urban area is considered. Based on river policy history in Japan, the waterside of rivers has been constructed or improved without regard to residents' preferences. Recently, not only central government but also local governments have been obliged to pay attention to residents' preferences when formulating public policy, particularly in the construction or improvement of amenities.

Currently, no method of environmental valuation is absolutely reliable. Consequently, the value obtained from any type of valuation method must be used only to evaluate alternative plans that reflect residents' preferences.

In this study, we presented a model that provides a means for obtaining not only an environmental valuation but also information useful for planning a waterside. Three variants of the discrete choice model were used to obtain information for a plan aimed at improving the waterside in a manner actually desired by residents. Although the benefits of the three model variants can be calculated easily, the obtained values should be used only to evaluate the alternative plans in comparison with each other. The absolute values for some plans may have no meaningful significance at all. Thus, the role of environmental valuation should be limited in public policymaking, although the models themselves, as shown in this paper, yield useful information for construction or improvement of the waterside.

Acknowledgements Part of this study has originally published in Environment and Planning C: Government and Policy 2004, volume 22, pages 3–13, Pion Limited, London; www.pion.co.uk and www.envplan.com (Hagihara and Hagihara 2004). We would like to thank the publishers for their permission to use the material here.

References

Adamowicz W, Swait J, Boxall J, Williams M (1997) Perceptions versus objective measures of environmental quality in combined revealed and stated preference models of environmental valuation. J Environ Econ Manag 32:65–84

Bollen KA (1989) Structural equations with latent variables. Wiley, New York

Duncan OD (1975) Introduction to structural equation models. Academic Press, New York

Environment Agency (1985) 100 best bodies of water. Ministry of the Environment, 1-2-2 Kasumigaseki, Chiyoda-ku, Tokyo 100-8975 (in Japanese)

Freeman AM (1993) The measurement of environmental and resource values: theory and methods. Resources for the Future, Baltimore

Hagihara K, Hagihara Y (1990) Measuring the benefits of water quality improvement in municipal water use: the case of Lake Biwa. Environ Plann C Gov Policy 8:195–201

Hagihara K, Hagihara Y (2004) The environmental valuation in public policymaking: the use of urban waterside area in Japan. Environ Plann C Gov Policy 22:3–13

Hagihara Y, Hagihara K e (2010) Planning for water and green. Kyoto University Press, Kyoto. (in Japanese)

Hagihara Y, Hagihara K, Takahashi K (1998a) Urban environment and planning for waterside: with the aid of systems analysis. Keiso Shobo, Tokyo. (in Japanese)

Hagihara K, Hagihara Y, Zhang SP, Shimizu S (1998b) Environmental valuation on waterside in urban area. J Appl Reg Sci 3:133–141. (in Japanese)

Hagihara Y, Takahashi K, Hagihara K (1995) A methodology of spatial planning for waterside area. Stud Reg Sci 12(2):19–45

Hanley N (2001) Cost-benefit analysis and environmental policymaking. Environ Plann C Gov Policy 19:103–118

12 Environmental Valuation Considering Dual Aspects of an Urban Waterside Area

Hanley N, Barbier EB (2009) Pricing nature: cost-benefit analysis and environmental policy. Edward Elgar, Cheltenham

Ministry of Land, Infrastructure and Transport (Ed.) (1983) Kasen-kaishuu-jigyou-kannkei-reikishuu. Nihon-kasen-kyoukai, 2-6-5 Kojimachi, Chiyoda-ku, Tokyo 102-0083 (in Japanese)

Ministry of Land, Infrastructure and Transport (Ed.) (1990) Kasen-kaishuu-jigyou-kannkei-reikishuu. Nihon-kasen-kyoukai, 2-6-5 Kojimachi, Chiyoda-ku, Tokyo 102-0083 (in Japanese)

Mizokami S, Kakimoto R (1999) A new estimation method of discrete choice models with serially correlated plural data. J Japan Soc Civil Eng 618(IV):53–60. (in Japanese)

Morikawa T, Moshe B-A (1992) Method of estimating a disaggregate behavioural model with combined RP data and SP data. Trans Eng 27(4):21–30. (in Japanese)

Morikawa T, Sasaki K (1993) Discrete choice models with latent explanatory variables using subjective data. J Japan Soc Civil Eng 470(IV):115–124. (in Japanese)

River Council (1981) River environment management policy. Ministry of Construction, Japan (in Japanese)

River Council (1991) Policy for future river improvements. Ministry of Construction, Japan (in Japanese)

Chapter 13
Economic Evaluation of Risk Premium of Social Overhead Capital in Consideration of the Decision-Making Process Under Risk

Chisato Asahi and Kiyoko Hagihara

Abstract Japan has experienced a number of large-scale natural disasters, and social demand for effective infrastructure to manage risks related to these disasters is increasing under the constraint of public financial drought. In practice, benefits under risk only account for the expected value of the physical and human damages, and therefore, the integration of the idea of 'risk premium' and 'vulnerability' into cost-benefit analysis needs to be addressed.

This chapter utilizes data from a questionnaire concerning municipal water cut-off risk as a case study to investigate the decision-making process for the valuation of risk premium. We focus on two decision-making frameworks: decision-making under risk and the prospect theory. We examine whether risk prevention behaviour or risk-cost trade-off choices concerning water cut-off risk are affected by the risk aversion index, risk perception, and the reference point effect or not by using a logit regression and an interval regression analysis.

The main conclusion is as follows: risk preference in terms of monetary scale does not affect the choice of a household in the case of water cut-off risk, whereas risk perception does. The reference point effect in the combination of loss aversion and probability evaluation is observed in the household's choice experiment.

Keywords Risk premium · Vulnerability · Infrastructure · Cost-benefit analysis · Prospect theory · Reference point effect

---

C. Asahi (✉)
Department of Urban Science and Policy, Faculty of Urban Environmental Sciences, Tokyo Metropolitan University, Hachioji, Tokyo, Japan
e-mail: asahi@tmu.ac.jp

K. Hagihara
Tokyo Metropolitan University, Kyoto, Japan
e-mail: khagi@tb3.so-net.ne.jp

© Springer Nature Singapore Pte Ltd. 2019
C. Asahi (ed.), *Building Resilient Regions*, New Frontiers in Regional Science: Asian Perspectives 35, https://doi.org/10.1007/978-981-13-7619-1_13

13.1 Introduction

Since Japan has been suffering many natural disasters, the demand for construction, maintenance, and the renewal of social overhead capital to reduce disaster risks is of great importance. On the other hand, the social security budget has been decreasing, and the government debt burden has been increasing due to population decline and rapid population ageing. Therefore, the investment capacity available for social overhead capital has decreased.

One of the difficulties concerning social overhead capital is 'a more accurate appraisal and maintenance for social overhead capital', and the importance of an appraisal of both quality and efficiency—especially concerning coping with risk—has been crucial issues during this decade (Cabinet Office policy unification official 2012).

Generally, the benefit of a project under uncertainty is evaluated by the amount of expected damage, where the money-based evaluation of 'risk premium'—that is, 'the mitigation effect of the uneasiness on uncertainty'—is not counted (Ministry of Land, Infrastructure, Transport and Tourism 2009). The appropriate evaluation method for risk premium in social overhead capital should be dependent on whether the risk is distributable or collective (Kobayashi and Yokomatsu 2002). We can ignore risk premium in the evaluation of a public project with a risk, since the risk is distributed among many households (Arrow and Lind 1970). However, a risk cannot be distributed when the risk is collective (i.e. a large-scale disaster), because correlation occurs among households' damage. Therefore, the amount of the risk premium should be added to the amount of expected damage.

According to the benefit evaluation theory under uncertainty in welfare economics—given that a risk is collective and the cost of the project is fixed—the appropriate welfare measurement is option price. The option price is the willingness to pay for the aversion of uncertainty, where it is assumed that an economic agent can know the exact result of the risk beforehand (complete foresight). However, it is difficult for a household to predict the frequency and loss of the risk, since a disaster or the environmental risk is characteristically catastrophic or unknown. In other words, the revealed or stated preference for risk aversion is based on incomplete foresight. The household may therefore suffer from damage that is caused by the gap between a prior prediction and the ex post result, which Asahi and Hagihara (2012) defined as vulnerability.

Since the social overhead capital service is a basic service to preserve life, an ex post result should be the criteria for valuation. However, the basic information used to evaluate the cost-effectiveness is the ex ante choice of a household, which is why we need a framework to evaluate this vulnerability. To that end, factors influencing household choice under uncertainty—for instance, how it recognizes probability or how it values loss—should be examined.

In this chapter, we empirically examine the cut-off risk in the municipal water infrastructure as an example of households' choice for risk aversion using theoretical knowledge about decision-making under uncertainty. We aim to reach an implication concerning the benefit valuation model for the vulnerability improvement effect provided by social overhead capital. The next section provides an outline of the benefit valuation model for vulnerability improvement. In Sect. 13.3, the prospect theory is compared with the term decision theory in risk-averting behaviour. In Sect. 13.4, the vulnerability valuation model that exhibits the decision-making process is shown, and it is consequently investigated empirically in Sect. 13.5. Section 13.5 shows the survey on households concerning risk preference, risk awareness, and actual choice about the storage of drinking water. Furthermore, the relationship between a WTP (willingness to pay) for the water cut-off risk reduction and decision-making properties of the prospect theory is examined. Section 13.6 discusses the findings, before Sect. 13.7 concludes the study.

13.2 Economic Evaluation of Vulnerability Improvement by the Provision of Social Overhead Capital

Consider an investment in waterwork service as an example to measure the welfare of vulnerability (Asahi and Hagihara 2012).

A household optimizes water consumption, y. Next, let us suppose that the household recognizes a risk in the water consumption as an ex ante probability, π, and makes the optimal choice concerning private investment, R. Vulnerability, V, is left even if the household chooses optimal water investment, R^*, under income M, and probability θ, when consumption z—which is a minimum water consumption for living—is not met. Vulnerability (V) is described as follows:

$$V = V(M, y(R^*, G), \pi, z, \theta)$$

1. The welfare of improving vulnerability by public investment G (marginal change of the provision) is described in Eq. (13.1). Here, term 1 in parenthesis in Eq. (13.1) is the effect of public investment reducing vulnerability through a change in water consumption. Term 2 is the effect of public investment reducing the ex ante probability of the damage, π. The former is an effect of the investment to secure capacity, and it can be evaluated by using a normal project evaluation method. The latter is the effect on probability, and the valuation technique based on the choice of the household has not been established. We therefore build an evaluation model for term 2.

$$\frac{dM}{dG} = -\left(\frac{\partial V}{\partial y}\frac{\partial y}{\partial G} - \frac{\partial V}{\partial \pi}\frac{\partial \pi}{\partial G}\right) / \frac{\partial V}{\partial M} \ for \ dz = dR = 0 \qquad (13.1)$$

13.3 Decision-Making Properties in Averting Behaviour

13.3.1 Decision-Making Theory Under Risk

When the demand function of the social overhead capital service cannot be observed directly, the benefit is evaluated by a revealed preference for the substitution goods or stated preference. One of the revealed preference methods is the averting behaviour method, which posits that the benefits from households' consumption choice to evade the risk by oneself—instead of by social overhead capital—can approximate the benefits of the social overhead capital concerned (Hagihara 2013).

Next, we address the decision theory under risk. The traditional expected utility theory has been dominant for approximately two centuries since the 'St. Petersburg paradox' (Bernoulli 1738). The expected utility theory takes the axiomatic approach, meaning that it does not describe the psychological process of reaching a choice but assumes a decision-making process meeting axioms—such as independence axioms—to approximate a choice. Using such a traditional decision-making model supposes that the household has a risk preference, evaluates a recognized risk according to this preference, and takes risk-averting action.

13.3.2 Prospect Theory

Because an action cannot be accurately predicted in expected utility theory, prospect theory—which was proposed by Kahneman and Tversky (1979)—has been developing in the field of behavioural economics. Prospect theory consists of two important concepts: 'reference point effect' and 'non-linearity in evaluating the probability'. A decision-maker compares their choices with a reference point of their own. If they get more (or less) than the reference point, it is a gain (or loss). The loss is psychologically seen as worse than the same amount of gain. Additionally, it is assumed that the decision-maker reacts nonlinearly to the probability given to the result of the choice.

The prospect theory can explain an anomaly which the expected utility theory cannot explain. This is because it largely focuses on the psychological process, unlike the expected utility theory, which makes use of an axiomatic concept. The decision-making process is divided into two stages: the 'editing stage', where they recall a reference point of a choice, and the 'evaluation stage', where they perform loss aversion based on the reference point and a nonlinear interpretation of the probability (Table 13.1).

Table 13.1 Characteristics of the prospect theory

Decision-making phase		Prospect theory	Examples of evaluation and behaviour
Evaluation	Value function	Loss aversion Diminishing sensitivity	A gamble, of which the expected value is zero, is avoided The choice that may cause either big loss or big gain is evaluated as low Endowment effects or status quo bias For example, the 'willingness to accept' of the goods becomes higher than the 'willingness to pay' when the goods are not given
	Probability weight function	Subjective probability	Probability is overestimated in a situation that has 'very low probability' Zero risk effects: people hope that a risk becomes zero

Source: Based on Jantti et al. (2012) and Takemura (2006)

13.3.3 The Reference Point Effect (Loss Aversion) and Evaluation of the Probability

Risk aversion behaviour is comprised of three factors: ① the degree of the utility function curve, ② an evaluation of the probability, and ③ loss aversion based on the reference point. Many previous experiments show that ③ explains at least 50% of risk aversion behaviour. This suggests that choice is explained better by the reference point effect of the prospect theory (③) than risk preference in a traditional decision-making model (①). The appropriate explanation of a choice—the expected utility theory or the prospect theory—depends upon the experience and the information provided by the contexts (List 2004). The factors affecting the reference point itself also need to be determined in an economic experiment (Wakker 2010). It is often supposed that the present condition (status quo) is a reference point. Concerning the evaluation of the probability, the 'overestimation of low probability' and 'zero risk effect' are well-known factors.

Concerning risk aversion behaviour related to social overhead capital, it can be assumed that a situation where security—which is secured in daily life—is not kept should be avoided. Therefore, it is necessary to determine a characteristic of the choice in an atypical situation. Since this choice needs to be made in a situation with little information and experience, it can be expected that the endowment effect is big. Additionally, the difference between this choice and a daily choice pertaining to the effect of the risk preference should be considered. Since the reference point concerning the consumption of social overhead capital is not clarified in the theory, we need to empirically investigate which can be the reference point at present, a minimum or a safety standard.

Figure 13.1 illustrates the difference between traditional decision-making theory and prospect theory.

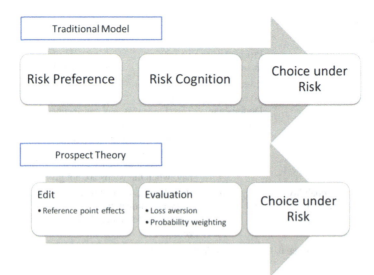

Fig. 13.1 Decision-making process

13.4 Vulnerability Valuation Model

13.4.1 Vulnerability Valuation Model

A household makes an optimal choice based on a subjective ex ante probability. However, as a result, a shortage may occur compared to the minimum requirement of the social overhead capital service. The probability of the occurrence of such an event is an ex post probability. Even though a household makes decisions using an ex ante probability, the decision of a social project is made based on an ex post or posterior probability. Therefore, we need a valuation model that can describe the gap between an ex ante probability—as recognized by the household—and the posterior probability. The chosen model should be capable of predicting what kind of choice the household will make based on an ex ante probability. Next, we propose which decision-making model (or decision theory) should be used in the analysis.

The traditional decision-making model is characterized by risk preference and risk recognition, while the prospect theory-based model is characterized by the reference-dependent effects and weighted probability function. These factors—which affect choice under risk—are incorporated into the chosen model, and parameters are estimated using data obtained through a questionnaire survey. This enables us to determine which of the two decision-making models can explain the choice better according to the significance of the parameters. Furthermore, it enables us to evaluate the posterior probability and the degree of the vulnerability that the household faces after optimal choice.

13.4.2 Choice Model

A household's utility function is assumed to be a general value function. The value function has two variables: private payment, R (negative consumption), and damage, A. According to the choice model based on Viscusi and Huber's (2012) work, it is expressed as follows:

$$u(R,A) = v(R_1) + \mu[v(R_1) - v(R_0)] + \pi_1 \cdot w(A) + \lambda(\pi_1 - \pi_0) \cdot w(A) \quad (13.2)$$

The parameters of the reference point effect—which is set in not only private payment R but also probability weight π—are estimated. μ and λ, respectively, represent the reference point effects for loss aversion and for probability appraisal. Subscripts 0 and 1 represent decision-making points in time. $v(\cdot)$ is a loss function, and $w(\cdot)$ is the appraisal of loss caused by damage A. Additionally, $v < 0$, $v' < 0$, $v'' \leq 0$ and $w < 0$, $w' < 0$ $w'' \leq 0$ are assumed.

Equation (13.3) is derived by first-order condition and total differentiation concerning private payment and ex ante probability.

$$du = \frac{\partial v}{\partial R_1} \cdot dR_1 + \mu \cdot \frac{\partial v}{\partial R_1} \cdot dR_1 + w(A) \cdot d\pi_1 + \lambda \cdot w(A) \cdot d\pi_1 = 0$$

$$(1 + \mu)v' \cdot dR_1 + (1 + \lambda)w(A) \cdot d\pi_1 = 0$$

$$-\frac{dR_1}{d\pi_1} = \frac{(1 + \lambda)w(A)}{(1 + \mu)v'} \quad (13.3)$$

WTP is represented in terms of the trade-off between risk and private payment (the left-hand side of the equation). It is explained by the parameter of the reference point effect for private payment (μ), the parameter of the reference point effect for probability (λ), the magnitude of the risk (A), and the marginal utility of private payment (R). We suppose that both the value function $v(R)$ and loss evaluation function $w(A)$ are CRRA-type utility functions and that the relative risk aversions are constant (η). The constant relative risk aversion-type utility function is specified so that the degree of risk aversions is equal in R and A.

$$v(R) = V \cdot R^{1-\eta}, w(A) = W \cdot A^{1-\eta}$$

Therefore, Eq. (13.3) is used to construct Eq. (13.4), in which risk aversion (η) is introduced for WTP (Saito 2006).

$$-\frac{dR_1}{d\pi_1} = \frac{(1 + \lambda)W \cdot A^{1-\eta}}{(1 + \mu)V(1 - \eta)R^{-\eta}} \quad (13.4)$$

Using revealed preference and stated preference data, the parameters of Eqs. (13.3) and (13.4) are estimated. Comparing the results enables us to determine which decision-making model can explain the factors that prescribe a choice based on ex ante probability better.

13.5 Empirical Analysis

13.5.1 Questionnaire

The case being used for this study is the cut-off risk of consumable tap water. We carried out a web questionnaire to procure data concerning the recognition of cut-off risk, personal measures, willingness to pay, and the clarification of the relationships between these factors. The questionnaire targeted respondents from across the country that are 20 years or older. It was carried out from March 12 to March 14, 2014 (consigned to MACROMILL Co. Ltd.). It was sampled on equal distribution by generation, considering that a web questionnaire generally tends to collect more answers from the 30–40 age group. There were 840 completed questionnaires and 19 investigation items: ① risk preference (three), ② risk cognition (four), ③ risk/risk aversion choice (two), ④ the option for the change in risk and in the burden of a water pipe replacement (three), and ⑤ respondents' attributes (seven). The questions are shown in Table 13.2.

Questions 1 and 2 addressed risk response in daily life to obtain information concerning the degree of general risk aversion. Question 3 is aimed at calculating a parameter concerning the degree of risk aversion of the utility function (Lusk and Coble 2005). Questions 4 and 5 concern risk recognition, the water cut-off risk due to both the deterioration of a water pipe or due to disaster. Questions 6 and 8 are about the storage of bottled water, which is private risk-averting behaviour for water cut-off risk. In questions 7 and 9, we asked about the risk recognition in a case of choice. The probability in question 9 (15–1000) was calculated from the total number of water cut-off cases across the country and the data of the population with water supply (2011 water statistics). Note that the probability is likely to be bigger than the actual number, since the magnitude and overlap of the water cut-off areas are not considered in the calculation. In questions 10–12, hypothetical scenarios were presented concerning the replacement investment for water cut-off risk owing to the water pipe deterioration, and the respondents were asked about their WTP (double-bounded dichotomous model).

Fundamental statistics and the respondents' individual attributes are shown in Tables 13.3 and 13.4, respectively. Using this data, the prospect theory model of which the explained variable is WTP for risk change (question 10–12) and the traditional decision-making model of which the explained variable is risk choice behaviour (question 6) are estimated.

13 Economic Evaluation of Risk Premium of Social Overhead Capital... 231

Table 13.2 Summary of questions

No.	Categories	Questions	Data form
1	Risk preference	Over what percentage of precipitation of the weather forecast, do you go out with an umbrella?	Continuous (%)
2	Risk preference	You reserved a seat on the train for a trip. How long before the departure time do you arrive at the station?	Continuous (n minutes)
3	Risk preference	Choice experiments of lotteries A and B	Numerical (see Table 13.5)
4	Risk cognition	Do you think that the cut-off of water by the deterioration of the water pipe will occur?	Ordinal scale (9 scale)
5	Risk cognition	Do you think that the cut-off of water by an earthquake will occur?	Ordinal scale (10 scale)
6	Risk choice	Do you store some bottled water for cut-off of water?	Binary
7	Risk cognition	What reasons for the cut-off of water do you imagine when you store bottled water?	Binary
8	Risk choice	How many bottles of water per a family member?	Continuous (days)
9	Risk cognition	The cut-off of water risk caused by the deterioration of the water pipe is a ratio of 15 of 1000 on average. Do you think the risk is big or small?	Binary
10	Risk and payment	Do you approve, disapprove, or feel indifferent towards the investment of the reconstruction of water pipe? (For each contingent scenario)	Binary
11	Risk and payment	Asked again the respondents who replied 'approval' in Q10: Do you accept the increase of risk or payment? (Additional scenario)	Binary
12	Risk and payment	Asked again the respondents who replied 'disapproval' in Q10: Do you accept the decrease of risk or payment? (Additional scenario)	Binary
13– 19	Respondents' attributes	Sex, age, income, daily behaviour on drinking tap water, experience of water cut-off	Binary/ordinal scale

13.5.2 Empirical Analysis

13.5.2.1 Risk Choice and Risk Preference: Traditional Decision-Making Model

Model and Data

We apply the traditional decision-making model to determine the effects of risk preference and risk recognition on averting behaviour for water cut-off risk. The risk choice is expressed as follows from Eq. (13.4).

$$-\frac{dR_1}{d\pi_1} = F(f(\mu, \lambda), \eta, g(w(A), v(R))) \tag{13.5}$$

The marginal WTP for water cut-off risk—the left side of Eq. (13.5)—represents the valuation for a reference point effect ($f(\mu, \lambda)$), risk aversion (η), and $g(w(A), v(R))$,

Table 13.3 Fundamental data statistics

Variables	Obs	Mean	Std. dev.
Age	630	44.889	14.723
Sex	630	0.540	0.499
Risk preference (probability of precipitation)	630	48.848	17.065
Risk preference (reservation time)	630	17.051	11.025
Relative risk aversion	422	0.309	0.619
Absolute risk aversion	422	0.000	0.001
Risk cognition (deterioration)	630	4.943	1.632
Risk cognition (earthquakes)	630	3.903	1.534
Water storage	630	1.584	0.493
Water storage days	262	4.281	4.693
Income	536	2.780	1.335
Daily behaviour on drinking tap water	630	0.406	0.492
Knowledge on emergency hydrant	630	1.903	0.296
Experience of water cut-off	630	0.463	0.499

Table 13.4 Respondent attributes

Sex			**Districts**		
	N	%		N	%
Male	396	47.1	Hokkaido	52	6.2
Female	444	52.9	Tohoku	46	5.5
All	840	100.0	Kanto	306	36.4
			Chubu	142	16.9
			Kinki	150	17.9
Occupation			Chugoku	44	5.2
	N	%	Shikoku	24	2.9
Civil servant	27	3.2	Kyusyu	76	9.0
Manager	11	1.3	All	840	100.0
Company (administrative)	123	14.6			
Company (engineering)	73	8.7	**Income (yen, including tax)**		
Company (others)	81	9.6	(1$ = 15.79 yen, 2014)	N	%
Self-employed	56	6.7	−999,999	143	17.0
Freelance	24	2.9	1000,000–2,499,999	154	18.3
Full-time housewife	180	21.4	2,500,000–4,999,999	221	26.3
Part-time job	105	12.5	5,000,000–7,499,999	123	14.6
Student	31	3.7	7,500,000–9,999,999	49	5.8
Others	44	5.2	−10,000,000	29	3.5
Unemployed	85	10.1	Others	121	14.4
All	840	100.0	All	840	100.0

Table 13.5 Relative and absolute risk aversion

The number of safe choice	Relative risk aversion			Central value	Absolute risk aversion			Central value
1	−1.76	≦rr<	−0.97	−**1.365**	−0.0019	≦ar<	−0.0012	−**0.00155**
2	−0.97	≦rr<	−0.49	−**0.73**	−0.0012	≦ar<	−0.0006	−**0.0009**
3	−0.49	≦rr<	−0.13	−**0.31**	−0.0006	≦ar<	−0.0005	−**0.00055**
4	−0.13	≦rr<	0.2	**0.035**	−0.0005	≦ar<	0.0003	−**0.0001**
5	0.2	≦rr<	0.49	**0.345**	0.0003	≦ar<	0.0007	**0.0005**
6	0.49	≦rr<	0.79	**0.64**	0.0007	≦ar<	0.0012	**0.00095**
7	0.79	≦rr<	1.14	**0.965**	0.0012	≦ar<	0.0017	**0.00145**
8	1.14	≦rr<	1.61	**1.375**	0.0017	≦ar<	0.0026	**0.00215**
9–10	1.61	≦rr			0.0026	≦ar		

which is the function for loss and personal payment. The traditional decision-making model assumes that a reference point effect should be zero. Risk recognition is included in function g (/), since the choice is made according to the degree of risk aversion after having recognized the risk.

A logit model is estimated, setting a dichotomous variable of drinking water storage (question 6, Table 13.2) as the explained variable and setting risk preference, risk recognition, and the other attributes (sex, age, income, tap water drinking behaviour, and experience of water cut-off; see Table 13.2) as explanatory variables. The estimated model is Eq. (13.6), where p, η, g, and x represent the probability of drinking water storage behaviour, risk preference, risk recognition, and the other attribute vectors, respectively.

$$\text{logit}(p) = \alpha_0 + \alpha_1 \eta + \alpha_2 g + \boldsymbol{\alpha_3 x}$$

$$p = \frac{\exp(\alpha_0 + \alpha_1 \eta + \alpha_2 g + \boldsymbol{\alpha_3 x})}{1 + \exp(\alpha_0 + \alpha_1 \eta + \alpha_2 g + \boldsymbol{\alpha_3 x})} \tag{13.6}$$

The degrees of relative risk aversion and absolute risk aversion are calculated by the 'answer to lottery' of question 3 (refer to Lusk and Coble (2005) and to Table 13.5). Each representative figure is used for the estimates.

Result

Four types of risk preference data are assumed: probability of precipitation (question 1), reservation time (question 2), and the relative and absolute risk aversion by choice of lottery (question 3). The risk recognition data have three types: water cut-off by the deterioration (question 4), water cut-off by earthquakes, and the probability of water cut-off (question 9). The estimated results are shown in Table 13.6.

The parameters for risk preference (α_1) are not significant for any of the above cases. Additionally, the condition of risk aversion is not met in the case of using the risk recognition data for water cut-off probability by deterioration. However, the

Table 13.6 Results (logit estimation)

	Variables	Question	Risk preference: probability of precipitation			Risk preference: reservation time			Risk preference lottery (relative risk aversion)			Risk preference lottery (absolute risk aversion)		
Risk preference α_1	Probability of precipitation	Q1	−0.003	−0.003	−0.004	–	–	–	–	–	–	–	–	–
			(0.005)	(0.005)	(0.006)									
	Reservation time	Q2	–	–	–	−0.006	−0.006	−0.012	–	–	–	–	–	–
						(0.008)	(0.008)	(0.009)						
	Lottery (relative risk aversion)	Q3	–	–	–	–	–	–	−0.105	−0.092	0.009	–	–	–
									(0.151)	(0.151)	(0.172)			
	Lottery (absolute risk aversion)	Q3	–	–	–	–	–	–	–	–	–	−54.345	−47.866	28.778
												(98.089)	(98.452)	(111.824)
Risk cognition α_2	Deterioration	Q4	−0.084 *	–	–	−0.089 *	–	–	−0.063	–	–	−0.063	–	–
			(0.049)			(0.049)			(0.061)			(0.061)		
	Earthquakes	Q5	–	−0.097 *	–	–	−0.103 **	–	–	−0.136 **	–	–	−0.137 **	–
				(0.052)			(0.051)			(0.064)			(0.063)	
	Probability of deterioration cut-off	Q9	–	–	0.364 *	–	–	0.407 **	–	–	0.430 *	–	–	0.430 *
					(0.189)			(0.191)			(0.225)			(0.225)
Other attributes α_3	Sex (male = 0, female = 1)	Q13	0.391 **	0.375 **	0.535 **	0.393 **	0.376 **	0.536 **	0.514 **	0.524 **	0.574 **	0.512 **	0.522 **	0.572 **
			(0.176)	(0.175)	(0.207)	(0.176)	(0.176)	(0.207)	(0.216)	(0.216)	(0.249)	(0.216)	(0.216)	(0.249)
	Age	Q13	0.025 ***	0.024 ***	0.027 ***	0.025 ***	0.025 ***	0.028 ***	0.033 ***	0.033 ***	0.036 ***	0.033 ***	0.033 ***	0.036 ***
			(0.006)	(0.006)	(0.007)	(0.006)	(0.006)	(0.007)	(0.007)	(0.007)	(0.008)	(0.007)	(0.007)	(0.008)
	Income	Q14	0.126 **	0.121 **	0.205 ***	0.127 **	0.121 **	0.203 ***	0.175 **	0.172 **	0.220 ***	0.176 **	0.172 **	0.221 ***
			(0.061)	(0.061)	(0.071)	(0.061)	(0.061)	(0.071)	(0.074)	(0.075)	(0.085)	(0.074)	(0.075)	(0.085)
	Daily behaviour on drinking tap water	Q16	−0.471 ***	−0.473 ***	−0.492 ***	−0.479 ***	−0.481 ***	−0.499 ***	−0.475 **	−0.477 **	−0.680 ***	−0.477 **	−0.478 **	−0.683 ***
			(0.159)	(0.159)	(0.184)	(0.159)	(0.159)	(0.184)	(0.194)	(0.195)	(0.222)	(0.194)	(0.194)	(0.222)
	Experience of cut-off	Q18	0.115	0.118	0.005	0.112	0.116	0.011	0.261	0.220	0.267	0.261	0.219	0.267
			(0.209)	(0.209)	(0.239)	(0.209)	(0.208)	(0.239)	(0.263)	(0.263)	(0.294)	(0.263)	(0.263)	(0.294)

(continued)

13 Economic Evaluation of Risk Premium of Social Overhead Capital...

Table 13.6 (continued)

	Variables	Question	Risk preference: probability of precipitation			Risk preference: reservation time			Risk preference lottery (relative risk aversion)			Risk preference lottery (absolute risk aversion)		
a_0	Constant		-1.251 **	-1.256 **	-2.187 ***	-1.317 ***	-1.308 ***	-2.258 ***	-1.993 ***	-1.750 ***	-2.794 ***	-1.995 ***	-1.750 ***	-2.800 ***
			(0.506)	(0.498)	(0.551)	(0.470)	(0.463)	(0.481)	(0.538)	(0.524)	(0.542)	(0.538)	(0.524)	(0.542)
	Log likelihood		-470.4	-470.0	-356.1	-470.3	-470.0	-355.6	-320.0	-313.0	-251.0	-320.1	-318.3	-251.0
	Number of obs		719	719	552	719	719	552	495	495	399	495	495	399
	LR chi2		39.5	40.1	42.5	39.5	40.2	43.5	40.1	54.2	46.0	39.9	43.5	46.0
	Prob > chi2		0.0	0.0	0.0	0.0	0.0	0.0	0.0	0.0	0.0	0.0	0.0	0.0
	Pseudo R^2		0.040	0.041	0.056	0.040	0.041	0.058	0.059	0.080	0.084	0.059	0.064	0.084

Note: Figures in parentheses are standard error
Note: Significance level *10% **5% ***1%

parameter α_2 of risk recognition is significant at a 10% level. Particularly, the water cut-off risk due to earthquake is significant at a 5% level. The other attributes—except for water cut-off experience—are all significant at a 5% level.

13.5.2.2 Risk Choice and Reference Point Effect: Prospect Theory Model

Model

Equation (13.3) is specialized in Eq. (13.7) of the log-linear type. WTP for risk aversion (the left side of the equation) is a function of the reference point effect, f (μ, λ), the evaluation of loss, marginal private payment, and vector $\mathbf{x}$ controlling other factors. There are two reasons why the reference point effect should be explained by both loss aversion effect μ and initial endowment effect of probability λ; first, these factors will be solved by a combination of probability and private payment. Second, the relationship between the two is not known a priori.

$$\ln\left(-\frac{dR_1}{d\pi_1}\right) = \beta_0 + \beta_1 \ln\left(\frac{1+\lambda}{1+\mu}\right) + \beta_2 \ln w(A) - \beta_3 \ln\left(v'\right) + \beta_4 \mathbf{x} \qquad (13.7)$$

Data

Equation (13.7) is estimated by setting the explained variable choice of WTP as the risk (questions 10–12, Table 13.2: the burden on change of water cut-off probability). Three types of scenarios concerning the risk and burden (reference point effect) are set for explanatory variables (factor variables). Two regression analyses are conducted: one takes into account only the factor variables as explanatory variables and the other adds other variables such as loss evaluation (ln w [A]), private payment (ln [v']), and other factor vectors (x).

The explained variable is provided by each of the three scenarios concerning risk and burden. The first is the WTP scenario: water cut-off of risk decreases, but payment increases ($\mu+$, $\lambda-$). The second is the 'payment decrease or risk decrease' scenario, both water cut-off risk and payment decrease, ($\mu-$, $\lambda-$), and the third is the 'payment increase or risk increase' scenario, both water cut-off risk and payment increase, ($\mu+$, $\lambda+$).

The WTP scenario is explained here as an example. The scenario of water cut-off risk caused by the deterioration of a water pipe is shown in Fig. 13.2. Water cut-off risk is expressed as the likelihood of damage—'15–1,000'—and decreases in line with water pipe replacement. On the other hand, in this scenario, people will be subject to a water bill increase. The relationship between the change of the risk and the burden was shown to the respondents in both a figure and a table. The respondents were asked to choose either approval (yes), disapproval (no), or good (indifference). An answer indicating indifference meant that we can assume that the

13 Economic Evaluation of Risk Premium of Social Overhead Capital...

We would like to ask you about the policy about the water cut-off of risk.

* The following policy plan is based on a virtual scenario and is different from the real administration and policy.

Suppose your local water department is going to change a deteriorated water pipe. Since the renewal of the water pipe decreases the probability of accidental water leakage or a pipe burst, the water cut-off risk decreases. However, the renewal of the water pipe needs a substantial investment, and a part of these expenses are covered by the water bill.

Incidentally, suppose that damage from water cut-off by the deterioration of the water pipe in your district is the following: 15 water users out of a population of 1000 per year.

If the water pipe is replaced, the chance of damage decreases to the following ratio: three water users out of a population of 1000 per year. However, water rates are increased to cover the replacement investment.

Suppose the water bill in your household to be 4000 Yen (for one month, 20 m³). The replacement investment raises the water bill by 1000 Yen (25%), which results in 5000 Yen (for one month, 20 m³).

The next figure expresses the change in the water cut-off risk mentioned above. The green squares represent the number of people that avoided water cut-off damage by replacement investment. The table shows the relationships between the replacement investment and non-replacement, the water cut-off risk, and the water rate.

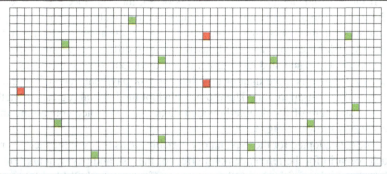

	With replacement investment	Without replacement investment
Water cut-off risk per year	3 to 1000	15 to 1000
Water rate	+ 1000 Yen (4000 Yen to 5000 Yen per month) (+ 12000 Yen per year)	±0 Yen (4000 Yen per month)

Fig. 13.2 WTP scenario: first phase

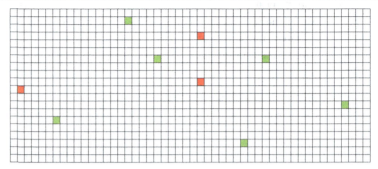

Fig. 13.3 WTP scenario, second phase

relationship between the change of the risk and the burden will no longer change and a WTP with a probability of 1 to 1000 was calculated.

If the respondents answered either yes or no, they advanced to the next phase, where an option of a more moderate change of the probability is shown. Figure 13.3 is the scenario that was shown in the second phase if the answer in the first phase was yes. The risk burden is calculated based on the 'indifference' replies, similar to the first phase. The calculated risk burden is censored data, since it can be assumed that the WTP shown is more than or less than the risk-payment trade-off in the case of 'approval' or 'disapproval'. Therefore, we adopt the interval regression method.

The structure of the double-bounded dichotomous choice concerning the WTP scenario is shown in Fig. 13.4.

The data adopted for the explanatory variable are as follows: the factor variable of each scenario for the reference point effect of the risk and payment are 'emergency water source recognition' and 'the water cut-off experience' (Table 13.2, respondent attribute) for net loss value ($\ln w[A]$), 'the bottled water stock days' (Table 13.2, No. 8) for the private payment ($\ln[v']$), and 'age' and 'tap water drinking behaviour' (Table 13.2, respondent attribute) for other factor vectors ($\mathbf{x}$).

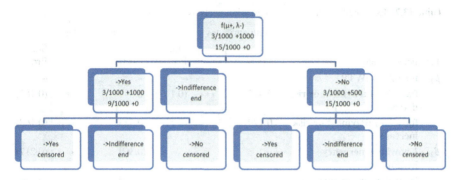

Fig. 13.4 Structure of the two-step dichotomous choice with the WTP scenario

Results

The estimated results are shown in Table 13.7. The parameters (β_1–β_4) in Table 13.7 correspond with the parameters of Eq. (13.6). The results are presented based on a reference point effect in the WTP scenario (risk decreases, but payment increases, $\mu+$ $\lambda-$). The reference point effect on risk payment is significant and positive in the scenario of 'payment decrease or risk decrease, $\mu-$, $\lambda-$' in both 'with attributes' and 'without attributes'. The reference point effect in the scenario 'payment increase or risk increase' is significant and positive in the case of 'with attributes', but not in the case of 'without attributes'. The WTP scenario is the choice of 'payment increase and the risk decrease', but for the choice of 'payment decrease or the risk decrease', the payment for the increase in water cut-off probability by 1/1000 grows bigger due to the reference point effect.

This implies that a respondent who is shown an option of 'payment increase, risk decrease' tends to see much more value in it than in the option of 'risk decrease or payment decrease'. Similarly, the fact that the reference point in the scenario of 'payment increase or risk increase' is positive would have a similar effect. In other words, the former desires a bigger payment (compensation). Both cases suggest that the 'trade-off' framing, i.e. whether risk increase (or decrease) or payment increase (or decrease) increases the evaluation for risk more than the framing of 'counter value', i.e. payment for the risk. However, the 'payment increase or risk increase' scenario does not show significant results in the 'without attributes' estimation, which implies that the endowment effects in probability evaluation (λ) are weaker than that in loss (μ).

Linearly predicting marginal effects using the estimated parameter, we determine the WTP for a water cut-off risk of 1 to 1000. Changing the water cut-off risk to 1 to 1000 is evaluated using the amount of 135.8 yen (US$1.3) in the 'payment decrease or risk decrease' scenario and 89.5 yen (US$0.8) in the WTP scenario with attributes. The valuation in 'payment increase or risk increase' scenario is 107.0 yen (US $1.0), which is smaller than the amount of the 'payment decrease or risk decrease' scenario. This again suggests that a loss evaluation is bigger than a probability evaluation concerning the initial endowment effect. The magnitude of the reference point effects has similar tendency in the estimate of 'without attributes' (Table 13.8).

240 C. Asahi and K. Hagihara

Table 13.7 Estimated results: section regression analysis

Parameter/Variables		With attributes			Without attributes		
		Coef.		Std. Err.	Coef.		Std. Err.
β_1	f(μ +,λ −) :WTP	−		−	−		−
	f(μ −,λ −) :**Payment or risk decrease**	0.417	***	(0.107)	0.348	**	(0.162)
	f(μ +,λ +) :**Payment or risk increase**	0.179		(0.110)	0.323	*	(0.168)
β_2	**Knowing emergency hydrant**				0.369	*	(0.217)
	No water cut-off experience				−0.181		(0.129)
β_3	**The number of water storage days**		•		−0.040	**	(0.016)
β_4	**Age**				0.010	**	(0.005)
	Daily drinking tap water				0.242	*	(0.135)
	_cons	4.494	***	(0.081)	3.502	***	(0.508)
	Log likelihood	−744.668			−296.34397		
	LRchi2(2)	15.84			28.33		
	Prob. > LR(chi2)	0.0004			0.0002		
	Number of obs	630			262		
	Censored observation						
	Left-censored	106			40		
	Uncensored	250			102		
	Right-censored	223			96		
	Interval	51			24		

Note: Significance level *10% **5% ***1%

Table 13.8 Marginal effects and payment

Scenario	Without attributes				With attributes			
	Marginal effects		Std. err.	Payment for 1/1000	Marginal effects		Std. err.	Payment for 1/1000
f(μ+, λ−), WTP	4.511	***	(0.125)	91.0	4.494	***	(0.081)	89.5
f(μ−, λ−), payment or risk decrease	4.860	***	(0.100)	129.0	4.912	***	(0.070)	135.8
f(μ+, λ+), payment or risk increase	4.834	***	(0.112)	125.8	4.673	***	(0.075)	107.0
Number of respondents	630				495			

Note: Significance level *10%, **5%, ***1%

13.6 Discussion

According to the results shown in Sect. 5.2.1, risk cognition affects the choice of storing drinking water to ward against water cut-off risk, but risk preference does not. However, some existing literature (i.e. Lusk and Coble 2005) and certain economy-based experiments have shown that risk preference has a significant influence on the choice of storing drinking water. Concerning the risk of water infrastructure or water availability, the risk preference according to a traditional decision-making model may not have an effect on choice. On the other hand, we observed that risk recognition had a direct influence on choice. Risk recognition is more significant for deterioration risk than for disaster risk with both significance and coefficients, when they are compared in scale. Additionally, probability cognition tends to be more meaningful than scale cognition in respondents' replies in the case of deterioration risk.

These results suggest two points concerning the decision-making model and benefit valuation. First, risk preference cannot be assumed naturally in the choice of social overhead capital service. Whether the assumption of risk preference is appropriate or not may depend upon the risk property. In other words, we should consider the difference between long-term daily risk such as genetically modified foods and non-daily but imaginable risks, such as disasters or the natural deterioration of infrastructure.

Second, we focus on the way that risk is indicated. By recognition of the risk, the cognitive burden will be less for a dichotomous choice than for a choice by a 9-unit scale. A simple risk indication method to decrease the cognitive burden is needed so that risk recognition can be improved for better averting action. Utilizing the prospect theory model, a reference point effect was observed concerning the trade-off between water cut-off risk and payment. It was shown that there was a difference in the combinatorial evaluation of probability and loss and the separation was explained by framing, which was payment of the risk or trade-off with the risk and compensation. Concerning the stated preference model in the evaluation of the risk and the environment, the psychological bias of the stated reply is well-known. Similarly, it was confirmed that a reference point effect occurred in the scenario concerning the contingent choice about the water connection infrastructure. Since the prospect theory is a descriptive theory concerning decision-making, there is not a universal standard by which to judge which reference point effect and framing are appropriate. However, the result of the reference point effect is important when the benefit evaluation is applied in a project evaluation. In other words, we should have employed a conservative payment framing in the questionnaire, using a reference point effect and considering framing for a sensibility analysis.

Should the traditional decision-making model or the prospect theory model be utilized to determine the unit value of the risk premium in a benefit evaluation? The estimated results imply that the framing of risk recognition and the scenario were significant factors in determining water cut-off risk by deterioration of the water connection. Therefore, the prospect theory model is more appropriate. This means that often, risk recognition rather than risk preference can clarify the influence of the reference point effect in the scenario.

13.7 Conclusion

In this chapter, we investigated the difference between a traditional decision-making model and the prospect theory model to evaluate the benefits of risk premium, using the case of water cut-off risk. The results were as follows. In evaluating the risk premium of infrastructure, the assumption of risk preference is not always appropriate, and the prospect theory model is more appropriate than the traditional model. Additionally, the framing of the reference point effects should be controlled in a survey and can be applied to a sensitivity analysis. These findings were determined by an experimental case study, and further examination would be beneficial.

Future studies could include a theoretically focused inspection of the reference point effect. Each reference point effect of probability and loss should be dealt with separately, or the probability evaluation should be modelled more explicitly. Furthermore, the risks related to the social overhead capital service is so extensive that the comparison with the evaluation of other social overhead capital services—such as roads or disaster prevention—should be performed and examined.

This work is supported by JSPS KAKENHI, Grant Number JP24730215 and JP16K03634.

References

Arrow J, Lind RC (June 1970) Uncertainty and the evaluation of public investment decisions. Am Econ Rev 60(3):364–378

Asahi C, Hagihara K (2012) Evaluation of the vulnerability of municipal water infrastructure. Stud Reg Sci 42(3):563–580. (in Japanese)

Bernoulli D (1738) Exposition of a new theory on the measurement of risk. Econometrica 22:23–36

Cabinet Office policy unification official (economic society system charge) Social overhead capital of Japan, it is 2012. (in Japanese)

Hagihara K (ed) (2013) Fundamental theory of the decision aiding for environment. Keiso-shobo, Tokyo. (in Japanese)

Jantti M, Kanbr R, Nyyssola M, Pirttila J (2012) Poverty and welfare measurement on the basis of prospect theory, UNU-WIDER Working Chapter, No.2012/109, United Nations University

Kahneman D, Tversky A (1979) Prospect theory: analysis of decision under risk. Econometrica 47:263–291

Kobayashi K, Yokomatsu M (2002) Disaster risk management and economic evaluation. Infrastruct Plan Rev 19(1):1–12. (in Japanese)

List JA (2004) Neotraditional theory versus prospect theory: evidence from the marketplace. Econometrica 72(2):615–625

Lusk JL, Coble KH (2005) Risk perceptions, risk preference, and acceptance of risky food. Am J Agric Econ 87(2):393–405

Ministry of Land, Infrastructure, Transport and Tourism (2009) Benefit Valuation under uncertainty. In: Project evaluation technique committee document. (in Japanese)

Saito M (2006) New macroeconomics. Yuhikaku, Tokyo. (in Japanese)

Takemura K (2006) Judgment and decision making in risk society. Cogn Stud 13(1):17–31. (in Japanese)

Viscusi WK, Huber J (2012) Reference-dependent valuation of risk: why willingness-to-accept exceeds willingness-to-pay. J Risk Uncertain 44:19–44

Wakker PP (2010) Prospect theory for risk and ambiguity. Cambridge University Press, Cambridge

Chapter 14
A Study of Nishihara Village's Disaster Response in the Kumamoto Earthquake and the Disaster Victims' Perception of Life Recovery and Assessment of Health

Sotaro Tsuboi

Abstract The aim of this study is to try to get an integrated understanding of the municipality's disaster response in Nishihara Village, Kumamoto Prefecture, and of the victims' perception of life recovery and assessment concerning health as well as to clarify the actual conditions and issues in the first year following the disaster, from the initial/emergency period of evacuation life to the early stages of recovery. The results of this survey make clear that the rapid response taken toward disaster victims in Nishihara Village was due to the flexible rearrangement of disaster response organizations and the way in which headquarters was established from the early stages of the disaster, as well as the creation of an original support system for rebuilding victims' lives. It was also revealed that of the victims' evaluations, assessment of perception of recovery was influenced by the *damage situation* and the *housing situation*. Furthermore, in health assessments, it was determined that deterioration of health among long-term shelter evacuees and in-vehicle evacuees has occurred.

Keywords Perception of life recovery · Health assessment · Disaster response · Nishihara Village · Kumamoto earthquake

14.1 Introduction

Knowledge and lessons learned in the restoration and recovery processes that take place in society in the aftermath of a disaster are vital to the effective support of victims and affected areas. In a survey of a previous study of victims in the aftermath of the Great Hanshin-Awaji Earthquake (1995), seven elements that constitute life reconstruction were identified and sorted in a time series for perception of recovery:

S. Tsuboi (✉)
Disaster Reduction and Human Renovation Institution, Saitama, Japan

© Springer Nature Singapore Pte Ltd. 2019
C. Asahi (ed.), *Building Resilient Regions*, New Frontiers in Regional Science: Asian Perspectives 35, https://doi.org/10.1007/978-981-13-7619-1_14

housing, social ties, townscape, preparedness and mitigation, physical and mental health, economic and financial situations, and relation to government. At the same time, it was revealed that a mindset of having "overcome the earthquake" was strongly related to the perception of recovery (Tatsuki et al. 2004). In addition, research on the aftermath of the Niigata Chuetsu Earthquake (2004) includes studies on intentions to continue residing in the area and on the impact on community activities (Mizumura 2010; Aoto 2006) as well a study of the recovery process organized as an ethnography and discussing the role of outside supporters in the disaster area (Miyamoto and Atsumi 2009).

The need for response in the following four aspects of recovery has been organized and recommended as the key to disaster recovery in recent years: *urban recovery* of damaged urban areas and infrastructure, *social recovery* of local communities, *employment recovery* to secure affected business and workplaces, and *life recovery* of affected families and housing (Nakabayashi 2016).

Valuable findings have been accumulated in this series of studies, and they are regarded as indicators for recovery policy and support in recent disaster response. In this study, however, the emphasis was on dividing and organizing the *external factors* of the initial/emergency response of the administration, and the *internal factors* of disaster victims' assessments including perception of life recovery evaluation and health evaluation, and getting an integrated understanding of them.

The decision to include victims' health in this study was due to the fact that worsening of symptoms of poor health and the occurrence of deaths related to the period of stay in evacuation shelters and kind of shelter have become an issue in disasters of recent years. The method taken to approach this issue was to create questions while referring to past research on subjective health and framing the responses of the disaster-affected residents as a "health evaluation" including health-related changes and symptoms before and after the disaster and status of hospital visits. For this study, a survey was conducted in Nishihara Village in Kumamoto Prefecture with the aim of clarifying the characteristics of the disaster victims' perceptions of life recovery and issues with the administration's disaster response as of April 2017, a year after the April 2016 Kumamoto earthquake. This particular earthquake disaster was characterized by a great deal of damage to houses, a prolonged stay in evacuation shelters due to repeated aftershocks, and a large number of evacuees living in their vehicles.

14.2 Research Methods and Overview of Survey Area

The target of this study was Nishihara Village, Aso County, located in the center of Kumamoto Prefecture on the western outer rim of the Mt. Aso crater (Fig. 14.1), with the Aso Kumamoto Airport located on its border with the adjacent town of Mashiki-machi. With its easy access to Kumamoto City and number one ranking as a "highly competitive village" in the Cabinet Office Economic Index Ranking (2015)

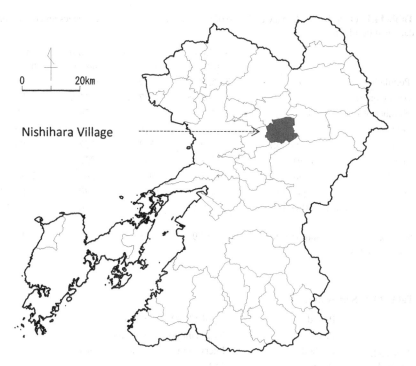

Fig. 14.1 Location of survey target area (Kumamoto Prefecture and Nishihara Village)

based on such indicators as agriculture and manufacturing industries and administrative financial power, the village had seen an increase in population in recent years.

Since Nishihara is located directly above the fault that runs below the Futagawa River, a river which flows right through the village, the foreshock that struck was recorded at a magnitude of 6.5 on the Richter scale in the village and the main shock at a magnitude of 7.3, resulting in 5 deaths and 56 injured and causing major damage to buildings including serious damage to more than half (56.6%) of the residents' 2408 houses. Looking at the overview of damage of the leading affected local governments due to the earthquake and the burden per local government employee (the ratio of employees to evacuees excluding support staff), based on the number of evacuees as of April 25th, the burden for Nishihara was largest after Mashiki-machi and Kajima-machi at 19.3 evacuees per employee, and the burden of damaged buildings was high at 16.4 buildings per employee, comparable to Mashiki-machi (Table 14.1).

This survey was jointly conducted a year after the earthquake over the period of April 13 to 22, 2017, at a consultation for residential land restoration and public housing tenant applications carried out by Nishihara Village. After attaining the consent of consultation visitors, the survey was carried out with an interview-style questionnaire form and responses received from a total of 212 people. Questions addressed the categories of "perception of recovery," "health evaluation," and

Table 14.1 Overview of damage and ratio of government employees to evacuees and to number of damaged buildings

	Mashiki-machi	Minamiaso-mura	Kashima-machi	Nishihara-mura
Population (2015:person)	33,639	11,912	8979	7075
Area (square km)	65.68	137.32	16.65	77.22
Number of government staff (person)	249	161	79	78
Number of dead (person)	21	16	4	5
Complete destruction (building)	2476	503	272	506
Half destruction (building)	2471	441	332	775
Total damage house (building)	4947	944	604	1281
Number of evacuees (April 25)	7328	1168	2070	1502
Rate of government staff (for evacuees)	29.4	7.3	26.2	19.3
Rate of government staff (for total damage house)	19.9	5.9	7.6	16.4

Table 14.2 Survey overview

Research method	Period	April 13, 2017 (Thu) ~22 (Sat)
	Place	Nishihara government building
	Method	Interview-type questionnaire survey
	Respondents	212
Question items	Basic attribute	Age/duration of residence/damage situation /evacuation period
	Perception of life recovery	Perception of life recovery(5 scale)
		Period of live recovery(every 2 months/6 scale)
	Assessment of health	Evaluation of health (5 scales)
		Hospital visits during evacuation
		Health insecurity (3 scale)
	Disaster response	Disaster response evacuation drills/earthquake insurance
		Neighborhood interaction
		People who experienced being approached/alerted for evacuation

"response measures." Investigators filled out the forms while explaining the contents to the subjects, as well as listening to additional details (Tables 14.2 and 14.3). Regarding the response of Nishihara's Disaster Management Headquarters, office employees were interviewed, and analysis carried out based on Disaster Management Headquarters' materials, photographs, etc.

14 A Study of Nishihara Village's Disaster Response in the...

Table 14.3 Overview of respondents (N = 212)

	Items	Number	Rate
Gender	Male	114	54.5%
	Female	95	45.5%
	Non-response	3	–
Current resident type	Repaired house	92	43.8%
	Relatives house	4	1.9%
	New house	5	2.4%
	Emergency temporary house	68	32.4%
	Rental temporary house	41	19.5%
	Non-response	2	–
Period evacuation	About 2 weeks	52	26.7%
	About 1 month	31	15.9%
	About 2 months	23	11.8%
	About 3 months	48	24.6%
	About 4 months	14	7.2%
	Over 5 months	27	13.8%
	Non-response	17	–
Age	Less than 30s	8	3.8%
	40s	28	13.2%
	50s	48	22.6%
	60s	76	35.8%
	70s	34	16.0%
	Over 80s	18	8.5%
Duration of residence	Less than 5 years	20	9.7%
	Less than 5–10 years	16	7.8%
	Less than 10–20 years	34	46.5%
	Over 20 years	136	66.0%
	Non-response	6	–
Damage situation	Complete destruction	97	46.4%
	Large-scale destruction	29	13.9%
	Half destruction	49	23.4%
	Partial damage	34	16.3%
	Non-response	3	–

14.3 Disaster Response in Nishihara Village

14.3.1 Status of Evacuees

Nishihara recorded its largest number of evacuees (1809 people) in the aftermath of the earthquakes on April 17, the day after the main shock, concentrated in 6 designated evacuation shelters in the village (Figs. 14.2 and 14.3). Moreover,

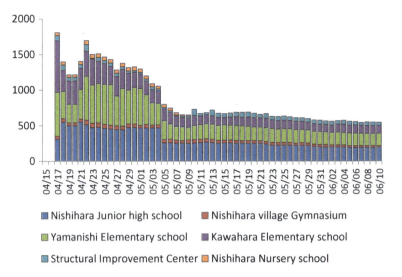

Fig. 14.2 Trends in the number of evacuees in designated shelters in Nishihara Village (people)

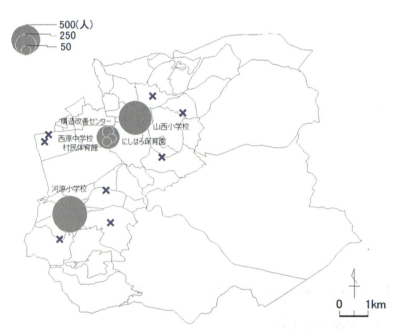

Fig. 14.3 Location of Nishihara Village's designated shelters and maximum number of evacuees (people). Note: X indicates non-designated shelters

14 A Study of Nishihara Village's Disaster Response in the... 251

9 independent evacuation shelters (non-designated shelters) were confirmed, and a maximum of more than 4000 people, or about 60% of village residents, were evacuated. Although the number of evacuees declined somewhat with the resumption of school in early May, the prolongation of evacuation due to the severity of damage to houses and lifelines meant that shelters continued operating for about 7 months until their complete closure on November 18, 2016.

14.3.2 Disaster Management Headquarters and Support Response for Reconstruction of Disaster Victims' Lives

Unlike in the restoration/reconstruction period, in the initial stage in the immediate aftermath of a disaster, municipalities are required to make prompt judgments and respond swiftly in emergencies, especially concerning human life and victims' support. In the Kumamoto earthquake, there were five municipalities (Otsu-machi, Mashiki-machi, Uto City, Yashiro City, and Hitoyoshi City) in which the government buildings were damaged and rendered unusable, and verifying the method of managing disaster management headquarters around the same time is considered to be an important issue as well as useful in the consideration of disaster response of municipalities of similar population scale and geographical conditions.

In Nishihara, a Disaster Management Headquarters was established immediately after the occurrence of the foreshock, and 15 employees were assembled and waiting in the office (assembly rate of 19.2%) at the time of the main shock. However, due to a power outage in the office, white boards, maps, and equipment were carried out to the parking lot, and disaster response consultations were held outdoors. Although the Nishihara Village Regional Disaster Prevention Plan specified that the peacetime departmental structure was supposed to shift as it was to disaster management teams (a 7-team structure), considering the severity of the damage, it was decided under the direction of the director (village mayor) based on a plan to expand response capabilities irrespective of the disaster prevention plan that from then on relocation of staff would be carried out beyond assigned departments as deemed necessary. Moreover, 3 days after the start of the disaster, in order to integrate all employees, a group chat was created on the instant messaging application LINE for information sharing and contact among staff. Reports, requests, and so on were also routinely done via LINE. Confirmation of residents' safety and number of evacuees was carried out promptly under the leadership of the 46 heads of the village wards following the procedures carried out in the "disaster response evacuation drill" held in the village every other year, and this information was reported to headquarters. A designated area for disaster management headquarters, which serves as a base for disaster response of municipalities, is permanently installed in prefectural offices, but in the case of basic municipalities, many are installed in large conference rooms or similar rooms in government buildings in the aftermath of a disaster. However, in the case of Nishihara, although there was a large conference room on the second

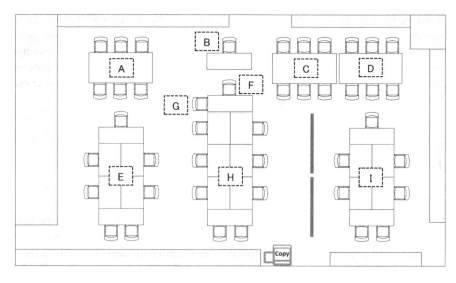

A	Self Defence Force · Cabinet office · Ministry of Health, Labor and Welfare		
B	Nishihara industry section	F	Nishihara Village head (Director)
C	Kumamoto Prefecture	G	Nishihara village vice head (Deputy Director)
D	Ministry of Land Infrastructure and Transport · Saga Prefecture	H	Nishihara (General team)
E	Nishihara (Information team)	I	Nishihara (Public Health Nurse)

Fig. 14.4 Seating chart of Disaster Management Headquarters setup in the Industry Division of the municipality office's first floor

floor of the municipal office, the headquarters was established in a space within the industry division on the first floor, taking into account the importance of immediacy of response and the morale of the "all hands on board" system. Because the industry division originally dealt with great deal of infrastructure information related to disaster response, this idea was devised in order to take advantage of the prompt decision-making and instruction-giving skills they had gained through training. In particular, stationed at the center of this arrangement was the director of headquarters (village mayor) and deputy director (deputy mayor) who remained in command until the end of July and November, respectively (Fig. 14.4). Moreover, since 2011 Nishihara had conducted personnel exchanges through reconstruction support work with Higashimatsushima City, Miyagi Prefecture, in an area affected by the Great East Japan Earthquake, and response in the Kumamoto earthquake was planned with Nishihara government employees who had support experience in the field playing a central role. Furthermore, Nishihara was the first among municipalities affected in the Kumamoto earthquake to decide on a construction site for temporary housing and start construction, beginning tenant application procedures in mid-June. It also constructed its own original "Disaster Victim Life Reconstruction Support System" for managing the issuing of Disaster Victim Certificates and the subsequent rebuilding of lives in a unified manner. Whereas the issue rate of Disaster Victim Certificates for Kumamoto Prefecture as a whole as of the end of

May was 47.9%, Nishihara achieved an almost 100% issue rate. This kind of prompt response toward victims characterized the village.

14.4 Disaster Victims' Perception of Life Recovery

14.4.1 Characteristics of Changes in Perception of Recovery

When measuring perception of recovery, especially regarding the definition of "recovery," it is important to resolve the discrepancies between the intentions of the investigators and those of the respondents and to minimize the deviation. For the purposes of this study, perception of recovery is based on the subjective evaluation of the disaster victims themselves, whose damage situations and living situations differ, measured against the "recovery achievement rate" indicated by the progress of public infrastructure development projects, etc. based on the reconstruction plans formulated by the government. Various methods and discussions have been carried out in past surveys and research on perception of recovery. These include methods that have set the reference point of perception of recovery as "a desirable life" or "life before the disaster," as well as questionnaires which asked for the "current recovery ratio (as a numerical value)" expressed on an observational scale prepared in advance or which asked about "the point when things had settled down to a certain degree" (Tsuchiya et al. 2016; Tsuboi 2014).

For this study, while following the methodology of past research and taking into consideration the sense of time and the comprehensibility of assessment measures regarding perception of recovery, a method of obtaining a "percentage" amount from responses to "the current ratio of recovery if pre-earthquake conditions are considered 100%" on a scale of 5 20% intervals regarding overall life at the time of the survey (1 year after the disaster) and a method of obtaining a sense of "time" from responses to "the point you felt the prospect of a certain amount of recovery and stability" on a scale of 6 2-month intervals regarding living environment, including resumption of water services, meals and work, a mental sense of calmness (psychological stability), and the vitality of the community were conducted and analyzed in relation to each attribute.

Figure 14.5 shows the results of the perception of recovery rate obtained from responses to the above "current ratio of recovery if pre-earthquake conditions are considered 100%" method cross-analyzed for age, damage situation (separated by Disaster Victim Certificate decisions) and current residence, and significant differences found using the chi-square test.

As seen in the figure, a significant difference was confirmed in the Disaster Victim Certificate decisions category where the greater the damage (severe damage deemed "complete destruction" or "large-scale destruction"), the lower the perception of recovery. In addition, according to data broken down by current residence, respondents who assessed their perception of recovery at "50 ~ 60%" (a perception of recovery of about half) or less accounted for 52.8% of the respondents residing in

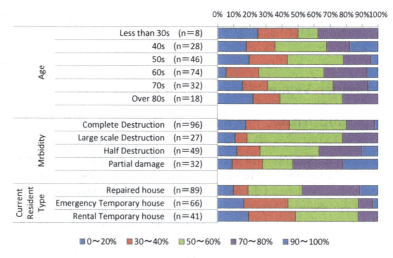

Fig. 14.5 Ratio of perception of life recovery by age, Disaster Victim Certificate decision, and current residence

repaired residences but accounted for 87.8% of the respondents living both in emergency temporary housing and rental temporary housing. This demonstrates that the *damage situation* (*disaster victim decision*) and *living conditions* (*current residence*) have an effect on the formation of perception of recovery. Figure 14.6 shows the changes in perception of recovery over "time" as a cumulative total ratio of respondents in the seven categories adopted for this study. It examines the change in speed of perception of recovery from the amount of change on the vertical axis with respect to the passage of time on the horizontal axis. As shown in the figure, a rise in perception of recovery in regard to the categories concerning living standards (water, meals, residence, work, transportation) can be seen in the period from June to the end of July 2016 when victims began moving into emergency temporary housing and infrastructure restoration projects were progressing, exceeding 80% in the period from August to the end of September 2016. However, for the categories of "psychological stability" (the point you felt a mental sense of calmness) and "community vitality" (the point you felt the community's vitality had returned), it was not until the period from December 2016 to the end of January 2017 that both categories exceeded 70%, demonstrating that cultivating an emotional perception of recovery takes more time. Although there are various kinds of relief aid available after a disaster for life reconstruction and recovery (financial support, loans, insurance premium waivers, etc.), their application requires the issuance of a Disaster Victim Certificate from the local government, making prompt issuance of these certificates essential. In many of the municipalities affected by the Kumamoto earthquake, however, there were delays in issuance of these certificates due to such factors as personnel shortages and the introduction of a unified system. In Nishihara on the other hand, issuance procedures were carried out at an early stage thanks to an original system created immediately after the disaster at the discretion of municipal

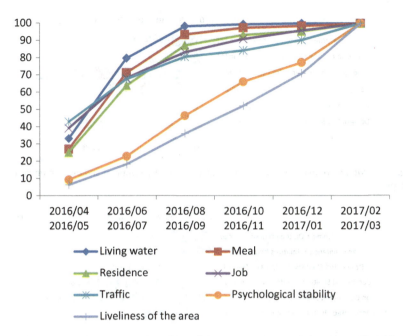

Fig. 14.6 Cumulative percentage of perception of recovery responses by category (%)

employees after consideration of the condition of the village. In regard to the evaluation of Disaster Victim Certificate issuance and response as related to reconstruction of disaster victims' lives and perceptions of recovery in this survey, on a scale of 5 degrees of satisfaction/promptness ranging from "dissatisfied/slow" to "satisfied/prompt" and "average" in the middle, 69.6% of all respondents (N = 195) answered "somewhat satisfied/fairly prompt" or "satisfied/prompt." This factor is thought to have promoted the start of life reconstruction at an early stage.

14.5 Characteristics of Post-disaster Health Evaluation

The condition of one's health may also affect one's perception of recovery after a disaster. In consideration of this point, this survey focused on victims' health problems as one of the elements that constitute perception of recovery, and questions were devised related to health such as about symptoms of poor physical health during the evacuation period and changes in physical health after the earthquakes. Figure 14.7 shows the total number of evacuees with symptoms of poor physical health by symptom for each type of evacuation destination, while Fig. 14.8 shows the rate of outpatient hospital visits for respondents who indicated symptoms of poor health. As seen in these figures, 63.8% of all respondents indicated experiencing symptoms of poor health from a set list of symptoms, of which the most common

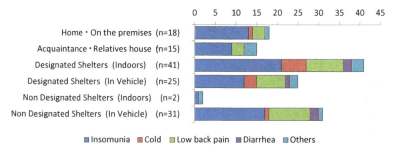

Fig. 14.7 Number of evacuees in poor physical condition by symptom and evacuation destination (people)

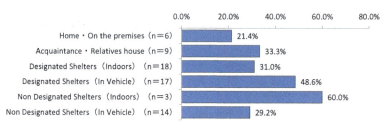

Fig. 14.8 Rate of hospital visits during evacuation period by evacuation destination (%)

one in all types of evacuation destinations was "insomnia." More than half of evacuees experiencing symptoms of poor health suffered from insomnia. With regard to "back pain/pain," 22% of those in designated shelters (indoors) and 16.7% of those at home or on the home premises suffered from this symptom, compared to 28.0% of those at designated shelters (overnight in vehicle) and 32.3% of those at non-designated shelters (overnight in vehicle), revealing that this symptom had a high rate of manifestation ($p < 0.05$). In the Kumamoto earthquake, the high number of evacuees who chose to stay in their private vehicles overnight ("overnight in vehicle") as a method of evacuation was particularly notable, and even in Nishihara, people choosing this evacuation method at not only non-designated shelters but at designated shelters as well were observed to a certain extent. From a health management standpoint with regard to evacuees in the village who stayed overnight in their vehicles, rounds by nurses and public health nurses were conducted in order to prevent the occurrence of economy class syndrome, as well as distribution of compression stockings to promote blood circulation and other measures. However, looking at hospital visit status by evacuation destination, except for non-designated evacuation shelters (indoor), a hospital visit rate of approximately 30% or more is seen. In particular, the highest rate of hospital visits, at 48.6% of all evacuees indicating poor physical condition, was seen at non-designated evacuation shelters (overnight in vehicle).

Figure 14.9 shows evaluations related to deterioration of health 1 year after the earthquake by attribute. The survey method consisted of respondents scoring their

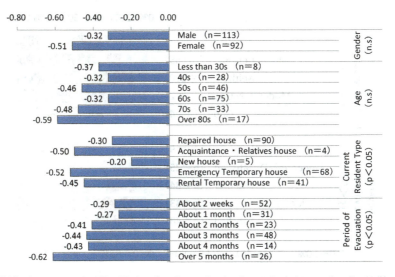

Fig. 14.9 Average score of health deterioration evaluation by attribute 1 year after the earthquake

state of health a year after the disaster (at the time of the survey) with their state of health before the disaster as a base (0) on a scale of -2 to 0 with 0 for no change, -1 for somewhat worse, and -2 for worse. These scores are averaged and shown in Fig. 14.9 by attribute. As seen in the figure, there were no significant differences attributable to gender or age, but broken down by current residence, results show points for health deterioration were higher for those living in temporary housing than in their own homes (repaired and new), and higher for residents of emergency temporary housing than rental temporary housing. In addition, broken down by period of evacuation, it was discovered that the longer the evacuation period, the higher the points for health deterioration were.

Figure 14.10 shows the results of cross analysis of perception of recovery (on a scale of 5 20% intervals) against health evaluation (on a scale of 5 from poor to good) and government evaluation (on a scale of 5 from dissatisfied to satisfied). The figure shows that the worse the present health evaluation is and the dissatisfaction with government is, the higher the proportion of low perception of recovery is. This suggests that maintenance and promotion of good health and prompt and polite government response to victims are essential for fostering a perception of recovery.

14.6 Evaluation of Self-Help/Mutual Assistance and Post-Disaster Administrative/Assistance Response

Figure 14.11 shows the number of respondents in this survey who took self-help steps against disasters. As seen in the figure, although the number of respondents who had earthquake insurance stood at 118 (58.4%) before the earthquake, the

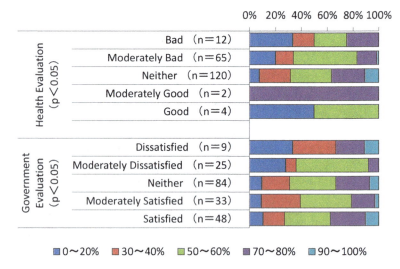

Fig. 14.10 Current evaluation of health/government and perception of life recovery

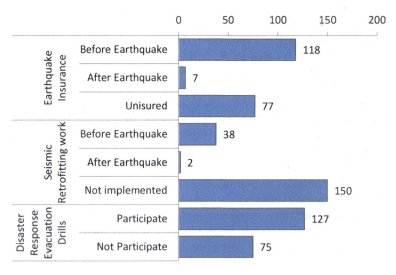

Fig. 14.11 Self-help disaster response before and after the earthquake (people)

number who had seismic retrofitting work done was low at 38 (20.0%). The number of respondents who had participated in disaster response evacuation drills (emergency drills) conducted every other year, however, was high at 127 (62.9%), and many of the respondents experienced being approached or alerted by district heads, fire brigades, and neighbors for evacuation as was practiced during the drills (Fig. 14.12). Moreover, cases of "mutual assistance" in which residents and fire brigades actually collaborated to carry out relief work from collapsed houses were

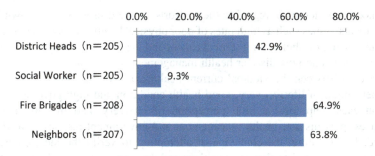

Fig. 14.12 Number of people who experienced being approached/alerted for evacuation (mutual assistance)

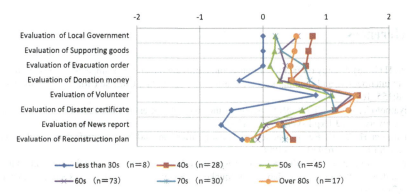

Fig. 14.13 Profile of average scores for evaluation of administrative/assistance response

revealed. Evaluation of administrative/assistance response broken down by age groups (on a scale of −2 to 2 with 0 in the middle) is shown in Fig. 14.13, and the average evaluation for almost every category is a positive number for every age group except the 30s and under group, showing that a certain level of evaluation was obtained because of public assistance.

14.7 Conclusion

Changes in perceptions of recovery of daily life and health of victims a year after the Kumamoto earthquake disaster were examined in conjunction with the disaster response of Nishihara Village in this study. Although the scale of damage was comparable to the neighboring town of Mashiki-machi in enormity, rapid response toward victims was carried out due to such factors as the operation of a disaster management headquarters which enabled top local government officials to take immediate action and the creation of an original support system for reconstruction of disaster victims' lives. It was revealed that a nearly 70% satisfaction rate was obtained from victims in regard to these efforts. In the disaster victims' own health assessments, issues such as high rates of poor physical health and hospital visits were seen in evacuation shelter long-term evacuees and evacuees who stayed overnight in their vehicles, and post-disaster health management remains an issue. However, in the relation between the victims' current health evaluation/government evaluation and perception of life recovery, good health condition and high government satisfaction each help form a high perception of recovery, and the importance of evacuees' post-disaster health management and government response was demonstrated. In the future, the challenge of attempting to verify the ideal cooperation policy among administrative organizations and the community in order to contribute to the improvement of perception of recovery at an early stage needs to be addressed.

References

Aoto H (2006) A study on factors of households' moving out and their impacts on the communities in intermediate and mountainous areas after the Niigata-ken Chuetsu earthquake. J Soc Saf Sci 8:155–162

Miyamoto T, Atsumi T (2009) Concerning the roles of stories and outside supporters in disaster recovery. Jpn J Exp Psychol 49(1):17~31

Mizumura H (2010) Reconstruction of housing after the mid-Niigata prefectural earthquake. J Archit Plan 75(654):1897–1906

Nakabayashi I (2016) Significance and prospects of disaster recovery research: from simultaneous studies of the great East Japan earthquake, recovery. Jpn Soc Disast Recover Revital 15 (7):34–41

Tatsuki S, Hayashi H, Yamori K, Noda T, Tamura K, Kimura R (2004) Model building and testing of long-term life recovery processes of the survivors of the great Hanshin-Awaji earthquake. J Soc Saf Sci 6:251–260

Tsuboi S (2014) Transitions of perception of recovery in the fishing industry in Miyako City on the Omoe peninsula of Iwate prefecture: a case study of Otobe/Omoe fishing port. In: Proceedings of the Japan Society for Disaster Recovery and Revitalization (Nagaoka Conference), pp 12–15

Tsuchiya Y, Nakabayashi I, Otagiri R (2016) Livelihood recovery in the victims of disaster in four years after the great East Japan earthquake: progress of housing reconstruction and its relevance to recovery, paper of workshop of the great East Japan earthquake. Inst Soc Saf Sci 5:79–84

Chapter 15
Smart Cities for Recovery and Reconstruction in the Aftermath of a Disaster

Yoriko Tsuchiya

Abstract As a measure against global warming, smart cities are being built to reduce the use of carbon by introducing renewable energy, securing dispersed and autonomous power supply, and managing energy at the scale of the city. Following the Great East Japan Earthquake of March in 2011, the concept of a smart city has gained considerable interest in Japan as a measure for controlling energy to improve disaster prevention ability and resilience to disasters. For shaping a smart city, energy-saving equipment and energy management systems should be introduced by using energy control technology, etc. Managing and controlling energy by means of a storage battery makes it possible to employ renewable energy sources such as solar power and to utilize energy potential. Furthermore, optimization and stabilization of energy supply and demand too can be contributed.

In this chapter, features of public–private partnership projects related to a smart city in the operational stage are described, which has been being developed for the reconstruction of afflicted areas. First, I will describe the concept and definition of smart city in Japan are explained, and then four cases of smart cities from Miyagi Prefecture are introduced. These four cases are "Alai Green City Project" as post-disaster public housing; "Tago West Project" as post-disaster public housing–general housing, mixed type; "Higashimatsushima Eco-Town Project" as post-disaster public housing–business complex type; and "Akaiwa Port Eco-Marine Processing Estate Project" as factory type.

In the planning stage of these projects, in addition to HEMS or BEMS for housings, also the networking of multiple facilities and introduction of large-scale energy infrastructure such as storage batteries and renewable energy are being studied. However, in Japan, presently, only limited part of the plan has been operationalized in power supply and its flexible distribution. In the next stage of operation, further improvement of the infrastructure, stability of profit structure, and reinforcement of the organization management to sustain electric power supply will be essential.

Y. Tsuchiya (✉)
Organization for the Strategic Coordination of Research and Intellectual Properties, Meiji University, Tokyo, Japan

© Springer Nature Singapore Pte Ltd. 2019
C. Asahi (ed.), *Building Resilient Regions*, New Frontiers in Regional Science: Asian Perspectives 35, https://doi.org/10.1007/978-981-13-7619-1_15

Keywords Resilience · Power supply, solar photovoltaics · Storage battery · Energy management system · Post-disaster reconstruction project

15.1 Introduction

As a measure against global warming, smart cities are being built to reduce the use of carbon by introducing renewable energy, securing dispersed and autonomous power supply, and managing energy at the scale of the city. Following the Great East Japan Earthquake of March in 2011, the concept of a smart city has gained considerable interest in Japan as a measure for controlling energy to improve disaster prevention ability and resilience to disasters. The municipalities affected by the earthquake in March 2011 have positioned the Smart City Project as the core of the reconstruction plan because this project contributes not only to environmental and disaster prevention but also to industrial promotion and employment creation.

Many municipalities are still planning of details along the concept; however, the development tasks have been completed in some of the leading districts, and the plan is proceeding from the verification to the practical application stage.

Evaluating each measures for smart city—its outcome, effectiveness, and contributions to reconstruction—is a time-consuming process. However, some of other municipalities that are not yet affected but are improving preparedness at high risk of tsunami may find it useful to be provided of a clear picture of empirical process from the initial stage to the operational stage for formulating their pre-disaster plan.

In this chapter, features of public–private partnership projects related to a smart city in the operational stage are described, which has been being developed for the reconstruction of afflicted areas. First, I will describe the concept and definition of smart city in Japan are explained, and then four cases of smart cities from Miyagi Prefecture are introduced.

15.2 Definition and Dissemination Measures

15.2.1 Background of Smart City Initiatives

Developed and emerging countries differ in terms of the background in which smart cities are developed. In advanced countries, including Japan, "efficient social infrastructure development and management" is required to respond to the decline of a city and financial deterioration due to aging and shrinking population. Meanwhile, for emerging economies, there is a need for "measures to cope with environmental deterioration and increase in energy demand due to sudden increase in population and overcrowding"(Izumii 2013).

Backed by the philosophy of sustainable urban management, a society of lower carbon footprints is a common target throughout the world to be achieved by reducing energy consumption and promoting cleaner energy. To realize such sustainability, there are two approaches as follows.

1. Utilization of information communication technology
2. Control and management of social infrastructure

15.2.2 Definition of a Smart City

Power device technology, power electronics technology, energy storage technology, energy control technology, security technology, etc. are essential for creating a smart city(Japan Smart Community Alliance 2015). The market size of the smart city industry, including such smart technologies, is estimated at about 4000 trillion yen by 2030. For many countries worldwide, the concept of smart cities is a part of industrial promotion other than environmental advantage(http://www.smartcity-plan ning.co.jp/index.html). In Japan, smart city industries are positioned as growth industries in the National Government's Growth Strategy (2008) and the New Growth Strategy (2010). Public and private sectors are addressing R&D and demonstrations of related technologies.

Figure 15.1 explains the means and goals of a smart city (NEDO 2014). First, introduction of energy-saving apparatus and energy management system realize to reduce carbon dioxide emissions and to introduce massive amount of renewable energy. Second, introduction of energy control technology and variable energy supply depending on the demand can supply energy stably and optimize supply cost. Finally, if they can provide new services targeting the elderly, they can contribute to improve their standard of living lives, convenience of transportation and lifeline service, and regional safety.

Thus, the objectives are not only to improve environmental property and restoration after disaster but also to include the convenience and safety of the residents in the goals.

For shaping a smart city, energy-saving equipment and energy management systems should be introduced by using energy control technology, etc. Managing and controlling energy by means of a storage battery makes it possible to employ renewable energy sources such as solar power and to utilize energy potential. Furthermore, optimization and stabilization of energy supply and demand too can be contributed. Energy management system, in particular, is important. The system is called home energy management system (HEMS) for households, factory energy management system (FEMS) for factories, and building energy management system (BEMS) for office buildings.

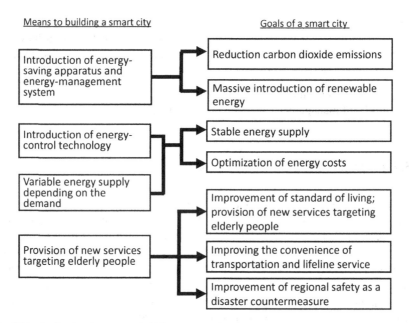

Fig. 15.1 Goals of and means to building a smart city.
Edited by the author from Smart City Project Official website (http://www.smartcity-planning.co.jp/index.html)

15.2.3 Policies of the Government for Promotion of Smart Cities

The Ministry of Economy, Trade, and Industry, the Ministry of Internal Affairs and Communications, and the Ministry of Land, Infrastructure, and Transport provide subsidies to private enterprises (mostly corporate consortiums) and local governments, which are the operation entities.

1. The Ministry of Economy, Trade, and Industry

The Ministry of Economy, Trade, and Industry covers the governmental energy policy including urban energy management.

The demonstration project promoted "smart community" which is implemented to city blocks, not to a whole city in scale. It encompasses a smart grid of the power system and includes heats of unutilized thermal energy. Basically a smart city is a concept that it consists a network of integrated, multiple block-sized smart communities.

The smart community is prescribed as a measure in the fourth Energy Basic Plan approved by the Cabinet concurrently with the National Government's Growth Strategy.

The promotion policy of smart community is described as follows: "As an effort to build a low-carbon society, we will realize" the 3Es (i.e., energy, economy, and environment) "by supplying energy stably with utilizing information and communication technology." In addition, as a promotion organization, "Smart Community Alliance" was established based on the public and private partnership organization including NEDO (New Energy and Industrial Technology Development Organization) designated as the secretariat.

The "Smart Community Initiative Promotion Support Project" is a subsidy to support private enterprises and local governments in formulating plans and initiatives, through assisting the formulation of business plans and implementing of project feasibility study according to regional circumstances or conditions in regard to renewable energy, energy conservation, supply and demand control of energy, etc. Either private enterprises alone or ones with local governments are eligible for the assistance.

Large-scale demonstration projects had been implemented in Yokohama City (Kanagawa Prefecture), Toyota City (Aichi Prefecture), Keihanna Science City (an unincorporated city on a border region between Kyoto, Osaka, and Nara Prefectures), and Kitakyushu City (Fukuoka Prefecture) since 2011.

2. The Ministry of Public Management, Home Affairs, Posts and Telecommunications

The Ministry of Public Management, Home Affairs, Posts and Telecommunications has a smart city policy aimed at the advancement of communication technology and its application to practical use.

As described below, the objectives are to address various problems in the region, to revitalize the region, and to create localities.

① Expansion of succeeded models in disaster prevention, medical/health, tourism, etc.
② Town development as a cross-sectional smart city with information and communication technology (ICT)

The ICT Smart City Improvement Promotion Project is aimed at subsidizing a part of the costs for initial stage and continuous improvement of system, likewise purchasing equipment, system construction, consultative meeting for system improvement, etc. Assistance is provided for introducing communication facilities, etc. to realize advanced energy management in a unit of region.

3. The Ministry of Land, Infrastructure, Transport and Tourism

The Ministry of Land, Infrastructure, Transport and Tourism is in charge of mobility-related policies such as policies related to roads, railway transportation, etc., and measures related to energy conservation of buildings, houses, etc. in relation to a smart city. The "Law on Promotion of Low Carbonization of Cities" (Low-Carbon Town Planning Act) has been in force since 2012 to promote development of a compact city and a low-carbon city.

① Conversion to realize intensive urban structures
② Promotion of planned use of energy at the district/block levels

③ Promotion of the use of public transportation

④ Promotion of urban greening

These policies have focused on, in particular, measures to reduce the impact to environment at the district or city block level in urban districts and other areas. In 2018, a guideline (in an interim report titled "toward the realization of Smart City"(NEDO 2014)) was announced, defining smart city as a city or district, sustainably addresses urban issues by management measures of planning, construction, management, and operation with new technologies such as ICT through intending total optimization.

Currently empirical investigations on incorporating advanced technologies of ICT such as implementation of automatic driving, artificial intelligence (AI), Internet of Things (IoT), etc. into urban infrastructure management has commenced. In addition, the Eco City Project Council (J-CODE), a council consisting companies and other agencies promoting urban developments in the overseas, has been established to support the promotion of eco-city projects in emerging Asian countries.

15.3 Status of a Smart City for Disaster Prevention and Post-disaster Reconstruction

Smart city in the disaster prevention and reconstruction plans are considered as the following: Firstly for the disaster prevention field, in the disaster prevention plan and the outline for earthquake countermeasures, the terms "smart city" and "smart community" are not explicitly stated. The central disaster damage prevention meeting announced, "Outline of disaster damage prevention and reduction measures for large-scale earthquakes" in March 2014, in which "1. Pre-disaster prevention, (5) measures to secure lifelines and infrastructure" and "independent and decentralized energy supply in the region" are stated. Although it is not positioned as a part of regional disaster damage prevention plan of local governments, securing electric power is an important matter in municipality BCP (business continuity planning).

Next, on post-disaster reconstruction policy, the Cabinet approved the basic reconstruction policy immediately after the Great East Japan Earthquake of 2011. This policy states that, as a part of reconstruction measures, it is important to introduce smart communities and smart villages with high efficiency of energy consumption in the affected areas and to realize environmentally advanced areas (eco-towns) in the affected areas. The introduction of renewable energy and energy conservation measures are also encouraged, based on lessons learned from the Great Earthquake disaster of 2011.

For a concrete reconstruction plan, let us consider the example of Miyagi Prefecture. The post-earthquake reconstruction plan formulated in October 2011 for Miyagi Prefecture includes "Formation of Eco-Town by utilizing renewable energy (Table 15.1)." In the reconstruction project, town planning incorporating

15 Smart Cities for Recovery and Reconstruction in the Aftermath of a Disaster

Table 15.1 Items in the Miyagi Prefecture reconstruction plan

Points of reconstruction
7. Development of eco-town with utilized renewable energy
Promotion of environment-friendly town planning
Dispersed power sources of high-energy-performance equipment, solar power, biomass power, geothermal power, waste heat power, small-scale hydroelectric power, wind power, etc. will be introduced to promote development of a town of resilient and well-prepared for disasters and to make an environmental friendly town
Full development of photovoltaic power generation in reconstructed houses
We (Miyagi prefecture, local government) will take initiative to introduce solar power generators and promote wider adoption of independent and dispersed energy to houses with fuel cell device and storage batteries for rebuilt and newly constructed houses
Encouraging transformation of communities advancing with smart grids and cogeneration
We will utilize functions to share dispersed energy, such as functions for efficient and autonomous photovoltaic power generation throughout the region, and to ensure the preferential treatment system by the government in purchasing power in the country. The goal for Miyagi prefecture is to be an advanced region for substituting fossil fuel and promoting renewable energy

renewable energy such as sunlight and biomass and equipment with high-energy performance in urban infrastructure are being promoted actively by the prefecture.

15.4 Case Study

Here, examples of four districts in Miyagi Prefecture are classified by the target facilities of energy management. In addition, the project descriptions are introduced. The characteristics of each case are described below.

1. Disaster public housing type: Disaster public housing, namely, apartments
2. Disaster public housing and general housing, mixed type
3. Disaster public housing–business complex type: Collaboration between hospitals, business buildings, and detached disaster public housing
4. Factory type: Efforts made by fishery processing business operators within industrial estates

East Arai area is located nearby the Arahama area on the coast of Sendai City where severely damaged by the tsunami. Located at the easternmost end of the region where the tsunami arrived, "East Arai" is a symbolic area for reconstruction as the edge of the land of safety. It is a section of a large-scale development district where land readjustment had been promoted since the time before the earthquake, as a part of the model project of environmental city distinctively subsidized by Sendai City. Large-scale public housing and disaster damage prevention groups with resettled housing complexes have been developed. Introduction of disaster reconstruction housing, energy management system, and renewable energy into business facilities, commercial facilities, hospitals, etc. is being planned for the surrounding area (Table 15.2).

Table 15.2 Outline of the disaster public housing type (Sendai City Official website; Ministry of the Environment, Sendai City and others 2012)

District name (Project name)	Arai East district (Arai Green City)
Plans/concepts	Sendai City eco-model town concept
Name of auxiliary project	Sendai City eco-model town promotion Project in 2013
Location (target area)	Arai East land readjustment Project area, Wakabayashi Ward, Sendai City
Promotion and management entity	Arai town management general incorporated association
Circumstances	From 2009 Developed by Sendai City Arai East Land Readjustment Project
Recovery and reconstruction business	Disaster public housing apartment (2 units/298 houses), detached houses (15 detached disaster public housing units, 60 general housing of detached houses by group relocation), medical and welfare facilities, commercial facilities, accommodation facilities, large-scale indoor facilities for sports and cultural activities, etc. (including facilities at the plan stage)
Energy system/equipment	Solar power generation panel (10 kW), storage battery (34 kW), HEMS
Renewable energy	Solar power
Planned population	3100 people
Business area	33.7 ha
Expenses	8.78 billion yen (total project cost)
Construction period	FY 2013
Operation period	FY2014–FY2022
Survey date	February 19, 2016

Currently, photovoltaic panels, storage batteries, and HEMS are installed in the reconstruction public housing, and energy systems are in operation. In the event of a disaster, electricity is to be supplied to meeting places, and the reconstruction public housing is to be used as an evacuation center (Fig. 15.2). Tablets are distributed to the residents of public housing for checking the power consumption of their households and generation in the district so that energy conservation behaviors are to be promoted through the visualization of energy generation and consumption. The administrator is Arai Town Management, a town planning organization working in the area which is designated as "Urban Renewable Corporation" by MLIT. And it is also responsible for delivering social services such as management of athletic parks in addition to energy management.

2. Disaster Public Housing and General housing, Mixed Type

Tago West district is located at inland of Sendai City's central district. Similar to the Arai East district, there has been a comprehensive project before the earthquake, and the public housing for victims is being developed by changing commercial and private operational systems (Table 15.3). This project utilizes the subsidies of the Ministry of the Environment and Ministry of Internal Affairs and Communications.

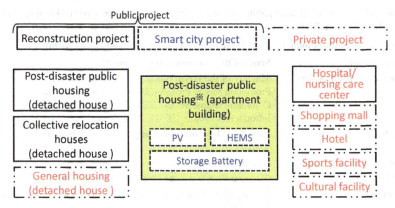

Fig. 15.2 Overall components of "Alai" Green City Project (post-disaster public housing)
Note: The concrete measures are as follows:
Distribution of tablets to residents in post-disaster public housing
Monitoring power consumption and generation
Adjustment to supply and demand using demand response system

The supply of electricity and water, power generation, and consumption of energy is monitored with equipment distributed in the residential areas of multifamily residential buildings and in two residential areas of general detached houses in the smart village block (Fig. 15.3). In the event of a disaster, electricity will be intensively supplied to meeting places so that they can function as evacuation bases. The utilization of electric vehicles was also considered; however, only two such vehicles have been introduced in the model project.

The administrator is not a local company but a council composed of larger, nationwide-scale private companies (International Kogyo Co., Ltd., as a construction consultancy company, and NTT Facilities Co., Ltd., as a communication company) based on a project focusing on technical demonstration.

3. Disaster Public Housing–Business Complex Type: Cooperation in Distribution of Energy Between Hospitals, Business Buildings, and Detached Disaster Public Housing

Higashimatsushima City is located at the middle part of Miyagi Prefecture, along the coast of Sendai Bay. In Higashimatsushima City Matsushima bay, known as a group of small islands in the bay, is a tourist destination representing Tohoku. Higashimatsushima City smart eco-town is a public housing complex developed as a reconstruction project of Higashimatsushima City (Table 15.4).

Four hospitals (General Hospital and hospitals for Orthopedic Surgery, Internal Medicine, and Gynecology) and Ishinomaki Driving License Center are connected by a self-serviced electric line to build a microgrid. Biodiesel generators and storage batteries are in place for emergency power supply in the district (Fig. 15.4). In the event of a disaster, these will supply electricity to hospitals and meeting places as usual for at least 3 days (Fig. 15.5). Public housing for victims is mostly of the

Table 15.3 Outline of disaster public housing–general housing mixed type (Kokusai Kogyo Co., Ltd Official Website 2016)

District name (Project name)	Tago West district (Green Community Tago Nishi)
Plans/concepts	Sendai City "eco-model town project"
Name of auxiliary project	Ministry of the Environment, Sustainable Urban Redevelopment Promotion Model Project (2011); Ministry of Internal Affairs and Communications, Smart Grid Communications Interface Introduction Project (2011), 2012 Sendai City Eco-Model Town
Location (target area)	Tago West land readjustment project area, Miyagino Ward, Sendai City
Promotion and management entity	Sendai green community promotion council
	(Kokusai Kogyo co., ltd., NTT facilities co., ltd.)
Circumstances	Developed by Sendai City Tago West land readjustment project from 2009
Recovery and reconstruction business	Four residential buildings (apartment, 176 units), 16 detached houses, large commercial facilities
Energy system/equipment	Disaster public housing:
	Energy center, solar power generation panel (40 kW), gas cogeneration system (25 kW), storage battery (50 kW)
	Detached house (general):
	Household energy management system (HEMS), installation of ICT terminal (visualization of power usage), photovoltaic power generation panel, storage battery, electric vehicle
Renewable energy	Solar power
Planned population	1000 people
Business area	16.32 ha
Expenses	2.4 billion yen (assisted area information aid project, full subsidy by earthquake reconstruction special allocation tax)
Construction period	FY2013 – FY2014
Operation period	FY2014 – FY2022
Survey date	February 19, 2016
	March 31, 2016

detached type, and smart meters are installed in each door. The management entity is a new agency owned by Higashimatsushima City. The agency was established to promote environmental measures including energy supply and reconstruction measures altogether.

4. Factory Type: Efforts Made By Fishery Processing Business Operators Within Industrial Estates

Kesennuma City is a fisheries community located along the Pacific coast of the northeastern tip of Miyagi Prefecture. Akaiwa Port District Development is a major project of industrial restoration in Kesennuma City. Kesennuma City is one of the cities where the central urban area has been suffered extensive damage and destroyed. Along with the reconstruction of Akaiwa Port, the industrial park for

15 Smart Cities for Recovery and Reconstruction in the Aftermath of a Disaster

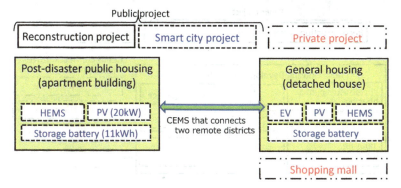

Fig. 15.3 Overall components of the Tago West Project (Post-Disaster Public Housing–General Housing, Mixed Type)
Note: The concrete measures within the Tago West district are as follows:
Distributing tablets to inhabitants
Monitoring power consumption and generation
Adjustment to supply and demand using demand response system
Community power improvements for disaster prevention through the collective supply of electricity and water service and continuing the supply of electricity and water after the disaster

Table 15.4 Outline of disaster public housing–business mixed type (Sekisui House Co., Ltd 2015)

District name (Project name)	Higashimatsushima City disaster-ready smart eco-town
Plans/concepts	Higashimatsushima City town reconstruction plan
	Environmental future city plan
Name of auxiliary project	Ministry of the Environment FY 2014 Promotion of Autonomy and Decentralized Low-Carbon Energy Society
Location (target area)	Higashimatsushima City
Promotion and management entity	Higashimatsushima Organization for Progress and "E" (economy, education, energy)
Circumstances	Designated as environmental future city in FY2011
Recovery and reconstruction business	85 disaster public housing units (70 detached houses, 15 units in total)
Energy system/equipment	Biodiesel emergency generator (500 kVA, 400 kW), solar power generation (disaster prevention adjustment reservoir, 400 kW; meeting place, 9.1 kW; apartment house, 49.9 kW); large storage battery (480 kWh)
Renewable energy	Solar power generation, biodiesel power generation
Planned population	247 people (public housing residents)
Business area	4 ha
Expenses	1.2 billion yen
Construction period	FY2014–FY2015
Operation period	FY2016–FY2020
Survey date	August 8, 2016

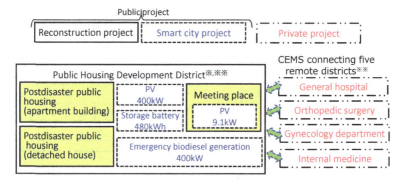

Fig. 15.4 Overall components of Higashimatsushima eco-town project (Post-Disaster Public Housing–Business Complex Type)
Note: Providing a system that distributes power collectively received at high voltage to consumers
Note: Securing the power supply supplying electricity to public houses, neighborhood hospitals, and public facilities just after the disaster

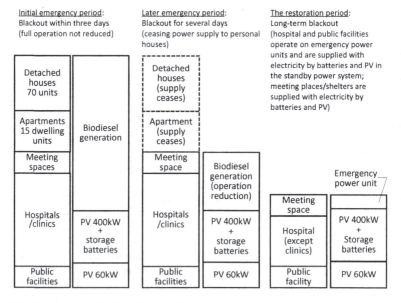

Fig. 15.5 Energy control in Higashimatsushima eco-town project post-disaster

the fisheries processing as the major industry of the city has been developed (Table 15.5). FEMS was introduced in 9 local enterprises and 11 facilities, where liquid crystal panels show monitored result of the electricity consumption and amount of electricity generated (Fig. 15.6). Furthermore, as a power supply for emergency, a V2F (Vehicle to Factory) system that utilizes in-vehicle storage batteries and PHVs (Plug-in Hybrid Vehicle) and EVs (Electric Vehicle) were introduced. EV and PHV are also useful as a regional transportation under the

Table 15.5 Outline of the factory type (Kesennuma City, Smart City Project 2012)

District name (Project name)	Akaiwa Port Fishery Processing Complex (Akaiwa Port Eco-Marine Processing Estate Project)
Plans/concepts	–
Name of auxiliary project	Kesennuma City Smart Community Building Project (Ministry of Economy, Trade and Industry 2013 Smart Community Introduction Promotion Project)
Location (target area)	Akaiwa Port in Kesennuma City, Miyagi prefecture
Promotion and management entity	Kesennuma marine products processing cooperative association
Circumstances	Fishery processing facilities of Akaiwa Port are integrally developed with fishing port facilities of Akaiwa Port as a core of industrial restoration in Kesennuma City
Recovery and reconstruction business	Akaiwa cold storage factory (refrigeration facility, freezing facility, detachment facility, management room, etc.)
Energy system/equipment	9 companies · introduced factory · energy management system (FEMS), visualization of power usage by liquid crystal panel, PHV · EV (total of 14 units) to 11 facilities ·
Renewable energy	–
Planned population	14 companies
Business area	20 ha
Expenses	14.4 billion yen (tsunami recovery center development project as a whole)
Construction period	FY2012–FY2014
Operation period	FY2016–FY2025
Survey date	February 18, 2016

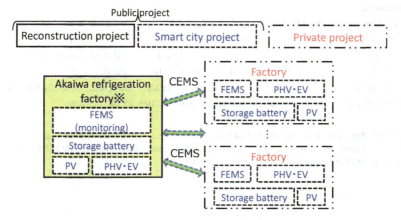

Fig. 15.6 Overall components of Akaiwa Port eco-marine processing estate project (Factory Type)
Note: Monitoring power consumption and the quantity of generation
Adjustment to supply and demand using demand response system

shortage of gasoline in emergency. The regional-specific electric utility company supplies electricity procured from a center for power generation by garbage heat in Soma City, Fukushima Prefecture, and a neighboring mega-solar power plant.

15.5 Future Prospects

Japan has adopted and developed the concept of smart cities as a reconstruction project through integral consolidation of factories or business facilities with public and private housings. These demonstration experiments' verification requires about 10 years for the evaluation. In the planning stage, in addition to HEMS or BEMS for housings, also the networking of multiple facilities and introduction of large-scale energy infrastructure such as storage batteries and renewable energy are being studied.

However, in Japan, presently, only limited part of the plan has been operationalized in power supply and its flexible distribution. In the next stage of operation, further improvement of the infrastructure, stability of profit structure, and reinforcement of the organization management to sustain electric power supply will be essential.

Although a rough estimate of the power supply for emergency has been obtained, how to optimize the actual use of the limited electric power during the recovery period after the disaster is not experimented fully. To establish a common recognition to use the power in the area, it is necessary to conduct the emergency measure simulation including a joint evacuation training with the residents and business operators.

Furthermore, except the case of the factory type, smart city operators are mere energy service providers offering electricity supply services only. It is expected that they would also provide various living services, equipped with actual driving force for encouraging a fully developed smart city; for example, sports facilities, real estate, residential complexes, transportation, nursing care, etc. or combinations of some services can be a solution for addressing issues in the region.

Acknowledgments I would like to thank the management companies and local governments of the afflicted areas who cooperated in the survey. This research was supported by JSPS KAKENHI, Grants-in-Aid for Scientific Research (S) 24221010.

References[1]

Izumii Y (2013) Development of smart community. J Inst Electr Install Eng Jpn 33(8):31–33

Japan Smart Community Alliance (2015) Smart community Japan's experience pp 1–66

Kesennuma City · Smart City Project (2012) Akaiiwa Port Project: (tentative name) Eco Maritime Processing Complex. December 2012, http://www.meti.go.jp/committee/summary/0004633/pdf/ 015_05_00.pdf (Reference date: September 25, 2016)

Kokusai Kogyo Co., Ltd Official Website: "Green Community Tago West"-Miyagi/Sendai City http://www.kkc.co.jp/pick_up/greencommunity_01.html (Reference Date: September 25, 2016)

Ministry of Economy, Trade and Industry Official website, http://www.meti.go.jp/ (Reference Date: October 25, 2018)

Ministry of Internal Affairs and Communications Official website, http://www.soumu.go.jp/ (Reference Date: October 25, 2018)

Ministry of Land, Infrastructure and Transport Official website, http://www.mlit.go.jp/ (Reference Date: October 25, 2018)

Ministry of the Environment, Sendai City and others (2012) Sustainable Urban Redevelopment Promotion Model Project, Tago West District Environmental Disaster Prevention City Urban Development Project Report. March 2012

NEDO (2014) Renewable energy technology white paper version 2 pp 3–27

Sekisui House Co., Ltd. (2015) Press Release: "Disaster Public Housing Yanagi-no-Me -higashi Completed, Moving in Town (Higashi Matsushima Smart Disaster Prevention Eco Town)." August 7, 2015

Sendai City Official website Eco Model Town Promotion Project. (Updated on July 15, 2016), http://www.city.sendai.jp/business/d/ecomodel.html (Reference Date: September 25, 2016)

Smart City Project Official website, http://www.smartcity-planning.co.jp/index.html (Reference date November 26, 2015)

---

[1]All in Japanese.